MAPPING CRIMINAL JUSTICE DELIVERY IN INDIA

MAPPING CRIMINAL JUSTICE DELIVERY IN INDIA

Towards Development of an Index

PRAMOD KUMAR
RAINUKA DAGAR

INSTITUTE FOR DEVELOPMENT AND COMMUNICATION

A Founding Member of Altus
altus GLOBAL ALLIANCE

MANOHAR
2009

First published 2009

ISBN 978-81-7304-791-6

Published by

Ajay Kumar Jain *for*
Manohar Publishers & Distributors
4753/23 Ansari Road, Daryaganj
New Delhi 110 002

Typeset at

Digigrafics
New Delhi 110 049

Printed at

Salasar Imaging Systems
Delhi 110 035

Contents

List of Tables

List of Graphs and Map

GRAPHS

MAP

List of Boxes

Applied Indicators

Preface

The twenty-first century has thrown up major challenges to human security. These have added new dimensions to the principles and scope of accountability of the criminal justice system. With the globalisation of rights and crimes, the threat posed by terrorism, technological revolution and the emergence of diaspora, the nature and scope of criminal justice system have been transformed.

The new global order with its emphasis on globalisation of capital and restricted mobility of labour without ensuring distributive justice has brought into focus issues relating to national and human security. Further, the state having abdicated to the market its responsibility to meet the survival needs of the people, its role has been reduced to performing regulatory functions. The regulatory state has to depend excessively on the security apparatus to provide a semblance of being effective and efficient. Moreover, the world over violent conflicts are dominated by intra-state conflict leading to excessive reliance on the police to maintain order and peace.

The criminal justice system has to acquire skills relating to prevention and management of crime in this new order while maintaining a fair dispensation of justice with corresponding accountability. It has also to function in convergence with the cultural needs of the people without disturbing their cultural sensibilities.

We have learnt from our experience that fragmented interventions and piecemeal solutions remain part of the problem as such an approach precludes the examination of the very system, which breeds crime. It may be more realistic to view criminal justice system in a holistic framework and against the broader social context.

The present effort is to provide parameters to measure performance, with an inclusive approach along with justice outcomes.

The approach followed in this document was first presented in an international research meeting on Internal Systems of Police Performance Measurement in June 2003. Thereafter, the effort was to comprehensively document the delivery of justice in the states of India. Unfortunately, this venture could not reach fruition as there were huge data gaps and absence of sufficient documentation. This continues to be a challenge.

Nevertheless, it was thought prudent to bring these challenges in public discourse and at the same time provide a handy instrument to stakeholders and policy planners to assess the delivery of justice.

For this work, we are thankful to experts and colleagues at IDC for their sustained patience and support. In particular, we are grateful to Prof. J.N. Joshi for his insights into statistical analysis. And Sangeeta Puri and Harsh Chopra for collection and compilation of data. We are thankful to Sunil Arora for data processing, Sisham Bala for Library assistance and indexing and Ashwini Kumar for secretarial assistance.

PRAMOD KUMAR
RAINUKA DAGAR

Abbreviations and Acronyms

ASI	Assistant Sub Inspector
BC	Backward Class
CAD	Community Affairs Division
CBI	Central Bureau of Investigation
CEDAW	Convention to Eliminate All Forms of Discrimination Against Women
CH	Culpable Homicide
CHRI	Commonwealth Human Rights Initiative
CJS	Criminal Justice System
CLG	Community Liaison Group
CPRC	Community Policing Resource Centre
CS	Constables
FGD	Focus Group Discussion
FIR	First Information Report
HC	Head Constable
ICT	Information and Communication Technology
IDC	Institute for Development and Communication
IPC	Indian Penal Code
ISO	International Organization for Standardization
IT	Information Technology
NGO	Nongovernmental Organization
NHRC	National Human Rights Commission
NJA	National Judicial Academy
NOC	No Objection Certificate
OECD	Organization for Economic Cooperation and Development
PC-PNDT	Pre-Conception and Pre-natal Diagnostic Techniques Act
PCR	Police Control Room
PIL	Public Interest Litigation
PIS	Punjab Istri Sabha
PSVW	Police Station Visitor Week

SC	Scheduled Caste
SHO	Station House Officer
SI	Sub Inspector
SLL	Special and Local Laws
ST	Scheduled Tribe
TADA	Terrorist and Disruptive Activities Act
UN	United Nations
US	United States
UT	Union Territory
VCR	Video Cassette Recorder
WAN	Wide Area Network

1. Introduction

Safety, security and equitable access to justice are prerequisites for a functional democracy, for generation of material wealth, for reduction of poverty and elimination of social exclusion. It is, therefore, essential to address the fear and risk of crime, improve provisions for the security of individuals and their living environment by creating effective justice institutions and mechanisms that aim at the creation of a crime free society. The focus has to be on prevention of crime and victimisation through a multi-pronged approach that includes improving performance, efficiency, integration of efforts across agencies and the involvement of diverse stakeholders ranging from public service providers to civil society activists.

The UN Guidelines on the Prevention of Crime reinforce the need for a holistic approach with a multi-disciplinary knowledge base and intervention strategy. 'Crime prevention strategies, policies, programmes and actions should be based on a broad, multi-disciplinary foundation of knowledge about crime problems, their multiple causes and promising and proven practices'.[1] This broad mandate requires multiple and multi-staged efforts through an appropriate institutional framework and strategic approach.

To begin with, a systematic mapping of the criminal justice system leading to the development of an index shall help in setting clear priorities, linkages and indicators for crime prevention.

This instrument, in turn, shall provide a framework to strengthen the delivery of justice. It uses an inclusive approach and links local cultural needs of justice with global standards of

[1]United Nations, Economic and Social Council, 2002, *Guidelines for the Prevention of Crime*, New York: United Nations, Economic and Social Council, Office for Drug Control and Crime Prevention.

human rights. It can also be used to assess, improve and monitor the efficiency and accessibility of justice and the physical security of citizens. It highlights democratic alternative mechanisms that have been institutionalised in the justice sector incorporating interventions outside the conventional legal system. The instrument maps the delivery of justice in the formal criminal justice system and identifies the informal mechanisms wherever relevant.

PERSPECTIVE OF THIS INSTRUMENT

This document has been prepared with the following boundary conditions:

1. INTEGRATED JUSTICE DELIVERY SYSTEM

The criminal justice system is viewed holistically.[2] The institutions of police, courts and prisons are taken as part of the system performing specialised functions. Performance accountability is attributed to specified functions rather than being competitive with each other. Coordination mechanisms within agencies have been given recognition for effective networking. To rate the performance of agencies in a segregated manner would, in effect, isolate the institutions from the system and limit its relevance to a contextual analysis. The delivery of justice is viewed as more than a sum of each individual institution's performance. Separating an institution for scrutiny or allowing single agency initiatives to lead, strengthens one institution, but weakens the system and propels the agencies towards contention with one another.

[2]The police and prisons, together with courts, and now called the criminal justice system, an expression which was only invented in the second half of the twentieth century.

Graeme Newman and Gregory J. Howard, 1999, 'Introduction: Data Sources and Their Use', in Graeme Newman (ed.), *Global Report on Crime and Justice*, New York: Oxford University Press for United Nations; Office for Drug Control and Crime Prevention, Centre for International Crime Prevention, pp. 1-11.

2. MULTI-CULTURAL APPROACH

Access to justice is an integral component of a fair justice delivery system. The extent to which the system mainstreams the rights of the vulnerable groups is gauged with each available measurement indicator. In particular, it maps the policy initiative of specific needs: in representation of various groups and, more qualitatively, the extent to which the policy is implemented and integrated with all spheres of institutional functioning. The extent to which the staff at the point of service delivery are implementing this directive; collection of disaggregate data pertaining to various groups and its reflection in documents; resource allocation according to the needs of the groups and if a monitoring system is in place to regulate the policy imperatives are discussed.

3. BRIDGING THE LOCAL WITH THE GLOBAL

Human rights enshrined in the United Nations are the established standards taken as a point of reference to measure the delivery of justice. The international standards, however, have to be related to a cultural context to provide meaningful justice. For instance, issues pertaining to gender, the Scheduled Castes, collectivity rights or the relevance of traditional systems may not be enstated in the international human rights, but in this document human rights are analysed in accordance with local considerations. However, while attempting this, it is necessary to draw a line between local considerations and localism.

Local experiences remain crucial in identifying needs and generating tailored programmes, which correspond to the distinctive characteristics of a given locality. However, a sensitivity to local socio-economic contexts and a recognition of a need for greater local autonomy should not hand a *carte blanche* to 'localism'. Decentralised local autonomy, which encourages bottom-up approaches to policy making needs to be bounded by principled and normative constraints of social, rather than local, justice.[3]

[3]Adam Crawford, 1999, *Local Governance of Crime: Appeals to Community and Partnership*, New York: Oxford University Press, p. 289.

It is in this context, the global standards have to act as normative filters for local needs for delivery of justice.

BOX 1.1: BRIDGING FORMAL RULES WITH SOCIAL NORMS

Institutions are 'the rules of the game in society or more formally, humanly devised constraints that shape human interactions. In consequence, they structure incentives in human exchange, whether political, social or economic.'[4] The application of *formal rules* and *procedures* in a context of divergent, different and pragmatic informal conventions and norms tend to produce *outputs* and *outcomes*, which are in contradiction with formal rules.[5] In another sense, at the implementation and cutting edge level the 'powerful interest groups, asymmetry of information, perverse incentives and high transaction costs' produce distortions in the delivery of justice. The importance of institutionalised rules and procedures varies from one cultural context to another. This variation needs to be captured to overcome the distortions and to harmonise cultural sensitive needs.

4. SUPPORTIVE DEMOCRATIC SYSTEMS OF JUSTICE

This document includes mapping of alternative mechanisms of justice delivery. These can be informal mechanisms or part of the formal justice procedures such as statutory bodies like the human rights commissions or the lok adalats. These institutions may perform parallel functions to the formal sector (lok adalats, family courts), or provide supportive functions (riot control programmes) or undertake the role of oversights. In particular, these pertain to functions performed outside the internal mechanisms undertaken by each sector of the criminal justice system. It includes external oversights of the state (legislature) and civilian oversights such as the human rights commission,

[4]Douglas C. North, 1990, *Institutions, Institutional Change and Economic Performance*, Cambridge: Cambridge University Press, p. 3.

[5]Yet because law and criminal justice remain expressions of the society in which they operate, subtle shifts in the logic and operation of social control are both emergent and inevitable. Identifying their symptoms and thinking through their implications will be the task at the centre of criminological agenda, both theoretical and applied, over the next few years.

Philip Smith and Kristin Natalier, 2005, *Understanding Criminal Justice: Sociological Perspective*, London: Sage Publications, p. 206.

women's commission, NGO forums and other socially codified procedures for justice delivery, accountability and transparency. A relevant issue is, are these oversights operating in a strong or weak internal system of justice delivery?

5. TREND REVIEW

This mapping is aimed at evolving a trend review of justice delivery by presenting a methodology for an index that ranks the performance of the criminal justice system on different aspects of justice demarcated for the states and union territories of India. While the index is based on quantitative measures, qualitative insights are used to raise vital issues of justice and provide a filter through which the index can be understood.

HOW THE INSTRUMENT IS ORGANISED

This instrument has four sections—the first deals with the aim, the broad parameters of analysis and cautions pertaining to the use of this methodology.

The second section deals with justice, reach and effectivity. The product indicators include both those of process and impact. As mapped here, the formal criminal justice system consisting of the police, courts and prisons has been addressed in terms of equal access to justice, crime data, performance measurement, responsiveness to the needs of the people on the margins and the rights of collectivities. In particular, the three sections include:

1. Accessibility and efficiency of criminal justice system
2. Level of physical security enjoyed by the citizens
3. Rights of populations affected by crime
    - Accused
    - Vulnerable groups

A number of issues highlighting the challenges faced in the application of the rule of law have been highlighted through qualitative narratives, micro survey findings, case studies and ethnographic analysis.

The third section attempts to capture the 'investment in safety' level indicators. Two aspects are dealt with here that pertain to:

1. commitment to justice, and
2. institutional alternatives to the orthodox criminal justice system.

As a legacy of the British colonial power, the criminal justice system was tuned to the enforcement of the policies of the rulers. The shift towards service delivery to the citizens of the country with their stakes in safety and peace is now the focus. But a number of changes in the perspective, mechanisms and protocols need to be brought about. This section attempts to address both the commitment and the potential available to revamp the criminal justice system towards this end.

The last section provides an index to the above five broad categories measured through a number of indicators. A standard score is computed applying a T score to allow each indicator to be summed with the others. This section is supported by data in Annexures arranged in accordance to the five dimensions used to classify the delivery of justice which are:

- Accessibility and efficiency of the criminal justice system
- Level of physical security enjoyed by the citizens
- Rights of populations affected by crime
- Commitment to justice
- Institutional alternatives

Aim of the Instrument

The instrument is aimed at policy makers, particularly in the context of inter-sectoral reforms underway in India with multilateral recognition of civil societies and criminal justice establishments. An assessment of the efficacy of the criminal justice system, its accountability and transparency, the distribution of security resources and their impact on security can be made on the basis of this index.

It can also be used by sectoral establishments as a performance management tool. It is a relevant instrument for replicability and is useful to interest groups. For instance, gender or civil society rights activists can identify the extent of resources, policy provisions and gauge the impact on gender or other vulnerable groups.

The index can be used in its totality to identify gaps in performance, variations in the delivery to different groups, co-ordination, etc. It can also be used themewise for purposes, such as specific states placement within the Indian spectrum or sectoral challenges.

Limitations of the Instrument: A Beginning

The approach recognises a number of cautions in the use of this instrument. Largely, these pertain to the methodology and issues that a quantitative analysis cannot capture. Also in terms of quantitative weightage each indicator has been taken as of equal relevance. Weightage may be given to contextual variations as and when captured.

PROBLEMS OF MEASUREMENT

Incorporating Qualitative and Quantitative Methodologies

Numerical data only exist for quantitative indicators in the context of the incidence of crime. Qualitative data, such as perceptions of security and safety in different groups, the context for non-reporting of crime and violations of the rights of collectivities do not find representation in the index.

Qualitative data reflect concepts that are yet being defined and conceptualised. These are exploratory in terms of codification of the issues into measurable means. Thus concerns that are evolving or have yet to be operationalised in terms of measurement are captured through qualitative techniques. The stigma to report a crime, the invisibility to perceive violence with brutality as the indicator of felt violation are common to people placed on the margins, particularly women and the Scheduled Castes. Availability of infrastructure and services may not be an indicator of accessibility for these populations.

Importantly, a qualitative analysis cannot be traded with quantitative measures in the realm of assumptions. Qualitative data are culture and local specific and standardisation both absolves their content and is limited in its capacity to reflect variations. For instance, in certain martial societies of South Asia it is considered manly to be an accused in murder cases; the police is perceived as a male bastion, an exclusive arena for representation of upper caste men—thus crime reporting, social support and staff diversity may be affected by non-typical issues. Delivery of services and policy making need to take these specificities into consideration to be effective and seen to be just.

BOX 1.2: METHODOLOGY AND DATA: WHAT IS USEFUL

Methodology and data that is simple to deploy, replicate and comprehend have wider applicability. Some considerations are listed here:

- *Policy relevant:* Data should be relevant for use in policy initiatives and change
- *Measures progress towards the target*: A performance management tool
- *Data* are available, cost effective and routinely collected
- *Disaggregate and standardised:* Data categories that are standardised by breaking down to sub-categories to reflect disaggregates is more reflective of multicultural contexts
- *Comprehensible to stakeholders:* A tool to help different interest groups make informed decisions
- Reflective of cultural concepts and variations
- Ability to incorporate change and range
- Can record good practices, civil society mobilisations, effective programmes
- Is interactive and inclusive

Standardisation of Data

Another associated caution pertains to the use of standardised[6] categories for data classification. Established nomenclature recognises activities in a given context and their replication in contexts not adjusted to cultural specificities provides a changed

[6]'Standardisation is the process of reaching agreement on common data definitions, formats, representation and structures of all data layers and elements.' OECD, *Glossary of Statistical Terms*, http://stats.OECD.org/glossary/search.asp

meaning to the operationalisation of the concept. For instance, dacoity in India is defined as 'five or more persons who co-jointly commit or attempt to commit a robbery'. In central tribal districts where barter exchange continues, giving primacy to commodities, the level of economic development continues to be basic and in tribal custom activities are co-jointly performed. Even the stealing of a chicken, if it involves five or more than five persons gets classified under dacoity with corresponding policing and punishment, which is more severe in its penalisation than the act warrants.

Also, standardised categories for data classification have traditionally been along administrative divisions for compilation and mapping. In India data are collected according to administrative or revenue boundaries of the state, district or tehsil. These are only descriptive categories and cannot be interchanged with analytical categories—for instance, female foeticide has been declared as most rampant in a particular district in the country and all programmes to combat it find their genesis in that district—labelling Fatehgarh Sahib, a district in Punjab, with the lowest sex ratio in the country as most detrimental to female births, or its classification as an urban phenomenon, or concentrated in certain states absolving other areas from the same strictures in issues of female survival.

Aggregate Analysis

The use of aggregate[7] data indicators such as crime per capita or per lakh population blur the distinctions and are unable to represent a realistic analysis on injustice particularly in the context of India where the polity is highly divisive in terms of context (conflict/post-conflict, rural/urban), cultural groups and the extreme range that exists cannot guide policy in accordance with the needs of the populations. Where numbers and data classification allow a disaggregate analysis, it has been included.

[7]An aggregate is a sum of individual characteristics, experiences, or behaviours that is used to reflect a collective phenomenon for an entire population.

David Jary and Jilia Jary, 1991, *Collins Dictionary of Sociology*, London: Harper Collins, p. 11.

For instance, representation in staffing, crime against women, the Scheduled Castes, or crime against body, property, etc. However, this disaggregation is not 'standardised'. For instance, representation of staff may be undertaken in one institution (police) and not in another (courts).

Outputs and Outcomes

The OECD[8] defines outputs as the goods and services produced and outcomes are the impacts of the delivery of outputs on social, economic and other indicators. In India, the existing crime data only measures outputs in terms of crime processing, such as rates of disposal, chargesheeting, conviction, recovery of stolen goods, time taken in trial, etc., and does not measure outcomes in terms of improved security or perceptions of safety. It records the amount or the number of services available, but not their distribution in terms of needs of the citizens. Given this limitation, this document takes crime rates as a proxy for safety along with commitment to justice and labels these as 'outcomes'.

Primacy of Volume versus *the form of Injustice*

The extent of crime is a parameter of performance and does not reflect upon the nature of crime or its prevention. If low crime rates are recorded, can it be said that the state is performing well?[9] The recording of even one *sati* death is a reflection of social brutality and inequality (that allows a widow to burn in the funeral pyre of her husband) as is the existence of one communal riot, which reflects the existence of communal divides within society. Policy directions need to address issues for a crime-

[8]OECD, op. cit.

[9]Do the police detect problems that are important to most members of the community? And do the problems the police handle decline in magnitude or seriousness as a result? If the police do not detect important problems, then they cannot address them. But even if they address them, they may not reduce the harmful effects of the problems.

John E. Eck and Dennis P. Rosenbaum, 1994, 'New Police Order: Effectiveness, Equity, and Efficiency in Community Policing', in Dennis P. Rosenbaum (ed.), *Challenge of Community Policing*, Thousand Oaks: Sage Publications, p. 10.

free society rather than only focus on crime control, which involves a reduction in the volume of crime and does not address the existence of different forms of crime.

Issues of Mainstreaming

Data availability by disaggregate categories do not automatically mean that the analysis and incorporation of data has taken into account the inequalities and differences that exist in the disaggregate categories. Gender violence or crime against migrants have to be analysed in the backdrop of gender relations or assertions of 'Sons of Soil movements'. These continue to represent challenges.

NORMATIVE FILTERS

Data recording

The recording of crime data is based on social norms that may or may not classify a particular act as a crime. Also social norms may not allow a felt injustice to be processed and viewed publicly. Thus, registered crime is not always a measure of the extent of crime in society. 'Even if we adopt an orthodox position on statistics, the best that can be said of official crime statistics is that they do not measure the true extent of crime in society, but rather the extent of reported and recorded crime. Although most academic analysts, the media, politicians and the public rely on official statistics as "hard facts", the first and most paramount "fact" is that they are both partial and subjectively constructed.'[10] The recording of crime is not always a measure of the extent of crime in society. Victimology surveys can help to provide a more realistic picture.

Selection of Resolution Mechanisms

The selection of an agency for the delivery of justice may depend on the desirability of an outcome. For instance, informal justice

[10]John Muncie, 2001, 'The Construction and Deconstruction of Crime', in John Muncie and Eugene McLaughlin (eds.), *The Problem of Crime*, Thousand Oaks: Sage Publications, p. 25.

mechanisms may be approached by sections of society that are part of the informal systems themselves. Jat Sikh peasants may approach the panchayat, whereas the Scheduled Castes may approach the formal state police. Agency selection by complainant may also be done with a view to overwhelm (local bodies) or increase the cost to be borne (formal sector procedures) by the competing party and taking justice outside their scope. Thus meeting the expense of courts and police may automatically select certain sections who can approach the system and therefore, have a more viable outcome. Women may prefer a compromise since they may be challenged in financial capacity and social support to continue with procedures of the formal system.

Level and Nature of People's Participation

Participation of the community may be ad hoc and information may be shared without any opportunity to influence decision making processes. The foremost purpose is to make the delivery of criminal justice democratic. To assess this aspect it is necessary to capture the level, the nature and the extent of participation of communities. Accordingly, gaps identified can be targeted, for participation levels that will certainly influence in building the stakes of the community and 'communities of interest' for crime prevention. A stakeholder is defined as any individual, community, group or organisation with an interest in the outcome of an activity either as a result of being affected by it positively or negatively, or by being able to influence the activity in a positive or negative way.[11] At another level, the nature of participation may act as a proxy indicator particularly to assess the position of marginalised groups on issues relating to discrimination, oppression, alienation, etc.

[11] *Guidance on Local Safety Audits: Compendium of International Practice*, Paris: European Forum for Urban Safety (EFUS), 2007. www.urbansecurity.org/fileadmin/efus/secutopics/efus_safety_Audit_e_web.pdf

BOX 1.3: MAKING DELIVERY OF CRIMINAL JUSTICE DEMOCRATIC: ENGAGING STAKEHOLDERS		
Levels	Activity	Who all
I. Awareness generation	• Informing	All citizens
II. Sensitisation		
• Participatory		
• Co-opting (selective)	• Involving	Interest groups
	• Seeking inputs	
III. Capacity building		
• Training		
• Networking		
• Activating forums/ interest groups	• Delegating	
	• Influencing	Stakeholders
	• Selection of priorities	
	• Collaborating	
IV. Institutionalising	• Monitoring	Office-bearers
	• Accountability of stakeholders	

A Composite Overview

An index is a composite picturisation of a spectrum of indicators. It is a potent tool to provide contextual insights for prioritisation of tasks and activities corresponding to the allocation of resources. It also reveals the level of operation of the democratic process captured through the nature of participation of 'community and communities of interests'. It also builds sensitivities towards local cultural specificities and problems faced by the marginalised groups. It can act as a pointer for reprioritisation of crime prevention activities and opportunities to build a crime-free society.

> BOX 1.4: WHY AN INDEX
>
> - Can link dichotomous indicators with proportion and rates: Allows a comprehensive picture to unfold
> - Easy to deploy: Stakeholders, advocacy groups, policy specialists can comprehend the larger picture without a spreadout report
> - Identifies relevance of specific indicators for which data management and analysis can be focused upon

- A robust index can provide generalisations with an inclusive representation of local cultural specificities
- Can record progress and change in one measure itself
- Can check conflicting utilisation and mobilisation of resources (are efficiency and resources linked to crime prevention)
- Can locate opportunities and reprioritise objectives: Local community issues, contextual needs and risks/challenge areas can be refocused comprehensively (is there variation according to population—density, culture, festivals, location, crime type, etc.)

In a nutshell, the relevance of a composite index in the new era has multiplied. There is a reinforced need to use this index to restore the delicate functional balance between the judiciary, the police, correctional administration and civilian oversights. No doubt, the development of an index poses conceptual and methodological challenges, but at the same time, it has an ingrained potential to locate opportunities and reprioritise goals.

2. Justice: Reach and Effectivity

The state's instrumentality to safeguard the being and material interests of its citizens and people under its jurisdiction are addressed under this section. The criminal justice system has been mapped on three broad categories in terms of its *reach* and *effectivity:*

(i) accessibility and efficiency;
(ii) level of physical security enjoyed by the citizens; and
(iii) the rights of populations affected by crime, namely the accused and the victims.

Under the accessibility and efficiency issues, the capacity of the criminal justice system to discharge justice in an able and effective manner are captured. In other words, the process indicators to provide fair and effective justice are mapped and include resources and operational efficiency. Under the level of physical security enjoyed by the citizens, the safety of the population is measured through prevalence of crime and differentials in rates of total chargesheeting and convictions for vulnerable population groups. This set of indicators captures the impact of specific nature of crimes and deals with the level of crime in different sections of the population. In the third category, the rights of the populations affected by crime have been gauged to test the efficacy of justice for those in the most vulnerable conditions. These are divided into rights of the accused and the victims.

I. Accessibility to and Efficiency of the Criminal Justice System

This indicator measures the capacity of the criminal justice system to make available the necessary resources and services to avail fair treatment by law. Inputs and activities have been treated separately. Existing outlays in terms of staff, material resources and finances are captured under access to justice. Functioning capacity of the institutions is identified under efficiency levels. Time taken to dispose of crime cases falls under this purview. The instrument recognises that the availability of justice mechanisms may not be sufficient to provide accessibility to legal remedies. Social placement and norms influence the access to and use of infrastructure and services. Also, the cultural context can have an impact on the meaning and utilisation of the services. Efficiency measures the extent to which reported crime has been processed and justice delivered across different types of crime. It also captures disaggregate data for different types of crime. Operational effectivity is measured by chargesheeting rates, conviction rates, disposal rates, recovery of stolen goods and time spent in courts. These rates, where available are disaggregated for the five types of crimes listed and for population groups of women, children, Scheduled Castes/Scheduled Tribes. These are treated as impact variables under physical security of the citizens.

BOX 2.1: DISAGGREGATE CRIME CATEGORIES

Types of crime	Crime against vulnerable groups
Crime against body Crime against property Crime against public order Economic crimes Special local laws, which include particularly narcotics, arms and terrorist activities	Crime against women Crime against children Crime against Scheduled Castes and Scheduled Tribes (aggregated from all crime)

ACCESSIBILITY TO THE CRIMINAL JUSTICE SYSTEM

The deployed input pertaining to staff, material and finances and disaggregated in accordance with multi-cultural needs and local cultural specificities is listed under this parameter. It must be noted that all quantified data on all variables are not available. The index includes only variables on which data are documented. The other variables are discussed qualitatively.

BOX 2.2: LIST OF ACCESS INDICATORS

- Police infrastructure
  - Human resources
    - Staff density (area and population wise)
      - Number of policemen per 100 sq. km.
      - Number of policemen per 100,000 population
    - Staff diversity as representative of population groups
      - Representative percentage of SCs
      - Representative percentage of STs
      - Representative percentage of women
      - Representative percentage of minorities (Muslims)
  - Infrastructure resources
    - Budget/expenditure
      - Police expenditure (Rupees in crore) @ per lakh of population
    - Existing building
    - Existing equipment
  - Systems of management
    - Monitoring systems
    - Data management
    - Coordination with courts
    - Coordination with prisons
    - Networking
- Court infrastructure
  - Human resources
    - Staff density (area/population wise)
      - Number of high court judges per lakh population
      - Number of district court judges per lakh population
      - Number of judges per 100,000 population

    Other Staff
    - Staff diversity: As representative of population groups
    - Judges
      - Representative percentage of Women
      - Representative percentage of SCs
      - Representative percentage of STs
      - Representative percentage of Minorities
  - Infrastructure resources
    - Budget/expenditure
      - Court expenditure per lakh of population
      - Existing buildings
      - Existing equipment
  - Systems of management
    - Monitoring systems

- Data management
- Coordination with prisons
- Networking

- Prison infrastructure
  - o Human resources
    - Staff provisions
      - Number of jail staff per 100 inmates
    - Staff diversity: As representative of population groups
      - Percentage representation of women in jail staff
    - Infrastructural resources
      - Budget / expenditure on prisons per lakh population
  - o Systems of management
    - Monitoring systems
    - Data management
    - Networking

Capacity of Criminal Justice System to Discharge Justice

The wherewithal of the state to provide justice processes is measured under three capacities—human resources, infrastructural resources and systems of management.

❑ *Human Resources*

This parameter reflects the density of staff of the criminal justice system demarcated in the three institutions of police, courts and prisons to deal with crime. Both the number of staff per lakh population and areawise per sq. km. are presented. The capacity of the staff to provide the relevant services in terms of their training, education, motivation levels is supplemented through sample profiling and surveys. Additionally, policy initiatives for special needs have been listed through qualitative and detailed studies.

BOX 2.3: GOOD PRACTICES IN SERVICE DELIVERY

The following practices have been listed as useful in victimisation surveys conducted:

- *Awareness of and ready availability of services:* Visibility of services provided, awareness regarding rights of citizens, information on procedures, step-by-step guidance for availing services, lodging reports.
- *Programmes that promote community/police/legal aid interface:*

Regular contact with public, established networks of communication.

- *Transparency in functioning:* Information on processes, follow-up and contact points.
- *Integration of services:* Single point of delivery.
- *Collaboration of formal-informal mechanisms:* Traditional and customary services and state systems to be complimentary.
- *Responsive points of delivery:* Point of public interface to be interactive, receptive and efficient in dealing with complaints/services.
- *Population tailored and context-specific services:* Rural committees have different requirements as compared to the state-of-the-art functioning in the metropolis; SCs, women, migrants require friendly response, language support and assured privacy.

Staff competencies: Expectations of Citizens

From Police	
• Exemplary conduct	Disciplined, polite and non-hierarchical.
• No harmful action towards public	Should not take law in their own hands, no rash decisions.
• Non-discriminatory	Especially towards women, poorer sections or scheduled tribes.
• Honest	Non-corrupt.
• Vigilant	Ability to respond quickly in emergencies.
• Functions in accordance with law	Neutral and just in all situations, particular care during conflict and post-conflict situations.
From Courts	
• Deliver just verdict	Non-corrupt, not to be swayed by partisan politics at consideration and impartial in their conduct.
• Quick judgment	Delays should be avoided.
• Collaboration with higher authorities	In times of conflict especially, courts should be in tune with the larger priorities and aims of the constitution and priorities of the state.

Source: IDC Field Survey, 2006.

❑ *Infrastructural Resources*

Resource allocation in terms of a monetary budget and buildings and equipment to perform the necessary functions falls under this head. The index only includes financial outlays. A sample of infrastructural facilities required for efficient functioning has been included from the courts as prepared by the National Judicial Infrastructure Plan.

BOX 2.4: CURRENT STATUS OF JUDICIAL INFRASTRUCTURE IN INDIA[1]

A. *Number of Courts*

While district and subordinate courts are estimated to be located in 2066 towns, the number of court complexes in India is estimated at 2,500 (National Policy Plan and Action Plan for Implementation of ICT in the Indian Judiciary, August 2005, page 82) and the total number of courts at 12,323. Indian courts handle a case load of some 29 million (2.9 crores) cases. Some 20 million (2 crore) new cases are filed annually and some 19 million (1.9 crore) cases are disposed of annually. The bulk of this case load is at the local magistrate/civil judge court level. Although this is the level where the public has the maximum interface with the judiciary, this is also the level at which the judicial infrastructure is the weakest.

Details of court complexes with number of courts
For the District and Subordinate Judiciary
(*Source*: E-Committee Report, 2005)

Towns having...	Number of court complexes	Total number of courts
One court complex	750	750
Two court complexes	349	698
Three court complexes	210	630
Four court complexes	127	508
Five court complexes	61	305
Six court complexes	65	390
Seven court complexes	53	371
Eight court complexes	62	496
Nine court complexes	37	333
Ten court complexes	39	390

[1]*National Judicial Infrastructure Plan: Draft*, 10 November 2006, p. 9, www.supremecourtofindia.nic.in/NJIP.doc

Eleven court complexes	32	352
Twelve court complexes	33	396
=		=
Sixty-one court complexes	1	61
Sixty-six court complexes	1	66
Sixty-seven court complexes	1	67
Seventy-five court complexes	2	150
Seventy-eight court complexes	1	78
Eighty-three court complexes	1	83
One hundred three court complexes	1	103
One hundred four court complexes	1	104
One hundred nine court complexes	1	109
One hundred sixty-seven court complexes	1	167
Total	2066	12323

A systematic survey of the current status of judicial infrastructure is not available. It is well known, however, that the status of judicial infrastructure is in a state of acute crisis in a large number of courts. Many subordinate courts are working in crumbling buildings with sub-standard facilities for all participants in justice delivery—justice seekers, judges, lawyers, court staff, staff of lawyers and the public.

State of Judicial Infrastructure –
B. High Courts
(January 2005, based on information available to NJA)
A sample of the proposed infrastructure

High Court	Physical Infrastructure (Buildings & Equipment)	ICT and Document Management Systems	Human Resource and Staffing Pattern	Relevant Budget Head and Revenue Estimates
Andhra Pradesh	*Proposed:* - For construction activities, Government placing funds at the disposal of the High	There are 290 computers and 300 thin-clients and 15 servers in the High Court. The residences and chambers of the Justices are	The total sanctioned strength of the Judges of the High Court is 39, including Additional Judges.	Average Court Fee collected would be Rs. 47 crore per annum, including the subordinate Courts.

High Court	Physical Infrastructure (Buildings & Equipment)	ICT and Document Management Systems	Human Resource and Staffing Pattern	Relevant Budget Head and Revenue Estimates
	Court that can get the work done directly would reduce costs and improve standards. Presently, the Public Works Department undertakes the activities. - Fuel costs (of up to 200 litres each month) and regular maintenance of vehicles for officers transport is proving to be too costly. Sharing of vehicles; fuel allowance to personal vehicles – could be explored as feasible options.	provided with computers and are also provided with Laptops. All the Court Masters and senior officers, apart from typists are provided with computers. The Daily Cause List is being generated on computers and the Cause List is being placed on the net through two servers. Similarly, the orders/ judgments pronounced by the High Court are placed on the web. *Proposed:* Now computer information kiosks are working in the High Court. However, for providing more accessibility such Kiosks can be established at important places like the Secretariat & Collectorate, where even general public and govt. departments can have access	On the administrative side, the Registrar General heads a Registry of 34 Officers. The Registry is assisted by Officers consisting of Court Masters (senior stenographers); Court Officers and Section Officers. 6000 advocates are practising in the High Court. *Proposed:* - More ICT trained Staff	*Proposed:* - Post-expenditure audit should be undertaken

		and also at main railway stations, main bus stations, etc. Further, kiosks should also be in all district courts too. The cost of connecting all the courts on WAN (Wide Area Network) is to be examined.	
Bombay	*Proposed:* Steps for juvenile justice courts in every district. Every district shall have a family court.	*Proposed:* Steps will be taken to publish a 'Year Book' every year giving performance report of subordinate court judges, and particulars about pendency of cases, rate of disposal and steps taken by the High Court for court management.	

Source: National Judicial Infrastructure Plan: Draft, 10 November 2006, www.supremecourtofindia.nic.in/NJIP.doc

❑ *Systems of Management*

A third layer of capacity building pertains to the creation of systems of management such as performance management, data systems, coordinating structures and networking procedures. While coordination refers to inter and intra-agency interface, networking would be with other states and statutory bodies such as oversights, traditional systems, etc. Quantitatively this parameter has not been included due to data constraints. However an overview of systems as evolved by Punjab State Community Police Resource Centres (a police outreach programme) is included as an illustration.

BOX 2.5: MONITORING INDICATORS COMMUNITY POLICING RESOURCE CENTRE

	Administrative	*Brand Image*	*Services*	*Material Resources*	*Capacity Building*
• **Committee related (district, sub-divisional, police station/thana level)**					
• Formation of committee	•				
• Representative selection of non-official members	•				
• Frequency of meetings	•				
• Registration of CPRCs	•				
• Guidelines for running CPRCs to be passed by the committee	•				
• Information of decisions of the committee to be passed to the next level committee	•				
• Examination of proposals for new schemes by the committee	•		•		
• **Spatial factors**					
• Is CPRC a separate entity from the police station?	•	•			
• Accessibility from the major road			•		
• Ambience: cheerful and appealing		•	•		
• **Services provided by CPRCs**					
• Children library-cum-reading room	•		•		
• Victim Assistance Unit	•		•		
• Community-service-cum-information centre	•		•		
• Grievance redress unit	•		•		
• Economic offence cell	•				
• Traffic management			•		
• Coordination among units	•				•
• Networking with other government departments	•				
• Social security and women and child development	•				
• Rural development and panchayats	•				
• Welfare of SC/BC	•				
• District headquarters	•				
• Computerisation in CPRCs	•				•
• Software available for CPRCs	•				•

	Administrative	Brand Image	Services	Material Resources	Capacity Building
• **Physical resource management**					
• Communication facilities	•		•		
• Separate line for CPRC	•		•		
• Women hotline	•		•		
• Child hotline	•		•		
• Are the women's cell, child line and CPRC number standardised?	•				
• CPRC banner		•			
• CPRC letterhead		•			•
• CPRC logo		•			•
• **Grievance redress unit**					
• Furniture		•		•	
• Handbills for example duties of SHOs, duties of munshis, police contact numbers				•	
• Display information such as women's cell members, list of social welfare organizations				•	
• Procedure for registration of complaints			•		
• Follow-up and mode of grievance redress			•		
• Data bank available with centre			•		
• Feedback from staff regarding improvements and problems faced by them	•				
• Resource materials (reference manuals, books, reports)				•	
• Information materials/posters				•	
• Folder-CPRCs: overview				•	
• **Community service-cum-information centre**					
• Furniture		•		•	
• Computer system				•	
• Telephone				•	
• Display information such as list of travel agents, list of money conversion centres, list of government guest-houses, list of hotels and inns, what is an FIR, citizen's rights in a police station, after being arrested, torture in police custody		•	•	•	

	Administrative	*Brand Image*	*Services*	*Material Resources*	*Capacity Building*
• Information list, e.g., list of public peace committee, list of NGOs, handbills—women rights in police custody			•	•	
• Provision of single window system			•		
• Foreigner's counter			•		
• Verification counter			•		
• Crime counter			•		
• Data bank			•		
• Procedures for management of different counters	•				
• Time taken to Issue NOC/verification certificates, etc.	•				
• Is there a follow-up mechanism?	•				
• Record of services being utilised under each head	•				
• **Victim Assistance Unit**					
• Furniture		•		•	
• First aid kit			•	•	
• Access to ambulance			•	•	
• Display information: List of hospitals and dispensaries		•		•	
• Posters like cognisable crime against women and punishment, violence against women, what is dowry, female foeticide, female infanticide; gender crimes					•
• Folders like do not remain in the dark, what is dowry, rights of the unborn					•
• Professional staff available at victim assistance unit					
• Doctors, psychiatrists, counsellors					
• Specially trained women officers / volunteers					
• NGOs affiliated to the unit					
• Services provided by NGOs/affiliated group regarding relief/rehabilitation of the victim					
• Follow-up mechanism	•				
• **Child unit**					
• Furniture					

	Administrative	Brand Image	Services	Material Resources	Capacity Building
• Television & VCR					
• Recording procedure for help line					
• Child protection kit			•		•
• Special training of police/volunteers					•
• **Professional capacities**					
• Manpower management					
• Number of personnel posted in CPRC	•				
• Stability of tenure yet regular rotations	•				
• Knowledge of CPRC functions and community policing among staff					•
• Training					
• Training of senior officials by IDC					•
• Training of rank and file by Phillaur					•
• Knowledge and skills regarding services available					•
• Awareness regarding human rights					•
• Awareness regarding rights before and after arrest					•
• Gender sensitised					•
• Awareness regarding child rights					•
• **Community mobilisation**					
• Networking among community support structures	•				•
• Number of organisations affiliated to CPRCs (such as NGOs, volunteers, panchayats, mahila mandals, youth clubs	•				•
• Number of awareness camps regarding CPRC held					•
• Awareness campaign for CPRC					•
• **Funding and budget**					
• Financial resource allocation	•				
• Source of funding	•				
• Innovations undertaken			•		•

A qualitative mapping of resources and performance of some police stations in Haryana is also included to highlight the resource considerations that policy makers may find useful.

BOX 2.6: EVALUATION OF RESOURCES AND PERFORMANCE OF A POLICE STATION IN HARYANA

General Profile of Police Station											
Total Area of Jurisdiction											
Jurisdiction Pattern					Rural Area						
Sanctioned Strength					*Posted Strength*						
Inspector	SI	ASI	HC	Cs	Inspector	SI	ASI	EASI	HC	EHC	Cs
	2	5	4	32		1	6		9		24
Lady Staff					Nil						
Length of Posting											
Equipment					Helmets, Cane Shield, Baton, Body Protector, Tear Gas						
Transport					1 Gipsy, 1 PCR, 7 Motor Cycles						

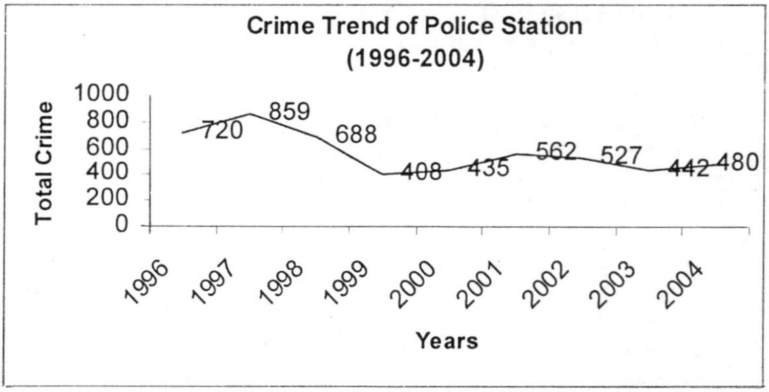

The police station was centrally located and easily approachable, but not easily identifiable. It was inside a ruined fort, though in a newly constructed building but it is sinking because the outer boundary wall, especially the back of the building, is constructed in a ditch.

Just at the entrance of the outer boundary, there was the canteen. Visitors used it as a waiting area. On the other side, the boundary wall of the fort was falling, and there was a narrow escape some time back for a policeman.

This police station bagged a score of 19 out of 50 and stood at the 3rd position.

Performance of Police Station

Approachability	Poor
Ambience	Poor
User friendliness	Average
Humanitarian facilities	Below Average
Staff welfare	Average
Resources management	Average
Modernisation	Below Average
Public dealing	Below Average
Community policing	Poor
Awards or commendations	Poor

All the rooms were properly marked. On the right side of the entrance, there was the lock-up, clean and hygienic. There was no one in the lock-up as an arrested person, so there was nothing on the notice board. Some posters of criminal and missing persons with their photographs were posted on both the right and left side of the wall of the entrance. The separate record room, evidential property room and ammunition room were properly managed.

The staff sat in the verandah and listened to complaints. Recovered and other vehicles were parked away from the building but within the boundary wall. There was a *dargah* of a Muslim *pir*, managed and taken care of by the police personnel, especially the cook (Langri).

There was no public utility service for visitors, or separately for females. Even the toilet and bathroom portion was sinking. So, they had made a separate public utility service and had to go far away for this purpose. Also, these were unhygienic, stinking and unclean.

There was no building map, map of crimes, jurisdiction area, suggestion box or visitor register. A list of important telephone numbers was placed under the glass on the table of the officer-in-charge. On being asked about the station house officer's frequent transfer, as obviously visible on the name board of the in-charges, the team was told, 'Sometimes corruption complaints, political approaches and pressure of criminals is the main reason behind this'.[2]

2. Provisions to Address Multi-cultural Needs

India is a multi-cultural society with different population affiliations to ethnicity, caste, language and culture. Social structures,

[2] *IDC Field Survey on Haryana Police Station Walkthrough*, 2004.

values and norms influence the acceptability and utility of infrastructure and services. Accessibility to these resources needs to reflect group concerns. (Lack of information about certain categories is a curtailing factor in compiling the index). Both the policy and its operationalisation in terms of representation of diversity, sensitisation of staff (training, awareness material) and service delivery in accordance with multi-cultural needs is gauged by qualitative data included here and some pointers for multi-cultural responsiveness.

BOX 2.7: INDICATORS OF MULTI-CULTURAL REFLECTIONS

1. Representation	Is there staff representation in accordance with population groups?
2. Sensitisation of staff	Are the staff trained on rights of minority/ vulnerable groups?
3. Awareness material	Is there any documentation, audio-video material?
4. Documentation of data according to disparate needs	Are data classified in disaggregate indicators – SES, groupwise, etc.?
5. Service delivery in accordance with multi-cultural needs	Are there provisions for use of language, customs, festivals of multi-cultural groups?
6. Inclusive Policy	Is there a comprehensive policy and analysis in accordance with the rights and issues of vulnerable groups?
7. Monitoring	Is there an interactive monitoring system?
8. Analytical inferences	Are disaggregate data and categories analysed in accordance to conceptual considerations for each cultural/group category?

The parameters of service delivery are inclusive rather than exclusive. In other words, the provisions for distinct groups have to be mainstreamed in the existing delivery system.

3. Local Cultural Specificities

Standardised categories can blur distinctions and special needs of disparate population groups. Here regional/local agencies, special laws or provisions to deal with distinct needs are elicited. For instance, certain towns have a historical religious significance; there are tourist zones with distinct needs. Border areas and riot prone sectors also have to be equipped specially. Certain states such as Uttarakhand have rural police stations that are run under local revenue officers and traditionally it is the revenue administration that oversees the police functioning. How far these have been integrated with the formal system while maintaining their traditional significance? This analysis remains in the domain of qualitative inquiry.

THE EFFICIENCY OF THE CRIMINAL JUSTICE SYSTEM

This category deals with the operational aspects of crime control and redressal. Indicators under this head map the extent of crime under the Indian Penal Code (IPC) and the special laws and local laws (SLL) which can be state specific and include amendments to the IPC. Operational functioning such as disposal of cases, chargesheeting rates, conviction rates and time taken to discharge these functions is mapped here.

Operational Functioning

Crime data have been accessed from the National Crime Records Bureau of the Home Ministry. This is annually published in the document—*Crime in India*. A major focus in the index pertains to crime rate and its processing. The speed of disposal of cases and extent of convictions are indicators used to rate the efficacy of the justice system. An overview of the categories used is presented.

The rates of disposal, chargesheeting and conviction have been included for all crime in totality. While crimes are classified under five categories of crime against body, property, public order, economic crime and special local laws that include crime related to narcotics and terrorism. Chargesheeting and conviction rates are only available for each type of crime (homicide, kidnapping, narcotics) and not for sub-categories. A range of crime within each section can be gathered and against these crimes chargesheeting and conviction rates can be computed as required. However, for this edition of the index, operational efficiency is not measured disaggregated by the nature of crime since this needs to be computed. But data disaggregated by groups is computed and used as an impact. For example, chargesheeting/ conviction rates for SC/ST, women and children. This is reflected as the differential rate of performance for vulnerable groups under the category of physical security of citizens.

Disposal Rate

The total number of cases investigated by the police is referred to as the disposal rate of the police and the total number of cases tried by the courts in a year refers to the disposal rate of the courts.

Chargesheeting

Chargesheeting cases refer to such cases where charges are filed by the police and fall under the final report. Reports cancelled due to withdrawal by the complainant or where evidence is lacking fall under the category of Case Fault or Untraced Reports. Only the final report is chargesheeted by the police.

Conviction Rates

This reflects the ratio of cases convicted to the total number of cases tried by courts in a year.

Recovery Rate

The stolen property that is recovered by the police against the total reported stolen property is measured under recovery rate.

BOX 2.8: LIST OF INDICATORS FOR EFFICIENCY OF THE CRIMINAL JUSTICE SYSTEM

- Police Function
  - Clearance/ Disposal rate of cases by Police
    - IPC
    - SLL
  - Recovery rate of stolen property
  - Chargesheeting rate of cases by the Police
    - IPC crimes
    - SLL crimes
    - Chargesheeting rate of crimes against body

- Crime Against Body
  - Homicide per 100,000 population (murder)
  - Serious assault per 100,000 population (attempt to murder)
  - Culpable homicide not amounting to murder
  - Kidnapping and abduction per 100,000
  - Hurt
  - Causing death by negligence
- Crime Against Property
  - Dacoity
  - Preparation and assembly for dacoity
  - Robbery
  - Burglary
  - Theft
- Crime Against Public Order
  - Riots
  - Arson
- Economic crimes
  - Criminal Breach of Trust
  - Cheating
  - Counterfeiting
- Cognisable crime against Special Local Laws
  - Rate of Total Cognisable Crimes SLL per 100,000 Population
  - Percentage change in SLL crime in 2005
  - Arms Act per 100,000 population
  - Narcotics and drugs offences per 100,000
  - Explosives and Explosive Substances Act per 100,000 population
  - Terrorist and Disruptive Activities Act per 100,000 population

- Court functions
  - Disposal rate of cases by courts for
    - IPC
    - SLL
  - Conviction rate of cases by courts
    - Conviction rate of IPC
    - Conviction rate of SLL
      - Crime against body
        - Homicide per 100,000 population (murder)
        - Serious assault per 100,000 population (attempt to murder)
        - Culpable homicide not amounting to murder

        - Kidnapping and abduction per 100,000 crime
        - Hurt
        - Causing death by negligence
    - Crime Against Property
        - Dacoity
        - Preparation and assembly for dacoity
        - Robbery
        - Burglary
        - Theft
    - Crime against public order
        - Riots
        - Arson
    - Economic crimes
        - Criminal breach of trust
        - Cheating
        - Counterfeiting
    - Cognizable crime against special local laws
        - Rate of total cognizable crimes SLL per 100,000 population
        - Percentage change in SLL crime in 2005
        - Arms Act per 100,000 population
        - Narcotics and drugs offences per 100,000 population
        - Explosives and Explosive Substance Act. per 100,000 population
        - Terrorist and Disruptive Activities Act per 100,000 population
- Average time taken for trial of cases in all courts (in years)
- Average time taken for undertrials in prison (in months)

Note: For computing the index total IPC and SLL crimes are used for disposal, chargesheeting and conviction rates. Specific crimes are mentioned under sub-heads to allow for user particular computations. The specific crimes have also been used to present a disaggregate analysis, where required. Under SLL only a few selected crimes are mentioned here.

BOX 2.9: ACCESSIBILITY AND EFFICIENCY OF POLICE STATIONS: AN INITIATIVE

Police Station Visitors Week (PSVW) :
A community assessment of police stations

In 2006, the Altus Global Alliance working across continents and from a multi-cultural perspective to improve safety and justice initiated a project in which local residents from 23 countries visited their local police stations. The aim was to assess the quality of services delivered in the participating police stations, to identify some of the best practices in use by the police and to strengthen the accountability of the police to the local community. The visitors provided a feedback on five categories of assessment. These categories fall in the domain of the process outlays, the police as an institution of the criminal justice system provided to the population in its jurisdiction. These five indicators were:

(i) *Community orientation:* This assessed how geared the police station was towards the general public. It captured if the station was easy to locate, if there was staff allocated to serve the public that seeks police intervention? If there was clear information of how to procure services in the station.

(ii) *Physical conditions:* This component rated the material condition and equipment present in stations necessary to perform the given functions. It did not measure how humble or how spruced up the building itself was, but captured the basic provision of space and facility in the station which were available to perform the required operations. For instance, if there were different spaces for interviewing suspects or facilities for witness protection, a reception area demarcated, armoury storage, etc.

(iii) *Equal treatment of public without bias on age, gender, ethnicity, nationality, minority status or sexual orientation:* Growing awareness in a multi-cultural world makes equal opportunities for all a basic requisite of service delivery. This dimension assessed the availability of these considerations in police stations. If there were the required facilities for vulnerable and minority groups such as a women's desk/room, facilities for the handicapped, adequate representation for different minority groups, use of linguistic information and services in accordance with immediate contexts.

(iv) *Accountability and transparency:* This criteria judged if there was visibility regarding the functions performed and the existence of checks and balances for violations and gaps in given protocols. Easy identifiability of the police staff, performance of the police stations in terms of crime statistics and their dissemination, complaint boxes form the range of measures assessed.

(v) *Detention conditions:* Citizens rated the police stations in terms of safety and protection measures for the detainees. Hygiene, sanitation and basic rights of the suspects as citizens were gauged. In India, states that participated in PSVW were in itself an indication of the police partnership with the community and those who gave recognition to the police accountability to its citizens.

'It is interesting that the states that participated in the police station visitors week were those that either had strong community policing initiatives or had undertaken police reforms at the police station level. For instance, in Andhra Pradesh a two-month training for police personnel on Culture Change Management and Practice that included training on team and personality building, conflict resolution and handling of technology had been implemented in Cyberabad areas where the visits were approved. Cyberabad is the electronic capital of Andhra Pradesh, a leading state on Information Technology. Police services in this pocket of Cyberabad have evolved in accordance with the needs of global professionals and IT culture. In Rajasthan, police stations that were visited were ones that had been or were being upgraded under the international norms of ISO systems of management to improve service delivery. Punjab has a programme of community policing resource centres (CPRCs) through which certain services in the police stations are provided under a joint community-police mandate. Meghalaya is a state, which has perforce historically close ties with community leaders. Most of the police stations visited were in the tribal Khasi dominated areas and all police interactions with the tribals had traditionally been via the tribal leaders.'[3]

It must be mentioned that in this event the Shipra Path police station in Jaipur, Rajasthan, was selected as the global best police station out of the stations that participated. It could outcompete stations in the US, one of which even had its own helipad with four helicopters at their disposal. While the infrastructure at Shipra Path was adequate to meet the needs of its population, special initiative for crime prevention and structured networking with its community were the clinching issues in the selection of Shipra Path.[4]

II. Level of Physical Security Enjoyed by Citizens

Indicators of citizen safety have been mapped through proxy variables of crime rates. These have been tapped disaggregately for both IPC crimes and the SLL. This section also serves to measure the impact of safety and security measures undertaken

[3]*Police Station Visitors Week: Report of Results in India – 2006*, IDC-Altus Global Alliance, p. 10.

[4]*Police Station Visitors Week: Global Report 2006*, The Hague, The Netherlands: Altus Global Alliance Secretariat.

by the states as a rate of crime per lakh population for vulnerable groups. This disaggregated crime data is undertaken for vulnerable populations namely women, children, Scheduled Castes and Scheduled Tribes. The crimes against women and children pertain to specific types of crimes against these populations, such as rape, dowry deaths, infanticide or foeticide. However, crimes against body (such as murder, hurt) or against property, (such as theft, or against public order (such as rioting or cheating) under economic crimes, are not segregated according to gender, but only for Scheduled Castes and Scheduled Tribes.

BOX 2.10: LIST OF INDICATORS FOR LEVEL OF PHYSICAL SECURITY ENJOYED BY THE CITIZENS

- Reported rate of crime
  - Total IPC crimes
  - Crime against body
    - Homicide per 100,000 population (murder)
    - Serious assault per 100,000 population(attempt to murder)
    - Culpable homicide not amounting to murder
    - Kidnapping and abduction per 100,000 population
    - Hurt
    - Causing death by negligence
  - Crime against property
    - Dacoity
    - Preparation and assembly for dacoity
    - Robbery
    - Burglary
    - Theft
  - Crime against public order
    - Riots
    - Arson
  - Economic crimes
    - Criminal breach of trust
    - Cheating
    - Counterfeiting
  - Reported rate of crime against women
    - Rape per 100,000 population
    - Kidnapping and abduction of women and girls per 100,000 population
    - Dowry deaths per 100,000 population
    - Cruelty by husband and relatives per 100,000 population
    - Molestation per 100,000 population

- Eve teasing (sexual harassment) per 100,000 population
    - Importation of girls per 100,000 population
    - Immoral Traffic (P) Act per 100,000 population
    - Indecent Representation of Women (P) Act per 100,000 population
    - Dowry Prohibition Act per 100,000 population
  - Reported rate of crime against children
    - Infanticide per 100,000 population
    - Murder per 100,000 population
    - Rape per 100,000 population
    - Kidnapping and abduction per 100,000 population
    - Foeticide per 100,000 population
    - Abetment to suicide per 100,000 population
    - Exposure and abandonment per 100,000 population
    - Procurement of minor girls per 100,000 population
    - Buying of girls for prostitution per 100,000 population
    - Selling of girls for prostitution per 100,000 population
    - Child Marriage Restraint Act per 100,000 population
  - Crime against SC/ST
    - Crime against Scheduled Castes per 100,000 population
    - Crime against Scheduled Tribes per 100,000 population
  - Cognisable crime against Special Local Laws
    - Rate of total cognisable crimes SLL per 100,000 Population
    - Percentage change in SLL crime in 2005 [(+) increase (-) decrease] over 2004
    - Arms Act. per 100,000 population
    - Narcotics and drugs offences per 100,000 population
    - Explosives and Explosive Substances Act per 100,000 population
    - Terrorist and Disruptive Activities Act per 100,000 population
- Difference in chargesheeting rate for specific population
  - Women (totals from the following)
    - Rape per 100,000 population
    - Kidnapping and abduction of women and girls per 100,000 population
    - Dowry deaths per 100,000 population
    - Cruelty by husband and relatives per 100,000 population
    - Molestation per 100,000 population
    - Eve teasing (sexual harassment) per 100,000 population
    - Importation of girls per 100,000 population
    - Immoral Traffic (P) Act per 100,000 population
    - Indecent Representation of Women (P) Act per 100,000 population
    - Dowry Prohibition Act per 100,000 population

- Children (totals from the following)
  - Infanticide per 100,000 population
  - Murder per 100,000 population
  - Rape per 100,000 population
  - Kidnapping and abduction per 100,000 population
  - Foeticide per 100,000 population
  - Abetment to suicide per 100,000 population
  - Exposure and abandonment per 100,000 population
  - Procurement of minor girls per 100,000 population
  - Buying of girls for prostitution per 100,000 population
  - Selling of girls for prostitution per 100,000 population
  - Child Marriage Restraint Act per 100,000 population
- Scheduled Castes/Scheduled Tribes (totals from the following)
  - Crime against Scheduled Castes per 100,000 population
  - Crime against Scheduled Tribes per 100,000 population

- Difference in conviction rate for specific population
  - Women (totals from the following)
    - Rape per 100,000 population
    - Kidnapping and abduction of women and girls per 100,000 population
    - Dowry deaths per 100,000 population
    - Cruelty by husband and relatives per 100,000 population
    - Molestation per 100,000 population
    - Eve teasing (sexual harassment) per 100,000 population
    - Importation of girls per 100,000 population
    - Immoral Traffic (P) Act per 100,000 population
    - Indecent Representation of Women (P) Act per 100,000 population
    - Dowry Prohibition Act per 100,000 population
  - Children (totals from the following)
    - Infanticide per 100,000 population
    - Murder per 100,000 population
    - Rape per 100,000 population
    - Kidnapping & abduction per 100,000 population
    - Foeticide per 100,000 population
    - Abetment to suicide per 100,000 population
    - Exposure and abandonment per 100,000 population
    - Procurement of minor girls per 100,000 population
    - Buying of girls for prostitution per 100,000 population
    - Selling of girls for prostitution per 100,000 population
    - Child Marriage Restraint Act per 100,000 population
  - Scheduled Castes/Scheduled Tribes
    - Crime against Scheduled Castes per 100,000 population
    - Crime against Scheduled Tribes per 100,000 population

A number of constraints can be mentioned under this category of mapping the extent of crime. It must be noted that the level of physical security is gauged *vis-à-vis* reported crime, but a large number of crimes do not fall under the purview of crime statistics.

SOME FILTERS FOR THE COMPUTED INDEX

1. *Unreported Crime*

A number of considerations may influence non-reporting of crime.

- Nature of crime
  - Brutality of crime
  - Invisibility
  - Stigma
  - Tactical concerns
- Difficulty in registration of crime

(i) *Nature of Crime*

Gender crime is particularly influenced by the social structures that colour the perception of crime. A wide range of personal and social factors is likely to affect both whether an incident is perceived as criminal and whether the observer then decides to report the incident to the police.[5] For instance, wife beating, dowry harassment, if not brutal, would fall under the realm of a historical relational paradigm as an accepted practice. Thus, no violation may be perceived even by the victim, the perpetrator or the larger society.[6] In fact, exchange of dowry is an integral ritual of Hindu marriages. The brutality of the crime is also a factor in the reporting of crime. For instance, the more physically abusive a crime, the more its visibility. Thus dowry death is a more visible crime than dowry harassment and even reporting of incidents of dowry harassment may be higher as was found in a study in Punjab.

[5]Official statistics on crime do not indicate 'real' amounts of crime but how events are defined and processed by social control agents.

Eamonn Carrabine, et al., 2004, *Criminology: A Sociological Introduction*, London: Routledge, p. 267.

[6]Ibid., p. 26.

Tactical considerations in terms of social positioning may also be a factor in reporting or non-reporting of crime.[7] In a study on Farmers Suicides in Rural Punjab it has been noted that 'family members in the villages do not report suicides as it is seen as an act of cowardice in a patriarchal and martial society'. Additionally, farmers' suicides are largely attributed to indebtedness. If this becomes known, it adversely affects matrimonial alliances.

The stigma attached to a particular crime also acts as a hindrance to its reporting. Transgressions on the female body may not be reported as rape or molestation targets the victim through social stigma. Reporting of gender crimes is particularly low. A detailed analysis is provided from a research study in Punjab.

BOX 2.11: POLICE NOT APPROACHED FOR REDRESSAL OF GENDER CRIME

Reported data do not reflect the correct position of gender violence against women. While there has been a phenomenal increase in crime against women, certain forms of violence do not get reported at all. Wife-beating is one such form. The misuse of sex determination tests was declared a crime in Punjab in 1994 and in India in 1995, yet in 1996, only one case was reported. Social invisibility attached to crimes against women and the fear of social stigma contribute to the non-registration of such crimes with the police. While crimes like rape carry the fear of stigma, caste/rapes remain unperceived as violation in a caste hierarchical society. In a study of atrocities against women in Punjab,[8] non-reporting was found high and it varied according to the nature of the crime and its acceptability in society. For each reported case of rape, 68 went unreported. As many as 374 cases of molestation went unreported against one reported case. Eve-teasing is a relatively 'new crime' which was reported for the first time in 1992. The extent of unreported cases, however, reflects the widespread

[7]Changes in law enforcement and in what the law counts as crime also preclude much meaningful discussion over the extent of historical increases and decreases in crime. Legislative changes may mean that existing categories are redefined, thus rendering any historical comparison meaningless. Ibid., p. 27.

[8]Pramod Kumar and Rainuka Dagar, 1995, *Atrocities Against Women in Punjab*, Chandigarh: Institute for Development and Communication.

nature of the practice with 9177 unreported incidents against each reported case.

Ratios of Reported to Unreported Atrocities in Punjab

Reported		Unreported
1	Rape	768
1	Molestation	374
1	Eve-teasing	9177
1	Dowry death	27
1	Dowry harassment	299

Source: Atrocities Against Women in Punjab, 1995.

A comparison of unreported cases of dowry harassment and those that were reported reveals that for every reported case, an astonishing 299 go unreported. That a large number of dowry harassment cases remain unregistered is substantiated by a look at the cases that are brought to the women's cells, NGOs and panchayats for compromise or reconciliation. For example, in a study[9] of the women's cell at Ropar, it was found that of the 31 cases handled by it in five months (02-09-94 to 22-02-95), seven related to dowry harassment. Interestingly, these cases are brought to the women's cell of the police and yet these remain part of unregistered dowry harassment cases. Similarly, of the cases before the Faridkot Istri Sabha,[10] 61 per cent concerned dowry harassment, which are again a part of unreported cases.

CASES WITH PUNJAB ISTRI SABHA, FARIDKOT (1990-4)

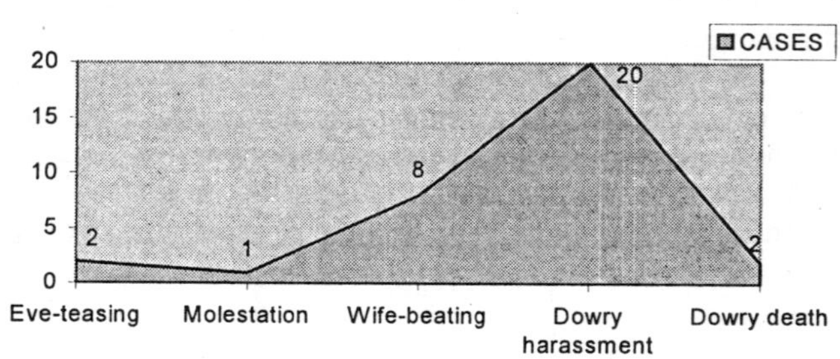

Source: P.I.S., Faridkot, 1995

A later study revealed that every fourth household in Punjab acknowledged having faced a dowry demand, while every 28th

[9] Ibid.
[10] Ibid.

household mentioned having faced dowry harassment and every 3rd household accepted the occurrence of wife beating.[11] This extent of crime against women is not reflected in the official reported data.

NTH HOUSEHOLDS THAT ACKNOWLEDGED FORMS OF VIOLENCE

Form of violence	Majha	Malwa	Backward Malwa	Doaba	Total
Dowry demand	5th	4th	4th	3rd	4th
Dowry harassment	19th	18th	45th	—	28th
Dowry death	56th	53th	—	—	100th
Wife-beating	3rd	3rd	2nd	3rd	3rd
Rape	56th	53rd	45th	—	66th
Molestation	56th	—	—	—	200th
Eve-teasing	28th	9th	5th	9th	9th
Sexual exploitation	—	—	11th	—	50th

Source: Combating Violence Against Women, 2001.

The problem which the enforcement agencies face while dealing with atrocities against women is that even when an atrocity is accepted as violence, it still may not be voiced. Perceived abuse against women may remain confined to the home or in the minds of the victims. Fear of a stigma, subjugative patriarchal structures, lack of legal literacy and even financial compulsions make it difficult for a woman to fight a legal battle.

(ii) *Difficulty in Registration of Crimes*

One of the reforms that civil society groups are asking for inclusion in the ongoing police reforms pertains to prompt stringent registration of the first information report (FIR).[12] Perception surveys provide some explanations for people not reporting crimes.

[11]Rainuka Dagar, 2001, *Combating Violence Against Women in Punjab*, Chandigarh: Institute for Development and Communication.

[12]Not all offences reported are recorded as offences by the police. The amount of resources available to the police and courts is limited and thus subjective and/or administrative decisions are made concerning which crimes to act against. John Muncie, op. cit., 2001, p. 25.

Table 2.1: Problems in Reporting to Police

Fear of harassment	Citizens resist visiting the police due to fear of harassment victimisation by the police and perception of being unjustly treated.
Complicated procedures	Lack of awareness and poor service delivery make public hesitant to visit police stations.
Corruption	Fear of having to pay bribes to the police.
Lack of faith in police	Inattention, lack of responsiveness.
Social stigma	Concerns that the image will be affected if they visit the police station and publicly acknowledge being victimised.
Less serious offences	Petty crime, which is not felt worth the trouble of visiting the police station.
Registration of cases related to performance of police	Low registration of cases is taken as less crime.

Source: IDC Field Survey, 2006

Although official crime statistics are driven primarily by the preparedness of the victim or witness to report crime to the police and by the recording practices of the police agency, it is known that some types of crime are more likely to be reported and recorded than others. For example, it is widely held that homicide is a highly reported and recorded crime, whereas it is also widely believed (and supported by victimisation surveys) that rape is poorly reported by victims and often not recorded by the police.[13]

In other words, citizens' hesitation both due to the fear of unfair treatment and perception of complicated and tedious procedures, the public does report some crime more than others. For instance, the following crimes have a higher rate of reporting:[14]

[13]Graeme Newman and Gregory J. Howard, op. cit. (1999), p. 11.

[14]Victimization surveys are an important method to better estimate the prevalence of victimisation by conventional crime. The International Crime (Victim) Survey has been carried out in more than 50 countries.

United Nations, 1999, *Guide for Policy Makers*, New York: United Nations; Office for Drug Control and Crime Prevention, Centre for International Crime Prevention, p. 2.

Victim surveys, such as the BCS, have suggested that in fact only about a half of known crime is reported. Thefts of vehicle and burglaries with loss are generally reported; vandalism, theft from the person and attempted

- *Brutal crimes:* Such as murder, attempt to murder, dowry death, etc.
- *Crime against property:* Burglary, theft, robbery, etc.
- *Assertions against state:* In times of turmoil, internal conflicts within the state or against competing identities reflect larger violations in public spheres.
- *Interest groups:* Assertive interest groups provide awareness of rights and the necessary support for higher reporting.
- *Victims of previous crimes:* Victims report a preference of keeping a distance from the criminal justice system after expectations of a speedy response are not met.
- *Breakup of traditional authority systems:* Crime reporting increases where traditional justice systems have deteriorated or become defunct.

Citizens' perception regarding police interface have been gathered from a number of field studies undertaken by the IDC. The above data are reflective of surveys conducted in four states of Andhra Pradesh, Gujarat, Meghalaya and Punjab.

Implications

Crime data are likely to be a reflection rather than actual violence in certain spheres particularly among population groups that are more disadvantaged than others.

> Clearly, victimisation and self-report surveys provide data on the amount of crime from a quite different perspective—an unofficial perspective, which provides an alternative measure that is not contaminated by the official practices of police agencies or other statistical reporting bodies. . . . Official data view the "dark figure" from the window of the police while victimisation surveys view the "dark figure" from the window of the victim.[15]

Victimology surveys need to supplement crime statistics for policy interventions to provide adequate services to victims and

---

motor vehicle theft less so. The main reasons given for not reporting a crime to the police were that victims felt they were not serious enough or that the police would be unable to take any effective action.

John Muncie, op. cit., 2001, p. 26.

[15]Graeme Newman and Gregory J. Howard, op. cit. (1999), pp. 16-18.

to strategise crime prevention. Linkages between Informal/ traditional system of justice can be strengthened for the private / culturally specific nature of crime, particularly in terms of gender violence and perhaps for populations such as tribals like the Garo and Khasi tribes in Meghalaya, who have their own traditional justice systems.

2. *Legal System as a Remedy or Redressal?*

Can social norms be addressed through rule making? In India, for instance, there has been a growing concern for the increasing number of atrocities against women. The state's response has been to make the laws on violence against women more stringent. Dowry laws have been bolstered,[16] sex determination has been made an offence[17] and efforts have been made to provide guidelines against sexual harassment at the work place.[18] The focus on the stringency of the laws directly puts the onus on the police, which as an enforcement agency is expected to implement these laws. A focus only on punishment rather than a multi-focused holistic perspective on gender violence that takes into consideration the socio-cultural conditions, questions the viability of enforcement itself. If the transfer of payments at the time of marriage (dowry exchange) remains integral to the hierarchical structures between the bride giving and receiving families, then enforcing dowry-related abuses becomes difficult, if not impossible, when the victims themselves do not perceive an abuse. Male child preference accords social acceptance to female foeticide and sex selection measures that are legally stated to be crimes. Social intervention in the hegemonic interaction only allows 'aberrations' of the prescribed conduct scrutiny by the legal periscope, be it dowry abuse, sexual violence, female foeticide or wife-beating. In other words, structural underpinnings make the law cognizable only to the manifestation and not the concept. Therefore, dowry exchange is an accepted

[16]*The Dowry Prohibition Act, 1961.*

[17]*The Pre-Conception and Pre-natal Diagnostic Techniques (Prohibition of Sex Selection) Act, 1994.*

[18]The Supreme Court judgement of 13 August 1997 Vishaka v/s State of Rajasthan provides guidelines prohibiting sexual harassment at the workplace.

custom, yet dowry harassment, its outcome, is an offence, thus promoting an outcry for enforcement if the crime has transgressed the sanctioned gender norms, such as dowry death. Therefore, allowing the police to practice non-interference if the abuse is perceived within the domain of gender structures, such as wife-beating. Gender bias permeates the police as a social institution and cannot, in fact, be insulated from social pressures while dealing with gender crime. In other words, this falls under the domain of commitment to justice and measures undertaken to sensitise community to link rule of law with criminal justice would be mapped under this purview.

3. *Legitimacy of Crime*

Certain labels of crime may be eulogised in a particular cultural context. For instance, manliness is traditionally eulogised in murder cases in some areas in Punjab. Violent masculinities form part of the cultural ethos of some societies. For instance, the evolved code for the Jat peasantry is to fight for land, woman and water. A hit pop song drawing from folk culture choruses on 'district courts are sites of Jat fairs'. It hails the large presence of Jat peasantry in the district courts where the accused in assault/ murder charges abound and portrays the legitimacy accorded to male peasantry facing charges of physical assault. This practice has a stamp of approval with traditional cultural notions that 'you are not a Jat if you do not have cases against you' or 'the more cases of murder you have on your head the more manly you are'. Thus, social status is linked to others being afraid of you since this entails control and influence, adding to influence and allowing the 'accused' word to be law within the immediate kinship. This crime is then viewed as a symbol of achievement. Again, this issue highlights the gap in promoting rule of law as recognised by international democratic standards. Where there are gaps in its adoption due to cultural or local traditions, linkages through supporting mechanism and alternative initiatives need to be strengthened to sensitise social norms.

4. *Cultural Barriers to Access*

Traditionally the criminal justice system is a domain of the male. Men as public beings formed the accused and dispensers of justice. All the institutions of police, courts and prisons are historically viewed as crime enforcement institutions, with crime itself an activity dissociated with the role and status of all women and also men of repute, barring leaders. Any interaction with these offices was a stigma. This cultural connotation continues and even women representatives of local bodies, who have an official mandate to use police services, are wary of visiting the police station. Studies reflect the distance women panchayat members maintain from the police. If required, women are accompanied by male family members and are largely limited to participation in domestic violence cases. Besides dealing with criminal activity, these institutions, particularly the police symbolise loud, brutal and inhuman traits reflected by the police staff. Police-community studies reflect peoples perceptions of the force as being brutal and crude.

BOX 2.12: POLICE AND WOMEN: CULTURAL INACCESSIBILITY[19]

Elected women representatives of local bodies also limit their dealings with the police, who they are expected to be in contact with. Surveys reveal the following practices adopted by women representatives in approaching the police:

- Only male members either from the family or local body represented by the women leader, deal with the police.
- Male family members accompany the female leader to the police station.
- Women leaders are only present in police presence when dealing with domestic violence cases.
- Women leaders may just provide their signatures as a representation.
- If women leaders have to be present, it is not considered socially desirable.

5. *Collective* versus *Individual Rights*

The inheritance of the formal criminal justice system through the British colonial powers have enshrined monistic responsiveness within the criminal justice system. The colonialists sharpened the distinction between collectivities and hierarchised the acceptance

[19]'Notion of Masculinity in Functioning of Panchayat', Chandigarh: Institute for Development and Communication, 2003, unpublished.

of a single collectivity as representative of the multitude cultures. Moreover, this notion of human rights was individual centered. In the context of the criminal justice system, collectivity rights are recognised largely through representation of staff and for women through special provisions. Do these inputs at inclusion of multi-cultural reality result in outputs of increased safety or perception of security or more equitable access to justice? Also, in a clash of collectivity rights, whose rights are given primacy? For instance, does the structural hegemony of castes reflect in discriminatory delivery of justice? Again, do collectivities impose their hegemonic control over their individual members or can the criminal justice system provide due protection in case of violation of rights—in a patriarchy does the police afford protection to victims of domestic violence? These are some considerations that need to be applied when analysing the performance and outcomes of the data.

6. *Segregation of Institutions for Hegemony of Political Order*

The agencies of the criminal justice system—the police, the judiciary and prisons are distinct in the nature of activity performed by the respective sectors and the function of each is integral to the performance of justice and safety of its citizens. In a democracy, the autonomy of each institution is expected to strengthen the quality of justice. The segregation at the operational level can lead to the institutions competing with one another, undermining the principle of collective systemic accountability. History is witness to political contexts providing primacy to a select sector, extending their role and space at the cost of the others. The failure of the delivery of justice then gets attributed to the functioning of institutions, which is more an effect of the nature of politics rather than the cause of poor safety. 'Police rule-bending and rule-breaking can be seen not only as a problem of individual deviance, but also as an indication of systemic failure. Systemic failures are related to the nature of police organisations, the character of occupational culture, and the particular opportunities and pressure presented by the environment that is policed.'[20] For example, during terrorism,

[20]Eamonn Carrabine, et al., op. cit. (2004), pp. 286-7.

political processes have been seen to be relegated to the background and administrative controls were unleashed through imposition of central rule (legislative assembly was dissolved). When such measures fail to control terrorism, security forces are unleashed and policing made the only vanguard of safety, and thus justice. When the security forces continue to hold sway after having restored peace, their functioning was seen through the prism of peace and coloured as abuse of power. The judiciary was then given primacy extending its reach outside its own functions, which was labelled as judicial over-activism. In a democracy, the role of each sector is essential in maintaining its vibrancy and giving supremacy to one over the other in a crisis situation undermines the criminal justice system itself. In fact, it is during crisis when the operational functioning and capacity of each sector is to be optimised. Reported data may not represent this skewed functioning of the system.

> *Systemic accountability* requires that institutions are :
> - *Complementary* and not *Competitive*.
> - Allocation of *roles*: Processes are linked with accountability for the final output and outcomes.
> - There is *systemic integration* with *functional separation* of various sectors.

7. *Public Safety* versus *Human Rights*

The war on terrorism is increasingly becoming a symbol of public safety. The dominant perspective on the war on terrorism tends to present public safety and citizen rights as a clash of interests. The priority accorded to the civil, political, social and minority rights may get diminished to ensure public safety from terrorist attacks. Sikhs may be expected to take off their turbans for security checks, political assembly of groups may be jeopardised as easy targets, racial profiling may increase. The civil and political rights especially the right to privacy and right to political protest and activism may get undermined. It has also indirectly affected people's right to various entitlements with the re-structuring of financial and material allocation. This concern has been expressed succinctly by Kofi Annan:

I do not believe there is or there can be a trade-off between the effective fight against terrorism and protection of civil liberties. If, as individuals we are asked to give up our freedom, our liberties and human rights, for protection against terrorism, and we do it, do we in the end have protection? I think we need to be careful not to undermine human rights and civil liberties in this fight against terrorism because if we do, we are handing the terrorists a victory they cannot win on their own.[21]

This poses a dilemma between public security and the human rights of the people. One standpoint such as the Commonwealth Human Rights Initiative (CHRI) considers national security and human security as synonymous. 'Democracy requires that national security cannot be achieved unless each and every person in the country feels safe. In other words, national security requires human security. Laws and actions that provide safeguards are necessary for the safety of the state and its people, where they protect life and poverty as well as liberty and rights.'[22] The present index gives primacy to human rights and fair delivery of justice as these acts as an insurance against violation of national security.

III. Rights of People Affected by Crime

The effectivity and fairness of the criminal justice system can be viewed cross-sectionally by analysing how the rights of people affected by crime are provided for by the state. Two types of population groups are focused in the section—the accused and the victims. It is perhaps a reflection of society's attitude towards the accused and those found guilty of crime that there is a dearth of documentation of data for the support of their rights.

[21]'War on Terror Equals War on Minorities', *IPS*, 8 September 2006 www.ipsnews.net/print.asp? Idnews = 34652

[22]Maza Daruwala and Tessa Boyd-Caine, 2007, *Stamping Out Rights: Impact of Anti-Terrorism Laws on Policing*, New Delhi: Commonwealth Human Rights Initiative, p. 9.

BOX 2.13: LIST OF INDICATORS FOR RIGHTS OF PEOPLE AFFECTED BY CRIME

- Criminal rights: *vis-à-vis* Police
  - o Arrest warrants
  - o Time period for which a person can be kept in police custody
  - o Average police remand time
  - o Undertrial's average time spent in jail
- Criminal rights: *vis-à-vis* courts
  - o Right to counsel
  - o Free legal aid (utilisation per lakh population)
- Criminal rights: *vis-à-vis* prisons
  - o Average remand time
  - o Facilities provided
    - ▪ Medical
    - ▪ Vocational training
    - ▪ Visitors

Rights of victims
  - o Medical support
  - o Economic provision / compensation
  - o Free legal aid
  - o Special provisions
    - ▪ Women's cell
    - ▪ Special law courts (family courts)
    - ▪ Special courts for SCs/special courts for STs
    - ▪ Human rights courts
- Violation by enforcement agencies (Police / courts / prisons)
  - o No. of complaints against the police per 100 policemen
  - o Percentage of police personnel convicted per 100 police complaints received during the year (-)
  - o No. of complaints against prison staff
  - o Percentage of prison staff convicted

Total death of inmates

RIGHTS OF ACCUSED

What kind of safeguards does the system provide for the rights of the accused and the convicted? The rights of the accused and victims are gauged as a process. Mapping the formal procedures that secure a citizen's rights as constitutionally given are applicable across states and are included in the indicators list while taken as inclusive in the index, since these rights are common and exist for the country as a whole. These include, if the accused are arrested according to certain procedures (arrest warrant, police custody procedures), and if their remand is sanctioned by a judicial decree. There are provisions of right to counsel extending to free legal aid where the case may demand. These rights are further captured in prisons where basic rights of food, hygiene, medical provisions, space and protection are warranted. While legal aid is measured in its operational capacity, reflecting use per lakh population, prison conditions need to be measured more qualitatively.

The average time in police remand and the rights maintained in prisons are yet to be reflected in crime and prison statistics published by the state. The average remand time in the prisons is one of the factors that have been listed in state documents. The rights of the criminals need to be examined through a qualitative analysis.

RIGHTS OF VICTIMS

The rights of victims have also seen a recent interest in the public domain with a number of provisions being put in place to address their needs. Prominent among these are the creation of women's cells, family courts, special courts for SCs and STs. Economic compensation is a case to case decision and medical support provided to the victims also varies. Largely medical support is provided through reference to government hospitals and doctors, which may not be timely and suffers from the vagaries of government hospitals.

Witness protection and compensation for victims are issues under debate. Under commitment to justice, victim rights and compensation issues are referred to through the intervention of oversights and civil society groups. However, the rights of citizens under difficult circumstances, such as in conflict and post-conflict situations, are reflected here with separate treatment. Since the issues raised are context specific and need to be highlighted for policy considerations.

RIGHTS OF CITIZENS IN CONFLICT AND POST-CONFLICT SITUATIONS

Conflict and post-conflict situations provide a challenge to the operative functioning of the criminal justice system—institutions may become defunct or others may acquire all encompassing powers of law maintenance, citizen protection, prosecution, retributive justice and even defining the priority of rights of the citizens and by default then rejecting some rights for protection of others (for instance, public safety compromising human rights). The functional capacities of the different sectors of the criminal justice system during and post conflict situations are no doubt a reflection of a robust democracy. However, conflict situations can throw up other challenges also. One particular issue refers to the rights of victims in conflict and post-conflict contexts. How does one define a victim in such contexts? How does one categorise the nature of violence suffered? What community confidence building measures need to be taken to ensure the rights of citizens?

Conflict and Post-conflict Situations: Issues in Categorising Victims and the Accessibility of their Rights[23]

From a human rights perspective, the extent of violence suffered by the victims forms the criterion for dispensing relief-rehabilitation. They include the victim-survivors, who have suffered abuse directly, dependents of the victims and those who are witness to violence. However, any intervention strategy, specially the one that focuses on rehabilitation and victim integration, needs to capture the social and political response of the victims rather than focusing only on the impact of violence. In order to implement human rights, the dominant trend is to hold the individual as the benefactor, without considering that collectivities are also human and have rights and they, in fact, may determine the context in which individuals are denied or provided the rights. The nature of terrorism in Punjab involved identity assertions whereby the victims' background (militant affiliate, state affiliate or other affected survivors) resulted in their victimisation in the first place and continued to fuel the feelings of revenge, guilt or marginalisation from the societal mainstream. In such a context, it is relevant to focus on victim

[23]For details refer to Pramod Kumar, Rainuka Dagar and Neerja, 2001, *Victims of Militancy: Punjab*, New Delhi: UNICEF. www.idcindia.org/conflict_studies/conflict.htm

affiliation rather than only on the act of violence as suffered by the victim. This allows to include the community in the plan of integration rather than only target individual victims for relief or rehabilitation. The content of the multi-staged strategies for intervention has to be evolved in response to the specific contextual requirements. These extend beyond the conventional strategies and have been formulated in the action plan to integrate victims of terrorism in Punjab to correct the visible effects of violence. Existing intervention by the state, civil society, oversights and human rights activists focus on financial relief and rehabilitation of the victims of violence. These are mainly material in nature, and the psychological, social and economic needs of the survivors are not paid adequate attention. The invisible effects such as hatred, trauma, feelings of revenge or addiction to past glory remain dormant and neglected. Another aspect that is often overlooked pertains to the partisan nature with which these rehabilitative measures deal with the effects of violence. The sufferings of the victims of violence belonging to the families of non-state actors, who have used violence against the state, are seen through the ideological prism and therefore, find negligible response in the rehabilitation plan of the state.

The relief measures responding to immediate survival needs, rehabilitation catering to the special needs of the victims and re-integration dealing with the resolution of conditions of violence, have to be operationalised as a continuum and in a synchronic manner.

BOX 2.14: ADDRESSING NEEDS OF VICTIMS: IN A FRAMEWORK OF RIGHTS OF COLLECTIVITIES

The relief and rehabilitation of the victims in terms of economic and health needs is essential, but conventional efforts only focus on the visible and direct effects of violence that are easily discernible as material and somatic damage. However, the victims are affected by trauma—specially pertaining to bereavement and sexual violence. They are also affected by glory or revenge addiction and reel under the violation of cultural ethos and norms that have damaged the social fabric. The community is imbued with mistrust that marginalises the victims and promotes insecurity. Therefore, rehabilitation must not only focus on the damage to individuals and families but also include the community to combat structural violence, to allow integration of the victims into the socio-cultural, economic and political milieu and disengage the conditions of conflict. The integration strategy needs to redress the effects of direct violence where relief is necessitated for survival and subsequently cater to the specific needs of the victims, such as provision of material sustenance, health and educational access, through rehabilitative measures. It also needs to address issues of structural violence to erase the conditions that caused the violence itself. Thus, an integration strategy has to target both the victim and the community, alleviate the needs (physical, psychological, social and economic) of the victim, and at the same time mobilise the community to provide support to the victims. It should undermine the culture of violence by sensitising all sections of society to victimisation. This will counter revenge or glory addiction, allay insecurity among the people and create an environment for conflict resolution. Involving the community also becomes important to enable targeting the specific needs of the victims without institutionalising them as a special category.

IMPACT OF TERRORISM ON VICTIMS
(DESCRIPTIVE CATEGORIES FOR INTERVENTION STRATEGY)

Visible effects	Invisible effects
• Somatic effects – Rape, sexual abuse – Physical ailments and disabilities (Backache, B.P., Migraine) – Psychological trauma – Education Break – Drop-outs – Lack of access Employment/Skill (loss or break) • Material – Assets – Income • Disintegration of family	• Isolation • Threat perception Trauma • Bereavements • Re-victimisation—backlash of patriarchy • Break in support base—kinship structures • Glorification of male victims, stigmatisation of women victims (Widowed/Abandoned) • Institutions—reliving experience • Status marginalisation—Impingement on cultural lifestyle – Curtailment of rights/choices • Culture of violence • Relational paradigm – Community – Kinship – Family • Ostracism

Note: Victims pertains to survivors only.

BOX 2.15: INDICATORS CAPTURING RIGHTS OF COLLECTIVITIES IN POST-CONFLICT SITUATIONS

Relief

- Material assistance (Monetary compensation, shelter)
- Health treatment
  - Physical illness
  - Disabilities

Rehabilitation

- Health and education
  - Access to health and educational facilities (surgery, health aids, immunisation, admissions, etc.)
  - Psychiatric assistance (hallucinations, depression)
  - Counselling (victim, parents, family)
- Material sustenance
  - Pension, material assets
  - Employment opportunities
  - Skill upgradation
- Administrative assistance
  - Increase victim categories, access to rehabilitation strategies (pension, compensation)
  - Special assistance (birth certificates, school certificates, etc.)
- Victims' awareness of available aid/schemes
- Freedom from police harassment

Integration

- Community sensitisation
  - Victimisation and its impact
  - Gender ideology
- Increase community interaction
- State policy to be convergent and integrative (Area focus rather than victim targeted)
- Activisation of support structures for conflict resolution

A strategy of relief or rehabilitation focuses on victim categories and provides physical resources to the victims according to their sufferings. However, integration is not only victim-oriented but also focuses on the community, taking cognizance of the victims' background (militant affiliate, state affiliate and other affected survivors) since their perceived identity made them the victims in the first place and continues to discriminate on this basis, thus building a reservoir of mistrust and fear. The victims continue to re-live the traumatic experience (prompted particularly in institutions). Social isolation, backlash of patriarchy, change in relational paradigm, which is suffering from break in kinship and community ties, etc. (examples of indirect violence) promote recourse to further violence. Prevention of both visible and invisible violence is a continuous process and involves community effort to undermine the impact of victimisation, thus necessitating the empowerment of community structures to resolve the existing and emerging conflicts democratically. The central thrust of the integration approach is to transform the culture of violence into a culture of peaceful co-existence. In other words, identification of self-perpetuating processes of violence (male world) and their demystification is needed. Not only this, the glorification of violence by referring to past glories and traumas has to be countered.

Victim oriented	Community focus

Provision of health and education facilities (Psychiatric assistance, counselling, health aids, enrolment, admission)
• Material sustenance—assets (Pension, employment opportunities)
  – Provision of skills
  – Housing
• Administrative assistance
  – Increase the victims' access to rehabilitation (compensation)
• Welfare/grievance redressal
  – Share in property
  – Adoption
• Awareness of available aid/schemes
• Freedom from police harassment
• Counselling for revenge/ glory addiction
	Community sensitisation
	  – Victimisation and its impact
	  – Gender ideology
	  – Counter revenge
	  – Glory addiction
	  – Allay threat perception
	  – Activisation of support structures for conflict resolution
	• State policy to be convergent and integrative
	  – Health
	  – Education
	  – Skill Upgradation
	  – Employment opportunities
	• Increase community interactions (utilise reservoir of peaceful co-existence)

Biases in the functioning of local support structures that continue to marginalise or glorify some sections of the victims also need to be brought into the ambit of this strategy. The intervention envisages that all victims are treated on a par, irrespective of their affiliation. Thus each victim needs to be helped by virtue of being a victim. Moreover, the strategy pertains to people who formed the families of the 'militants' or 'state heroes' and may not have themselves been involved in acts of violence. The victims' background is an important consideration in formulating the integration plan since it would reflect the nature of victimisation and revictimisation and the build-up of a threat perception. However, the victim targeted strategy should treat all victims alike, transcending the affiliate categories which propelled violence in the first place. No doubt, individual requirements will vary but all victims will require special access to health facilities, education, financial resources and security.

VIOLATIONS BY ENFORCEMENT AGENCIES

A second layer within this category is provided to record the violations by the agencies of protection themselves. The clarification of violations continues to be orthodox. 'The development of meaningful controls over officer use of non-lethal force lagged behind the controls over deadly force and began to reach a comprehensive approach only in the 1990s. In several important respects, physical or non-lethal force is more difficult to control than deadly force. Non-lethal force includes a wide range of behaviour and there is considerable ambiguity as to what actions constitute use of "force".'[24] In the index, violations include those by the police and prison personnel. The two issues that are dealt within the index are: (i) number of complaints against the police and prison staff and (ii) action taken on these complaints.

In response to international protocols, violation by members of enforcement agencies are registered. These data exist for police personnel, prison staff, and also the total number of deaths of inmates in prisons is recorded. Larger number of complaints come through the human rights commission and other human rights bodies.

To sum up, the index must not only address itself to assessment indicators, but also those which can help to identify resources and opportunities to evolve an holistic strategy for delivery of criminal justice.

[24]Samuel Walker, 2005, *The New World of Police Accountability*, Thousand Oaks: Sage Publications, p. 49.

3. Commitment to Justice: Initiatives

The evolving nature of this instrument is reflected most in this section. The Indian criminal justice system is characterised by 'practising from within the existing'. While globally the rights purview has also been on formal laws, it has included in its focus the democratic processes and democratic functioning of institutions. The multicultural context of the Indian polity further requires the reflection of particularism, i.e. the rights and interests of minority groups, vulnerable populations and the marginalised sections. This is in addition to the autonomy and robustness of individual institutions. Moreover, in India the primary accountability remains static at the state level and has to be evolved at the cutting edge level. It is in this background that the commitment to justice is being explored with the scope of additions to the existing quantitative index. This section is divided into two aspects. One features the *commitment to justice* in terms of:

1. Mainstreaming of international standards in the system;
2. Participatory and interactive policy formulations; and
3. Transparency and accountability initiatives.

The second section documents some of the *institutional alternatives* that have been successful in capturing dimensions of the above issues.

BOX 3.1: LIST OF INDICATORS FOR COMMITMENT TO JUSTICE

- Mainstreaming international standards in the system
  - Policy programmes
  - Operationalising the strategy
  - Outlays of staff/budget/systems
  - Consolidation of interest groups, networking, disaggregate data
  - Building stakeholder capacities
  - Fixing responsibilities and accountability
  - Monitoring mechanisms

- Participatory and interactive policy formulations
  - Legislative/select committee decision-making procedures
- Transparency and accountability initiatives
  - Internal controls
    - Police
    - Courts
    - Prisons
  - State controls
    - Legislative
  - State oversights
    - State Commission for Women
    - State Human Rights Commission
    - State Minority Commission
    - State SC Commission
    - Number of cases per lakh population
    - Cases received disposed from oversights by police/courts
  - Social controls
    - Media/NGOs/PILs
  - Right to Information Act

COMMITMENT TO JUSTICE

1. MAINSTREAMING OF INTERNATIONAL STANDARDS IN THE SYSTEM

Relevant international covenants that have been converted to law include, CEDAW, convention on the rights of child, convention against torture and other cruel, inhuman or degrading treatment, elimination of all forms of racial discrimination and the overarching convention on civil and political rights. (For Indian laws formed under international covenants, refer to Annexure III.) These laws *per se* are not included as part of the index, since these pertain to national policy and are covered by all states. However, a number of considerations need to be taken into account while gauging the penetration of these laws into operational facets. These can be grounded in the creation of a policy document and its implementation. But has it been operationally strategised in terms of provisions for resource outlays of staff, material and budget. This also includes creation of systems including setting up of an advisory group and consolidation of interest groups networkings, building capacities of the stakeholders to utilise and disseminate the evolved facilities, integrating an accountability mechanism within the formulated strategy and monitoring mechanisms to upgrade and improve delivery of services.

One of the most systematic efforts pertains to the elimination of all forms of discrimination against women. Commissions for women have been constituted at the national and state levels, womens cells in the police functioning, women's studies units in academic forums and the enactment of a number of laws including the Domestic Violence Act, upgrading of the Dowry Prohibition Act, PC-PNDT Act, the pending Women's Representation Bill in Parliament. Thus an encompassing body catering to women's rights, special provisions, such as women's cell and family courts and the creation of relevant laws and accompanying awareness campaigns and capacity building programmes reflect the state's commitment to provide justice to this vulnerable group. It is these measures that need to be captured in the section on commitment to justice. While certain initiatives have been undertaken such as for gender issues or by different states or institutions, these remain to be documented in a standardised format. For this index a qualitative analysis has been referred to. For instance, a more comprehensive mainstreaming procedure, an illustration of provisions for gender mainstreaming in police has been included.

BOX 3.2: MAINSTREAMING GENDER: CAPACITY BUILDING INDICATORS FOR POLICE ADDRESSING GENDER VIOLENCE[1]

Available facilities

- Is there a gender unit?
- Are specialised services provided for the target groups such as, adolescent girls, slum dwellers etc.?
- Is necessary infrastructure available to provide quality services (victim relief kit, ambulance, doctors on call, etc.)?
- Are counselling services provided professionally?
- Does the unit have a short-term and a long-term strategy to deal with gender violence?

[1]Rainuka Dagar, 2002, *Policing and Gender Sensitisation: A Strategy*. Chandigarh: Institute for Development and Communication.

- Has the unit tied up with NGOs/government agencies that provide similar services?

Gender sensitivity

- Are all police personnel trained to deal with gender issues?
- Is the training up to date. For instance, is the staff conversant with the emerging issues of gender violence?
- Why are life enhancing mechanisms resulting in life depriving outcomes (scientific technology and female foeticide)?
- Response to revictimisation of women rather than only providing justice?
- How does construction of masculinity affect gender violence?
- Does sensitivity to caste violence obliterate gender violence within caste groups?
- Are police personnel attentive to the needs and concerns of the victims and their families irrespective of legal provisions (referral services, etc.)?
- Is the police providing service similar to that of panchayats/NGOs.?
- What is the follow-up programme?
- Is the ambience of the gender unit friendly and comforting?
- What coordination mechanisms exist for the implementation of short-term and long-term strategies?

Effectivity of existing services

- Are the services of the gender unit being used?
- Is there an increasing demand for services?
- Is the service range provided being expanded (catering to women victims to provision of passports and licences)?
- What are the timings of the services provided? Are these available to all groups (for working women)?
- What activities have been initiated to spread awareness on gender violence?
- What support is forthcoming from the community/religious leaders and opinion-making sections for the programme?
- Have any outreach programmes been initiated?
- Is there a high dropout rate of cases being dealt with by the police?
- What management systems are existing?
- Is there provision for providing proformas for grievance redressal?

2. PARTICIPATORY AND INTERACTIVE POLICY FORMULATIONS

The rule of law and the principles of good governance seek to involve community, interest groups and stakeholders in the inception and functioning of governance systems. Reform of the criminal justice system in India is under debate and reflects some measures for consultative and participatory modes. However, this needs to be layered, made responsive and institutionalised. For instance, these levels can be further classified into three stages reflecting different levels of participation in the formulation of laws/policies. Ideally, the stages would refer to planning, formulation and finalisation. Laws and policies that already exist can seek participation through an institutionalised community interface. The levels of participation would vary from public awareness, i.e. where the public is informed, to consultations with interest groups, collaboration with stakeholders and empowering of multilateral representations. These processes are either yet to be put into motion or wherever they exist they are dormant, and, if vibrant they continue to be invisible in documentation.

BOX 3.3: LEVELS AND NATURE OF PARTICIPATION

Stages	Informing	Consult	Collaborative	Empowering
Planning	Informed by media, newsletters, gazettes	Submit inputs	Members of the planning process	Steer the group meeting
Formulation	Informed by media, newsletters, gazettes	Meeting with community groups, consultancy survey	Lead in certain aspects and influence in prioritisation	Assessing significance and deciding priorities
Finalising the feedback	Distribution of laws for community considerations	Feedback from community	Joint finalisation of laws	Decide the content of the law

Initiatives From Below: Building into Policy

A number of traditional or people-driven justice mechanisms exist and are initiated at the grassroot level. How can they be incorporated within the purview of formal policy and consequently in the domain of law? An excellent example of community participation and grassroot initiative can be drawn from the anti-alcoholism protest movement that was launched in

Haryana in the early 1990s. The initiative was widespread at the level of the community and the state was responsive to convert it into law. However, certain limitations, on account of both stakeholders—the protesting community and the law enforcing state agencies, left the initiative in doldrums and the policy had to be withdrawn. The overview that has been provided highlights the lack of collaboration at the level of planning, formulation, feedback and operationalisation of strategy within the key stakeholders. Also, an enforcement approach by the state agencies weakened the process.

BOX 3.4: BUILDING POLICY FROM BELOW

1. Broaden community-led base	• Building pressure groups • Bridging target groups and community representatives
2. Supplementing resources	• Involving state agencies/oversights • Seeking administrative support
3. Evolving a collaborative approach	• Developing forward-backward linkages
4. Instituting law	• Interactive participatory mode

BOX 3.5: A BACKGROUND OF ANTI-ALCOHOLISM PROTESTS[2]

A protest movement against alcoholism was launched in the rural areas of Haryana as a reaction to impoverishment of the family and increasing instances of wife-beating. The immediate causes were the increasing atrocities on women within the household and in society, rise in social crimes, disintegration of the family and other social risks.

The movement relied heavily on the socio-cultural reservoir predominantly against the consumption of liquor. Further, the older generation provided support to this movement because of their puritan values. Conspicuous consumption caused by affluence, had influenced the younger male generation, which had taken to excessive drinking.

Given the patriarchal context, women were allowed limited freedom and were forced to suffer male assertion including physical assault.

[2]Pramod Kumar and Rainuka Dagar, 1997, *Social Policing: Case of Prohibition in Haryana, India*, Chandigarh: Institute for Development and Communication.

The spread of education among women and awareness of their rights made the participation of young educated women possible in these protests.

Organisation of the Protest Movement

The protest movement was spearheaded by the victims and, therefore, remained centered around its impact on women, family impoverishment and crimes against women. In this case the women victims started organising themselves and demanded closure of liquor vends in the villages or at least shifting of these vends to the periphery of the village. The following course was adopted by the movement:

(a) Staging *dharnas* (sit outs) before the liquor vends;
(b) Punishment to the drinkers such as parading them in the streets, wearing *ghaghras*, garlands of worn out shoes, etc.;
(c) Incentives for giving information about persons consuming liquor to the organising committee;
(d) Networking with the media, political activists, panchayats, etc., to provide visibility.

Limitations of a Protest Movement

(i) The protest movement remains sectional.
(ii) Issues are reduced to those between the perpetrator and the victim and thereby the larger social implications are lost sight of.
(iii) Remedies, if confined only to the victim and the perpetrator, leave the root causes of the problem unattended.

If the remedies provide cover to the entire social domain, these are resented by the people who do not fall in the victim-perpetrator categories.

COMBATING ALCOHOLISM THROUGH
A PARTICIPATORY APPROACH

Rather than depending on only legal enforcement, a *democratic movement* can focus on the following aspects in an integrated manner for incorporating change in the criminal justice system.

Broadening Community-led Base

1. Community led initiatives
2. Communication with and awareness of the community
3. Broadening the theme to other affected interest groups: Inter-relating gender justice and women's development with the menace of increasing alcoholism.

Supplementing Resources: Seeking State Support

4. Social and peoples policing
5. Social fencing
6. Targeted and discriminatory approach

Evolving a Collaborative Approach

7. Building forward and backward linkages with development activities

1. COMMUNITY-LED INITIATIVES

The community should be encouraged, motivated and involved in the implementation of the programme as participants and stakeholders rather than as informers or controllers of alcohol distribution. The involvement of diverse sections of society needs to be ensured. To illustrate, in a protest movement it is the victims who rise against drinkers and the community as a whole is not mobilised.

On the other hand, a social collaborative movement is community-based and is a total movement directed at interrelated issues. For instance, to check excessive drinking it relies on generation of awareness, increasing access to education, health, employment opportunities, etc., with civil society groups and leadership from across the population divides.

2. COMMUNICATION WITH AND AWARENESS OF THE COMMUNITY

The community has to be mobilised on various fronts by generating awareness regarding the social cost of alcoholism and its related effects by drawing support from the existing cultural predispositions and by creating others.

(a) Creating awareness that alcoholism affects all sections of society, particularly the non-drinking population. This can be done by generating data on :
   (i) the number of non-drinking persons injured or killed in accidents caused by drunken drivers;
   (ii) the number of children of non-drinking parents who take to drinking;
   (iii) increase in the percentage of crime against non-drinking caused by drinkers;
   (iv) cost-benefit analysis of reducing the pressure on hospitals of diseases caused by excessive drinking.

(b) Its linkages with larger cultural organisations such as the Arya Samaj, etc.

(c) The impact of alcoholism on individual families and society in monetary terms. Therefore, a social cost benefit analysis to counter economistic interpretations should be undertaken.
(d) Its inter-connection with other social evils such as dowry, rape, social crimes, etc.

3. Interrelating Gender Justice and Women's Development with the Menace of Increasing Alcoholism

Awareness needs to be built in society regarding the social cost and impact of alcoholism as borne by women. What is most visible is physical assault, either in the guise of wife beating or social molestation and even the household burden borne by women with meagre income. Aspects that remain invisible are the burden of earning income, which fall on women and deprivation of family needs such as health and education of children. These issues could be linked with development activities related to women's issues.

4. Social and Peoples Policing

The concept of social policing means to encourage members of the community to participate and control the causes and symptoms of alcoholism within their localities. A group of law enforcing civilians can primarily function to provide guidance to erring individuals, protect society, maintain social codes and individual integrity.

5. Social Fencing

Rather than encouraging a physical fencing to block the porous state border, efforts should be made to initiate social fencing with the support of civil society members, NGOs, social activists and the media from across the communities' borders.

6. Targeted and Discriminatory Approach

Target groups and areas for intervention need to be identified and prioritising of strategies for different sections of community needs to be done. For instance, intervention may vary from deterrence to welfare to counselling to awareness.

Anti-alcoholism needs to be targeted at those aspects of alcohol intake, which lead to either creation of social nuisance, such as increase in crime or harassment of women; tackling the harmful effects of alcoholism on the individual and undermining the conspicuous consumption of alcohol that creates a culture of drinking.

In other words, anti-alcoholism is targeted to undermine the alcohol dependence of some individuals, abuse resulting from alcohol whether in the confines of the family or in society at large, checking the social nuisance factor of drunks and checking the rise in potential violation of the above three.

Thus anti-alcoholism is targeted as a specific type of alcoholism, which has a negative impact either on the individual, the family, society or the state.

IMPLEMENTING A TARGETED AND DISCRIMINATORY APPROACH: POINTERS FOR INDICATOR DEVELOPMENT

Target Areas	Focus Areas	Support Structure
Areas and people prone to liquor consumption	1. Direct enforcement 2. Drug de-addiction and counselling facilities 3. Community mobilisation	1. Social policing 2. Human resource development 3. Awareness generation 4. Gender justice and women's development
Moderate incidence of liquor consumption	1. Social policing 2. Human resource development 3. Community mobilisation	1. Awareness generation 2. Gender justice and women's development 3. Drug de-addiction facilities Enforcement support
Soft areas and occasional drinkers	1. Awareness generation 2. Human resource development 3. Gender development 4. Community mobilisation	1. Social policing 2. Drug de-addiction 3. Enforcement assistance

7. Building Forward and Backward Linkages with Development Activities

People have to be made aware of the material cost of alcoholism borne by society, the family and the individual and the extent to which it deviates resources from education and human resource development. Similarly, forward linkages could be built by providing health, education, etc. Human resource development needs should be the main thrust to undermine the culture of habitual drinking. The strategy would include calculating the economic cost of alcoholism borne by the families in terms of health services for the alcoholic, loss of education to the children, poor family health, etc. The loss of income to the family due to the diversion of funds, and loss of productivity to society should also be taken into account.

Such a strategy, therefore, is not restricted only to providing relief to the affected family from abuse within the family or from society. The participation of the community on this issue is not only of persons drawn only from identifiable victims of alcohol consumption, but from society as a whole since the negative effects of alcoholism are degenerative and are borne by the entire society. This approach provides the platform for instituting law.

Initiatives from below need to build support and state involvement before arriving at the stage of policy making. Stakeholders need to be effective in giving recognition to the changes sought. A wider base of networks, cross group representation, involvement of respective state agencies in activities leading to development of a collaborative approach with accountabilities fixed across layers of partners and which is coordinated with the required output can, help in initiating new laws.

3. TRANSPARENCY AND ACCOUNTABILITY

Integral to governance is the accountability of its institutions and transparency in the process of delivery of justice. Particularly in the criminal justice system, accountability is becoming the hallmark of the exercise of authority. While internal accountability referring to the hierarchical chain of command has been part of traditional authority systems, it is the accountability to the citizens and to the rule of law that is being strengthened. The need is to build institutional accountability structures that are democratic in their responsiveness, protective of rights and sensitive to the multicultures. Internal accountability within the institutions need to be made transparent and responsive rather than status quoist. Additionally, state controls such as, the judiciary and legislative bodies, autonomous constitutional controls, manifest in the national commissions (for human rights, women SCs/STs, minorities) are becoming proactive and need to be directional in their guidance rather than corrective and regulatory in their functioning.

> BOX 3.6: SOME PARAMETERS FOR ACCOUNTABILITY INDICATORS
>
> - *Multilateral and Multilayered mechanisms:* Layered and overlapping accountability to protect against stop-gap reactions.
> - *Follow-up and responsive:* Action-oriented and stakeholders informed on progress.
> - *Accountability fixed in accordance with responsibilities:* Each hierarchy, agency to be accountable for their range of activities.
> - *To be across board:* All stakeholders to be accountable, including oversights and social controls.
> - *Safeguarding complainant:* Anonymity, confidentiality to be maintained.
> - *Time-bound activity schedule:* Services to be provided in a time frame.
> - *Recognition of initiatives:* Rewarding of positive efforts encourages discharge of responsibilities.

These structured accountability mechanisms have a broader layer in the social controls reflective of interest groups, NGOs and the media. Internal controls in each institution of the police and judiciary are part of the internal hierarchy of controls.[3] The transparency of these controls is limited to the respective organisations. However, these follow the broad guidelines and respond to specific issues as complementary to state policies.

Providing justice is not an exclusive domain of the state. The functions to deliver services to the community and the attempts of the criminal justice system to function in an holistic manner have remained inadequate. The non-state civilian oversights both on the supply side of justice, i.e. National Human Rights Commission, National Minority Commission, National Women's

[3]The classification of accountability through control mechanisms in spheres of internal, external and social has been drawn from the Altus constructed definition. For details see http://nl.altus.org/altus/global_issues/global_issues_asp?section_id=28sub_section_id=468lang=en

Commission, etc., and on the demand side of justice civil society oversights, NGOs and the media have emerged to build bridges with state institutions.[4]

BOX 3.7: NATIONAL HUMAN RIGHTS COMMISSION AS A JUDICIAL OVERSIGHT

The institution has been created by an Act of Parliament called the Protection of Human Rights Act. (for details refer to Annexure V) The National Human Rights Commission is a statutory body chaired by an ex-Chief Justice of the Supreme Court and has ex-judges as members. In its authority to enact the powers of a civil court it can:

(i) Enquire into any petition regarding violation of/inaction to prevent human rights violation by any police institution or functionary in the country.
(ii) The commission can review and get action taken report on the existing policing safeguards and provide new guidelines/ procedures for custodial deaths/rape/police encounters, post-mortem examinations.
(iii) It can review policies/legislation/treaties pertaining to police accountability.
(iv) Provide sensitisation and training to the functionaries of the criminal justice system, NGOs, legislatures, judges.
(v) Monitor the functioning of the police in any state of India including insurgency affected areas.
(vi) It can provide recommendations for police reforms that would need to be considered.
(vii) Appoint human rights cells in each state police headquarters.

Given the above mandate, the NHRC has intervened in the following nature of instances related to police misconduct in:

(i) Custodial deaths
(ii) Police excesses (torture/death/misbehaviour)

[4]When police commitment is present, strong oversight can create a dialogue that will assist them in evaluating the steps they are taking, and keep them committed to, and focused on, achieving high standards. Effective and collaborative oversight further benefits police by reassuring policymakers, who provide the budgets to support high policing standards, that they are getting value for money.

David Bruce and Rachel Neild, 2005, *The Police That We Want: A Handbook for Oversight of Police in South Africa*, Johannesburg: Centre for the Study of Violence and Reconciliation, p. 8.

(iii) Death due to police firing/forceful charge/lathi charge
(iv) Women abuse/violations (allegation of connivance in trafficking in women)
(v) Inaction in case of atrocities against Scheduled Castes (see annexure)

The commission files an annual report of its activities with the Parliament. The report is, however, tabled according to the exigencies of Parliament. The report for 2003-4 was due to be tabled in Parliament in March 2006. For a detailed report for 2005 one will have to wait for another two years. Important cases addressed by the NHRC in 2005 are, however, listed. The number of cases can be vast—for instance the Punjab State Human Rights Commission has 7004 cases of alleged police misconduct reported to it for the year 2005.

For details refer to Annexure VI.

State controls have more or less been directed by the established social rules. These controls are at the most punitive. These non-state oversights have focused on correctional and transformatory agenda in relation to the marginalised groups, victims, common citizens and these have also sought explanations of violations in terms of reasons and behaviourial misconducts by building a reservoir of local resources. For the purpose of delivery of justice, the index maps the operational presence of external controls as state level oversights such as Human Rights Commission, Women/SC/ST/Minority Commissions. There is insufficient documentation to collate the per cent of beneficiaries and the focus for this edition of the instrument has only been on the processes of external control and does not include the impact. Also, social controls has been mentioned, but would only be included as an oversight if the efforts have been institutionalised and would then fall under the domain of institutionalised alternatives.

Right to Information Act

The Right to Information Act has been instated to provide freedom of information to the citizens as a basic right. It recognises the need for building institutional accountability structures, which are democratic and transparent. To arm the citizens with the right to demand information, however, may not be reflective of accountability and just governance. Multilateral linkages within the sectors, capacity building of staff and grievance redressal continue to be a challenge to the existing Act. These linkages and processes are yet to be developed, given the recent enactment of this law. The operational processes of this initiative would then form part of the index, followed by the impact analysis.

Institutional Alternatives

Gaps in the existing formal criminal justice system have been attempted to be filled with certain local specific initiatives. While some of these, such as *lok adalats*, may be national in character rather than local, this draws on the cultural traditions of the country dating perhaps to the Moghul era and can be labelled under a cultural mechanism. These institutional alternatives perforce function within the demarcated domains of the three institutions of the police, the judiciary and prisons. Two alternatives are explored under policing. One pertains to community policing, which has been adopted by the police in most states in India with an effort to involve the community as a participant in policing activities. The extent to which the community and the police work together for community needs of safety and crime prevention continues to remain debatable. Largely, community policing is being enforced rather than collectively conceived, implemented and monitored. Community policing experiments were initiated in the 1960s and 1970s in India. Some programmes like crime prevention weeks, setting up of boys' clubs and the Second Saturday Sports Meet were positive efforts for establishing police-public contact. The Delhi Police implemented schemes like Special Police Officers (1985), the Neighbourhood Watch (1989) through neighbourhood watch committees formed in each block, adoption of crime hot spots, and formation of anti-sexual harassment squads. To bring the community and the police closer, similar initiatives were taken in many other states—Madhya Pradesh, Tamil Nadu, Maharashtra, Rajasthan, Kerala, Punjab and Karnataka. These included the formation of Mohalla Committees to check communal violence in Bhiwandi (Maharashtra), Citizen Committees in Karnataka, and Village Vigilance Committees in Tamil Nadu.

Under the informal justice system certain programmes have been listed. These could be new initiatives such as the Near Zero Crime of the Rajasthan Police or the more traditional and steeped in history—the tribal dorbars of Meghayala. The Khap panchayat would also fall in this category but their democratic and just nature comes under scrutiny. In the courts, the *lok adalat* institution has been mentioned as an alternative, and under prisons, the open jail and the borstal schools are the provided illustrations. The index mapping is perhaps most inadequate in this sector since these initiatives are not well-documented and national police/prison/judiciary statistics are yet to include this classification. As mentioned previously, the index represents a methodology and initiatives are mapped as illustrations rather than data in the absence of readily available information.

BOX 3.8: LIST OF INDICATORS FOR INSTITUTIONAL ALTERNATIVES

- Police
  - Community policing
  - Informal justice systems
- Courts
  - Lok Adalat
- Prisons
  - Alternative to prisons
    - Borstal School
    - Open Jail

SOME EXAMPLES OF ALTERNATIVES THAT ARE INSTITUTIONALISED

COMMUNITY POLICING: COMMUNITY POLICE RESOURCE CENTRES[5]

The existing community policing efforts are directed to provide single window service and to use community representatives as facilitators for traffic management and security through neighbourhood watch groups. In other words, it is policing for the community and through the community and not policing along with the community. In view of this, there has been a felt need to evolve an institutionalised community policing through empowered community and culturally sensitive police.

[5]*Community Police Resource Centre: Punjab Police*, Chandigarh: Institute for Development and Communication.

An institutionalised version of community policing has been implemented in Punjab. The Community Policing Resource Centres (CPRCs) were formed through a notification by the Government of Punjab in 2003.[6]

It provides space for police-community partnership in crime prevention, grievance redressal, victim assistance and information related to law, rules and procedures, civic rights and duties.

It has a built-in mechanism of coordination with civil, judicial and non-government organisations.

The CPRC is a four-tier system of policing in partnership with the community, managed through committees having representatives of the civil society, specialists, NGOs, police functionaries and the civil administration.

At the state level, a Community Affairs Division (CAD) has been set up. The second tier consists of district level and the third tier the sub-divisional. The outreach is provided at the thana/police station level, the fourth tier.

All these tiers have forward and backward linkages. The state level steering committee provides policy guidelines, support for capacity building and strengthens the system of co-ordination. All other tiers provide backbone services and evolve their own local level and need-based schemes.

Each CPRC is an autonomous registered society collectively managed by representatives of the community and police functionaries. It provides citizens dignified access to police related

[6]Punjab has pioneered what is probably India's finest effort to improve relations between the police and local communities. In collaboration with the Ford Foundation, the Vera Institute of Justice and the Institute of Development and Communication, the government has opened community Police Resource Centers in most of the state's districts. These Centers provide a range of citizen services in a congenial atmosphere: A crime counter provides copies of first information reports (FIRs) and tracks the status of cases: a victim assistance unit provides professional counseling and support including advice on how to deal with the criminal justice system; a grievance redressal cell allows citizens' to file complaints against the police without having to go to a police station. As registered societies, the Centers have the right to raise money from external sources, although they are staffed by a mix of NGO activists and police officers.

World Bank, 2004, *Resuming Punjab's Prosperity: The Opportunities and Challenges Ahead*, p. 66.

services and a forum to implement community oriented programmes.

BREACH IN CITIZENS' SECURITY:
POLICING TO MANAGE COMMUNAL RIOTS[7]

The community policing approach has been adopted in many states to combat the eruption and management of communal riots. These efforts have been institutionalised in varying modes with some aspects more integral to policing and others conducted in an ad hoc manner as the situation demands. An illustration of managing these riots has been submitted to the central government with a frame of inclusiveness and participatory interactive approach by stakeholders. Included here are the indicators for stakeholders' engagements for three stages of riot prevention, management and social integration. The thrust of stakeholders activities shall change as per the situational context. For the prevention of riots in communally sensitive locations, the stakeholders would form part of the locality discussion groups to diffuse tension across the communal divides. In case of eruption of riots these stakeholders would perform the role of a riot defence committee and post-violence this group would emerge as the community nucleus for the integration of the victims and regenerator of the violence-torn social fabric.

BOX 3.9: INDICATORS FOR STAKEHOLDERS' ENGAGEMENT IN RIOT PREVENTION, MANAGEMENT AND SOCIAL INTEGRATION

- INDICATORS FOR EFFECTIVE STAKEHOLDER ENGAGEMENT: RIOT PREVENTION
  - Representative leadership of diverse social groups
    - Communities affected by communal tensions are represented on this group.
    - Community representatives are willing and voluntary participants.
    - Do the stakeholders have the capacity on the following:
      - Skills to identify alternatives on contentious issues which have a basis in historically perceived antagonisms.

[7]Pramod Kumar, 1998, *Youth for Social Harmony: Ek Aur Manthan: Facilitator Manual*, Chandigarh: Institute for Development and Communication.

- Willing to redefine goals and interests of the conflict situations.
- Are dovetailing issues of social harmony with development concerns (example—development work on roads is taken up in localities of both the Hindus and Muslims).
- Are committed to peaceful resolution of underlying conflicts.
  - Are willing to counter communal myths, stereotypes and rumours.
  - Protect society and maintain social codes and individual integrity.
  - Have deployed techniques of social fencing
    This involves efforts to build people's and ideological fence rather than physical fence of one locality from the other. Social fencing can be initiated with the help of the youth, students, NSS volunteers, NGOs and social activists from across the community borders.
- Through dialogue with group members they are creating social measures to undermine communal thinking and action.
  - They are creating confidence among the community members for peaceful and productive existence.
- They are constantly monitoring the situation.
- They are meeting in a timely manner to undertake follow-up action.
- They are moving towards change by identifying roles and discussion for agreed actions within the stakeholders' group.

- INDICATORS FOR EFFECTIVE STAKEHOLDER ENGAGEMENT: RIOT MANAGEMENT
  - Stakeholders agree to work together to manage the riot and control the violence at the earliest.
  - Undertake social fencing and policing. The concept of social policing means to encourage members of the community to participate and control elements of population participating and instigating riots.
  - The stakeholders have created youth groups for policing at the checkpoints in the locality.
  - Are working to protect the safety and security of each locality member irrespective of their religion or other divides.
  - Have undertaken Patrolling by defence groups of sensitive localities where anti-social elements are located. People of the locality, irrespective of their religion, should be protected from these anti-social elements.
  - Are sensitising the community to incidents leading to riots.
  - Are reducing hostilities by dispelling insecurity among the clashing groups, generated by rumours, stereotypes and generalisations.
  - De-communalisation and de-politicisation of incidents are being undertaken with locality centric dealing of the situation.

- Have gauged the level and nature of stakes and actors in the disputes to diffuse incidents.
- Have created security groups, which will protect religious processions, festivities.
  - Have undertaken tight vigilance in localities prone to riots (checking the spread of rumours, myths, containing small spats, etc.).
  - Are protecting the community from anti-social elements. Has vigilance been provided to symbols and religious places, which could be potential targets for sabotage or demolition?
- Are providing protection to sensitive points, which have experienced recurrence of rioting and also targets religious places, houses of prominent personalities such as leaders, cricketers, etc.
- Are collaborating and networking with the security system.
- Are mobilising the local, traditional and institutional authority systems to control the outbreak and escalation of antagonism, hostilities and violence.

- INDICATORS FOR EFFECTIVE STAKEHOLDER ENGAGEMENT: SOCIAL INTEGRATION
  - Identification of victims and families affected by the riots (victims include not only those who have been targets of physical violence, but also their dependents, witnesses to violence and those who have lost property in the violence).

❑ *Rehabilitative Measures*

- Liaisoning with health centres and hospitals.
- Organising health camps.
- Promotion of mobile health units in localities which have faced widespread violence.
- Provision of educational assistance such as tuition to students who may have missed a number of school days.
- Recreational activities.
- Sports and cultural activities to be started in localities to initiate interaction and act as stress relievers.
- Assistance in rehabilitation through administration's support.
- Checking harassment of women who may have been traumatised, abused and are susceptible to harassment and exploitation

❑ *Community sensitisation and mobilisation*

- Sensitisation and training of Community support structures such as NGOs, civil society network on:

- Victimisation and its impact.
- Conflict resolution: Strategies and skills.
- Gender sensitisation.
- Mobilisation of community to integrate victims and spread awareness to counter the culture of violence.
- Assistance to the victims (for further details refer to addressing needs of victims in a framework of rights of collectivities).

BOX 3.10: STEPS IN MANAGEMENT OF COMMUNAL RIOTS

- An assessment of the nature of interaction between the groups involved in the conflict.
- An understanding of the role of various actors involved in disputes like teasing of a girl, route of a procession, etc.
- Gauging the level and nature of stakes of the actors in the dispute.
- Mobilisation and involvement of the members of the community with a positive orientation towards the value of welfare, peace, justice and social development.
- Matching the values of the parties to the dispute for early prevention.
- Community sensitisation for insulation of dispute.
- De-communalisation and de-politicisation.
- Community mobilisation and awareness.
- Social fencing and policing.

INFORMAL MECHANISMS: DORBARS; RANGBA SHNONG

The tribal hill state of Meghalaya in north-east India has traditional institutions of communities that have been functioning as parallel justice providers and also in overseeing the functioning of the police force on a case to case basis.

The Khasi tribe has a tradition (prior to British Rule) under which criminal justice was delivered by assemblies of adult men. It has a pyramid structure with a chief, an intermediatry group of selected members and a larger group of men at the bottom. Prior to the installation of the Indian criminal justice system, the Dorbar pronounced judgments on disputes. While the Dorbar continues to function as a parallel adjudicating system to police and courts, it has drawn on its reservoir of traditional legitimacy to oversee police functioning in cases involving tribal members.

The Dorbar has approached the police for its slow investigation, inhuman treatment, questioned police excesses and inadequate protection of the rights of citizens. All interventions have been in specific cases.

ALTERNATIVE DISPUTE RESOLUTION: NEAR ZERO CRIME[8]

In order to provide justice which is timely and accessible, Rajasthan Police involved its citizen based community liaison groups (CLG) to be part of a programme, which resolves petty cases through the involvement of community representatives that are mutually settled. Through this programme, the aim was to settle disputes amicably and fairly in a matter of days in contrast to five or 10 years' delay the people face in courts. This programme combines the services of the police and the judiciary. The need for a community-based alternative for dispute resolution was felt, keeping in mind that:

- Only 2 per cent of the cases disposed by the courts were severe enough to be penalised by imprisonment. A large majority i.e. 98 per cent end in discharge, acquittal or a fine.
- In all, crime by professionals/habitual criminals and falling under the heinous offences, is only 20 per cent of the total cases going to courts. The remaining 80 per cent fall under the category of petty offences and arise from local disputes between relatives, neighbours, partners, etc.

Operational Features

- A close watch is kept on events in villages through frequent visits by beat in-charge and beat officer (constable).
- Consent of parties to the dispute for counselling and mutual settlement, taken by CLG members.
- Provision for counselling in the village rather than police station.
- Counselling is supported and assisted by beat in-charge and officer.

[8]Harsh Chopra, 2007, *Alternate Dispute Resolution: A Case Study of Rajasthan, India*, Chandigarh: Institute for Development and Communication.

- No registration of case if counselling results in voluntary and satisfactory compromise.
- Even after registration of a case and during investigation and trial, counselling continues.
- Heinous offence and offenders with criminal background are not part of this programme.

Evaluation of this scheme found that the stakeholders were provided with relief and there was a reduction in the reporting and registration of petty crime. Low registration of cases in police stations reduced the number of cases instituted for trial in courts.

A crude analysis of crime statistics since the launch of this programme reflects that the share of petty offences in reporting was reduced to 28.0 per cent.

To strengthen the existing delivery of justice mechanism, alternative justice delivery initiatives as a supplement will create an enabling and encouraging participatory institutional framework. A commitment to this shall contribute to building a crime-free and just society.

BOX 3.11: INSTITUTIONAL ALTERNATIVES: HOW DEMOCRATIC AND EFFECTIVE?

- Are institutional alternatives integral to policing?
- Are their institutional arrangements to support mainstreaming of activities?
- Are integrative mechanisms flowing from macro policy framework to micro enterprise at the regional and local levels?
- Are their coordinating structures with other government departments and NGOs promoting an integrative model of delivery of justice?
- Is there political ownership to the programme?
- Are participatory systems structured for planning and management to promote transparency, accountability and ownership?
- Is there a dedicated monitoring mechanism?
- Is representation of diversity reflected in planning and operational functions?
- Nature and level of community response to services provided.
- Have community representatives become stakeholders?

4. Towards Development of an Index

A criminal justice system index has to reflect the complex interrelationship between the phenomena of divergent sorts and interrelationship of performance of various sectors like the police, the courts, prisons, etc. To operationalise this across the five dimensions mapped, indicators have been classified as Performance, Inclusive and Outcome oriented. Performance indicators include efficiency and transparency and inclusive indicators comprise of participation of cultural and equal justice dispensation to diversities and outcome indicators include reduction in crime and commitment to justice.

Under each of the three operational indicators, all sectors involved in the delivery of criminal justice system like the police, the court and prisons have been covered by using multiple indices analysis.

These indices have been used to formulate a criminal justice composite index of its performance, inclusive approach and outcomes.

For building a comprehensive policy regime, the outcomes have to be placed in the local context while keeping in view global standards.

Gauging What Affects Safety

Controlling the crime rate is the endeavour of the police, improving the disposal of case loads is a major concern of the Judiciary and managing prison populations a pre-occupation of the prison staff. These institutions have their corresponding parameters of performance within an enforcement oriented framework. In other words, investigation is the exclusive domain of policing, prosecution is with Director Prosecution, and litigation and conviction trials remain with the courts. The whole process of delivery of justice is demarcated with each institution performing its own assigned role with no ultimate accountability towards the end result.

For the police, the assumption is that lower the reported crime rate (even if the occurrence of crime may be high), more efficient the policing. Whereas, for the prosecution and the courts, the measure is high conviction rate even if the quality of trial and justice dispensed may be poor. Thus, 'The deeper we delve into the processes of criminal justice and the more we rely on prosecution, court and prison statistics, the more we reduce our chances of saying anything straightforward about the nature and extent of crime.'[1]

These multi-agencies perform different functions within the domain of criminal justice. How do these help in improving the safety or the perception of safety and the delivery of justice among citizens? Does participation in community policing programmes, strengthening of informal and customary justice mechanisms, and easy approach to courts overhaul the perception of criminal justice functioning in the country?

Besides the issue of accountability for citizen safety, a pertinent issue, also refers to 'whose safety'. In India, myriad differences of ethnicity, region, caste, gender, language, mark social reality. Do these differences then constitute a composite citizen? While equality of citizens of India is the hallmark of the constitution, these differences do place some citizens unfavourably in context to others. In practice, it is the formal equality that is envisaged with the provision of equal access to the resources for safety and protection of human body and property. Unfavourably, placed groups such as Scheduled Castes, migrants, minority and women have relatively poor access to services and facilities than the average population. To presume that the prism of equality sees no differences may, in fact, discriminate against minority and unfavourable groups by being insensitive to their concerns. For instance, if the policy of gender equality treats both male and female on parity, then the special needs of women, for instance, privacy to report domestic disputes, of bodily violence like rape

[1]John Muncie, 2001, 'The Construction and Deconstruction of Crime', in John Muncie and Eugene Mclaughlin (eds.), *The Problem of Crime*, p. 29, London: Sage Publications.

or molestation would not be included as part of a neutral initiative to treat each citizen alike. A homogeneous language, personal laws or cultural practices, in fact, selects one choice (generally of the dominant group) while denying others. Rather than being identity neutral, sensitivity to the identity of the gender, religion or other primordial groups have to be part of the delivery of justice. Further, in a multicultural context, the recognition of difference may not be able to prioritise what difference or whose difference needs to be accorded primacy. Do the criminal justice institutions have parameters on the basis of which one group's differences stand higher in hierarchy over others? This issue emerges as one's collectivities rights conflict with that of another's collectivity or when the rights of an individual conflict with rights of its collectivity. The infamous Shah Bano Case is an example of an individual right in conflict with collective identity. The practice of personal law, symbolically proclaims a group's distinct identity. Shah Bano, as a divorced women, had the right to demand maintenance under Indian Civil Law, which the Muslim Personal Law did not provide. Resorting to the Indian Civil Law was perceived by certain sections of Muslim as interference in undermining the Muslim identity. The right of the Muslim collectivity was supported by an act of the Parliament and Shah Bano relegated to a gender unjust verdict of the Muslim clergy. Are these considerations part of the justice system when it strives to protect the rights of citizens in their individual, collective and distinct identities?

A related matter pertains to prioritising the criminal justice outlays and initiatives. For instance, what are the necessary and what are the additional measures to improve the delivery of justice? When does commitment to justice gain relevance without sufficient investment in infrastructure, human and systemic support? How far can commitment to justice provide meaning to safety? Are the rights of population affected by crime less important than the protection of citizens untouched by crime? What kind of distribution and linkages need to be built between input of resources, output of capacities and outcomes in terms of crime reduction and commitment to justice? Some of these considerations have been clearly documented, for instance, in reference to community policing. To quote:

But discussions of community policing seldom distinguish effectiveness, equity, and efficiency, in part because these are often inseparable. Attempts to redress one deficiency, say equity, are often seen as addressing the other two. For example, it has been asserted, with little hard evidence, that involving members of the community in police decision making (equity) simultaneously makes people feel that the police are responsive (equity), helps reduce neighbourhood crime (effectiveness), and can reduce the police workload (efficiency). Similarly, it has been claimed that decentralising decision making (efficiency) makes officers better able to address community problems (effectiveness), makes officers more accountable to citizens (equity), and makes better use of police resources (efficiency).[2]

The discussion in this chapter tries to cull out some of these issues with the help of the index. These include issues in collective accountability; considerations of safety, provision of safety within the constitutional frame giving due recognition to differential placements of populations with equality of treatment as an outcome; linkages in different dimensions of safety and delivery of justice.

BOX 4.1: COMPUTING THE *z* AND STANDARD SCORE

The index is based on published macro indicators to help compare separate justice systems. (In India, law and order is a state subject and though the legal traditions are guided by the Constitution, enforcement and implementation are state specific.) The index is prepared on five dimensions:

1. Accessibility and efficiency of the criminal justice system
2. Level of physical security enjoyed by the citizens
3. Rights of populations affected by crime
4. Commitment to justice
5. Institutional alternatives

Diagnostic ratios are computed on the *z* scale for five dimensions. Further the *z* score is converted into standard score (*T*) to allow different indicators with varying nature to make them comparable. The average of the *T* scores represents each dimension and the index.

[2]John E. Eck and Dennis P. Rosenbaum, op. cit. (1994), p. 6.

Standard score for each indicator

$$z = \frac{X - M}{\sigma}$$

Convert z score into T score

$$z = \frac{T - 50}{10}$$

or Average of T on dimension T_1

Index: Average of all T scores on each dimension

$$= \frac{T1 + T2 + T3 + T4 + T5}{5}$$

An advance analysis of any of the five dimensions is also possible. For instance, correlations, rank difference correlations, cluster representation of indicators of policing, prisons or any other dimension can be undertaken. In addition, the centroid method of factor analysis can be employed on the inter-correlation matrix. Such a matrix will be generated from working out the inter-correlations between the sub-scores. This technique will be helpful in identifying 'common factors' and 'specific factors' leading to a constellation of variables clustering together and sharing a common factor variance. This will help in suggesting differential inputs to be provided in improving the justice index and in turn the delivery of justice.

The Five Dimensions of the Index

Different facets of justice are reflected in a composite manner through the index. It can be noted that there is no state that performs well or poorly on the five dimensions. Performance varies on various indicators.

I. ACCESSIBILITY AND EFFICIENCY

The indicators under this dimension are measures of the growing confidence of the people in the criminal justice system and internal efficiency of the multi-agencies assigned the task of dispensing justice. However, for this edition, due to limitations of data, accessibility has been reduced to availability of resources and should be analysed accordingly.

The ranking on this composite dimension shows that the

smaller and the peripheral states and union territories such as Mizoram, Andaman and Nicobar, Nagaland and Sikkim fall in the top four states providing the best access to and most efficient delivery of justice to people within their jurisdiction. In contrast, the central belt comprising states of West Bengal, Maharashtra, Bihar, Gujarat, Jharkhand, Uttar Pradesh and Orissa are among the ten low performing states. However, a disaggregate analysis provides further pointers and cautions to this broad picture. The efficiency ranking reveals that some of the southern and north-east states reflect the best efficiency in performance of the three core institutions of police, judiciary and prisons. Thus union territory of Pondicherry, Andhra Pradesh, Mizoram, Tamil Nadu and Nagaland are the top states in the gamut of process activities that include the performance measures, namely, disposal of cases (police and courts), recovery of stolen property, chargesheeting, conviction and time taken for trial. Maharashtra, Bihar and Jharkhand continue to have the lowest performance even in the subset of efficiency indicators. (Refer Table 1 in Annexure V.)

A number of configurations can be compiled within each dimension depending on the theme of enquiry such as resource deployment or more specific police personnel, equipment, diversity representation, etc. For instance, if the staff density as a composite of area and population is to be studied, data from both the number of police personnel per 100 sq. km. and per lakh population can be collated to give a better measure of police deployment. For instance, Delhi ranks number one on policemen per 100 sq. km., but falls to number twelve if police per lakh population is seen. On a composite scale, Chandigarh has the most staff density followed by Delhi with Jharkhand and Bihar having the least staff deployment. (Refer Table 2 in Annexure V.)

II. LEVEL OF PHYSICAL SECURITY

This composite indicator measures the level of physical security, constrained by the level of variation between the occurrence of actual crime and the reported crime.

Again the smaller and the peripheral states and union

territories of Lakshadweep, Andaman and Nicobar Islands, Nagaland and Mizoram registered high performance levels.

The mainland states like Delhi, Rajasthan, Orissa, Maharashtra, Madhya Pradesh figured among the lowest ten states and union territories.

A number of analysis can be made within this dimension, prominent among them being a study of statewise crime profile. For instance, the union territory of Delhi ranks 10th *vis-à-vis* the total crime rate. For crime against body it ranks 20th, but it is the most unsafe place for women and children. It is also the most unsafe place for material assets. On both crime against property and economic crimes, it ranks as the second most unsafe place after union territory of Chandigarh. It is relatively safer for crimes against Scheduled Caste populations and also on SLL crimes. (See Graph 1 in Annexure V.)

Another issue that is also reflected in the crime in India statistics is the percentage change in IPC crimes as compared to the previous year. Again the peripheral locations of Lakshadweep and Sikkim recorded the most change in their crime rates. But these figures need to be tallied with the total crime rate. While Lakshadweep has a relatively low crime rate ranked 34th, Sikkim has a relatively higher crime rate and ranks 25th in the overall crime rate. (Refer Table 3 in Annexure V.) However, when one compares Sikkim on all the five dimensions, it further falls to rank 18. Pertinently, it is important to explore the disaggregate, but within the larger context of justice.

III. RIGHTS OF POPULATION AFFECTED BY CRIME

This is an important dimension to measure the nature of the functioning of criminal justice system towards the creation of a sense of entitlement in justice delivery among the victims of crime.

It is revealing that the north-eastern states register the best performance in terms of safeguarding the rights of population affected by crime. The states ranked with the best performance on this dimension are Sikkim, Manipur and Meghalaya. The Naxalite troubled states of Andhra Pradesh and Madhya Pradesh and civil strife affected Mizoram fall in the last ranks. However, it is interesting to note that some of the smaller and peripheral union territories of Lakshadweep, Dadar and Nagar Haveli recorded a low performance on this dimension. Interestingly, the other three states that fall under this last ten category are Bihar, Punjab and Uttar Pradesh. A disaggregate analysis further reveals that Punjab has the most complaints registered against its security personnel (both police and prison staff), followed by Madhya Pradesh and Delhi. The least registering of complaints is in the peripheral union territories and the north-eastern region comprising Dadar and Nagar Haveli, Daman and Diu, Lakshadweep and in the north-east Mizoram, Manipur and Arunachal Pradesh. (Refer Table 4 in Annexure V.) If the record of performance of states in protection of affected population is further extended to rate of conviction of police personnel convicted and total death of inmates in the jail then the picture further intensifies with both Punjab and Madhya Pradesh continuing to be among the poor performing states. (Refer Table 5 in Annexure V.)

IV. COMMITMENT TO JUSTICE

This is a pointer towards making explicit the state's intentions to deliver justice through declarations of rights and providing constitutional remedies.

It is worthwhile to notice that mainland states of West Bengal, Maharashtra, Karnataka, Rajasthan and Assam are more explicit in their commitment to justice.

Whereas, the small and peripheral states and union territories of Lakshadweep, Pondicherry, Daman and Diu, Nagaland, Arunachal Pradesh and Sikkim registered low performance.

It must be noted that these two dimensions of commitment to justice and institutional alternatives suffer from data inadequacies. Institutions and commissions that have made themselves accessible to populations through the internet and other documentations have been included. However, certain trends do emerge, particularly that the state commissions most active are those for women, followed by human rights, minority and Scheduled Caste commissions, respectively. The commitment to justice is most prominent in context of women where not only the state commissions, but also supportive bodies, such as women cells in police stations, have been opened.

V. INSTITUTIONAL ALTERNATIVES

As the states and union territories become explicit in their commitment to justice, the efforts to make access to justice real can be gauged through the existence of legal institutions, participatory law-making and delivery of justice mechanisms.

The need and the practice that make delivery of justice democratic were more among mainland states like Rajasthan, Himachal Pradesh, Andhra Pradesh and Tamil Nadu.

On the other hand, small and peripheral states of Arunachal Pradesh, Manipur, Mizoram, Nagaland, Tripura, Dadar and Nagar Haveli and Daman and Diu have shown dismal performance. However, Bihar from among the mainland states, has shown less inclination to create alternative institutional mechanism to render justice to the people.

The most widespread alternatives that have been institutionalised are the community policing efforts. While majority of them are confined to the institution of police, some initiatives like that by Rajasthan cut across the judicial functioning (Near Zero Crime Programme). Even though, it is an extension of community policing into adjudication, it is only the institution of police that works with the local communities rather than a coordination between judiciary and policing.

For an indicatorwise scoring or ranking, please refer to tables in the annexure.

❑ *Why is the Composite Index and Ranking Not Filled?*

Readers would note that the composite index and its ranking of columns 11 and 12 have been left blank. The composite index has been included as part of the methodology that views the delivery of justice in a holistic manner giving due recognition to the various dimensions. However, to calculate and present the composite index in this edition would not be reflective of an accurate picture. However, a broad trend analysis has been undertaken to provide meaning to the conceptual framework

Table 4.1: Criminal Justice Index: Disaggregated on Five Dimensions

States	I. Accessibility efficiency of CJS	Ranking	II. Level of physical security enjoyed by the citizens	Ranking	III. Rights of populations affected by crime	Ranking	IV. Commitment to justice	Ranking	V. Institutional alternatives	Ranking	Composite	Ranking
	1	2	3	4	5	6	7	8	9	10	11	12
Andhra Pradesh	52.61	10	47.23	29	41.62	35	50.42	21	62.42	3		
Arunachal Pradesh	49.03	20	46.73	32	55.00	3	42.49	31	42.84	34		
Assam	45.69	30	50.02	16	51.40	16	59.27	1	55.38	11		
Bihar	44.98	34	54.26	4	44.37	33	55.32	6	42.87	33		
Chhattisgarh	49.88	16	48.16	27	46.83	29	50.60	19	51.14	15		
Goa	52.13	11	48.21	26	53.76	11	47.19	22	45.16	22		
Gujarat	46.55	29	50.74	12	48.35	22	55.28	7	55.50	10		
Haryana	49.45	18	48.30	24	46.61	30	47.19	22	47.96	17		
Himachal Pradesh	49.65	17	52.01	8	53.17	12	46.62	27	62.67	2		
Jammu & Kashmir	51.97	12	50.78	11	46.83	28	51.13	16	43.37	25		
Jharkhand	42.17	35	50.49	14	50.26	19	46.66	26	46.97	19		
Karnataka	48.06	24	50.99	10	48.67	21	59.27	1	56.35	7		
Kerala	49.27	19	49.85	20	54.19	9	55.28	7	57.58	5		
Madhya Pradesh	48.55	23	45.74	33	42.37	34	55.11	9	56.62	6		

Maharashtra	45.58	31	50.01	18	47.52	24	59.27	1	55.91	9
Manipur	50.46	14	52.69	7	54.45	7	50.60	19	42.94	32
Meghalaya	45.39	32	50.02	17	53.92	10	49.19	22	47.30	18
Mizoram	58.08	1	47.04	30	55.00	3	47.19	22	45.01	23
Nagaland	55.96	3	55.31	3	51.22	17	42.68	28	42.84	35
Orissa	47.10	27	50.41	15	47.42	25	51.13	16	52.77	13
Punjab	48.56	22	50.67	13	44.91	32	51.13	16	55.99	8
Rajasthan	48.61	21	48.10	28	46.98	27	59.27	1	67.46	1
Sikkim	54.96	4	48.72	23	55.72	2	42.49	31	46.22	21
Tamil Nadu	53.82	7	49.15	21	47.77	23	54.57	10	60.70	4
Tripura	50.70	13	49.88	19	52.41	13	51.34	12	42.96	31
Uttar Pradesh	48.05	25	53.57	5	45.62	31	54.57	10	43.34	26
Uttarakhand	49.95	15	53.07	6	52.13	15	51.17	14	46.89	20
West Bengal	45.22	33	55.87	2	50.76	18	59.27	1	55.35	12
UT Andaman & Nicobar Islands	58.05	2	51.49	9	50.10	20	42.68	28	43.23	27
UT Chandigarh	54.29	6	42.87	35	52.14	14	51.34	12	48.33	16
UT Dadar and Nagar Haveli	46.79	28	48.24	25	55.00	3	42.68	28	43.15	29
UT Daman and Diu	47.67	26	49.01	22	58.21	1	37.98	34	43.19	28
UT Delhi	53.06	9	45.24	34	47.21	26	51.17	14	51.91	14
UT Lakshadweep	53.34	8	58.14	1	55.00	3	37.98	34	43.06	30
UT Pondicherry	54.66	5	47.00	31	54.29	8	42.49	31	44.66	24

advanced and to present the viability of the instrument and relevance to criminal justice stakeholders. This is due to data inadequacies, absence of documentation in a systematic format, non-availability of victimology and citizen perception studies. The work on establishment of measurement equivalence is still in its infancy. The columns have been included since the instrument is a methodology towards the construction of a composite index, but its construction with the given data could lead to erroneous generalisations. Once these inadequacies have been addressed, the columns representing composite index can be printed.

Relevance of the Index

BOX 4.2: RELEVANCE OF THE INDEX

1. Focus on justice delivery
2. Justice as a composite service
3. Comparing inputs with outputs and outcomes
4. Addressing issues of vulnerable groups
5. Identifying indicators most effective for particular outcomes
   (a) Efficiency and crime rates
   (b) Relation between efficiency and staff representation
6. Measuring the utility of alternatives
7. Identifying patterns
8. Theme specific pointers

1. Focus on Justice Delivery

Conventional data reflect performance on individual indicators. For instance, conviction rates, staff deployment or the extent of crime. While these indicators are both process and impact based, they rate the performance on a single variable and are by default focused on the efficiency of the agency. The delivery of justice on the other hand is citizen-focused and measures the efficacy of fair, timely, effective, inexpensive and accountable justice. In addition to the performance levels, the outcomes are also measured. If the prosecution wing has been separated from the police, the departmental critique points to a fallout in terms of lower conviction rates, claiming a toll on efficiency—albeit of the prosecution wing. However, the scope of fair trial has been theoretically enhanced with specialised and focused input. In other words, the quality of justice provided to the citizen becomes central. At a secondary level efficiency can be improved by collective accountability where prosecution is bolstered by well investigated cases from the police. In fact, under this framework primacy is given to the outcomes of safety rather than outputs, which impact the outcomes.

BOX 4.3: EFFICIENCY *VERSUS* QUALITY OF JUSTICE

But the separation of the investigation and prosecution functions has resulted in no accountability for the end result. With the separation of functions of investigation and prosecution the conviction rate has declined in India.

DISPOSAL OF IPC CRIME CASES BY COURTS (1961-2001)

S.No.	Year	Total	No. of Cases		No. of Percentage of	
		cases for Trial (including Pending Cases)	Tried*	Convicted	Trial Completed (col. 4/ col. 3)	Conviction (col. 5/ col. 4)
1	1961	8,00,784	2,42,592	1,57,318	30.3	64.8
2	1971	9,43,394	3,01,869	1,87,072	32.0	62.0
3	1981	21,11,791	5,05,412	2,65,531	23.9	52.5
4	1991	39,64,610	6,67,340	3,19,157	16.8	47.8
5	2001	62,21,034	9,31,892	3,80,504	15.0	40.8

* Excluding Withdrawn/compounded cases
Source: Crime in India, 2001.

Demarcation of prosecution branch from police has conceptually enhanced the scope for a fair trial, but lack of logistic support has undermined trial quality and justice dispensed—Courts have to take a proactive role since this lacuna is glaring, e.g. Paras Yadav and others versus State of Bihar in (1999) 2 SSC. The court pointed out a lapse on part of the investigating officer and upheld the conviction of murder. The court held that on occasions, negligence or omission on the part of the police may give rise to reasonable doubt which would go in favour of the accused.

Source: Pramod Kumar, 2005, 'Mapping Police Accountability Spectrum: Issues for Building Quality Oversights with a Multicultural Framework', in Pramod Kumar (ed.), *Dimensions of Police Accountability in India*, Chandigarh: Institute for Development and Communication, pp. 1-36.

2. JUSTICE AS A COMPOSITE SERVICE

The sum total of the sectoral functioning is analysed in a single measure. Conceptually, the agencies' performance and roles are perceived as continuous and interlocked, but operationally demarcated in sectors, with specialised functions. Taken singularly or sectorally, the crime rate or the conviction rate reflects the efficiency levels of an agency on that particular variable and does not provide a composite reflection of the outcome, which is the delivery of justice. One department may perform exceptionally well on the recovery of stolen property but reflect poorly on its chargesheeting rate. Performance efficiency is meaningful in the context of the overall performance. In other words, a disaggregate data in itself is meaningless without the context, benchmarking or the totality of performance. For instance, Haryana ranks number one in the recovery rate of stolen property in 2005, but ranks 16th on the chargesheeting rate and its performance falls to number 30 for the average time spent by undertrials in prison. Yet on the Composite Index that covers all the five dimensions, Haryana ranks thirty-first.[3] How can one interpret the police functioning, and more importantly, the delivery of justice to the common man?

Sectorally, agency performance is the focus of attention rather than the citizen as a recipient of safety and justice. If conviction rates are high and occupancy rates of prisons are also high, and chargesheeting is low then the citizen suffers in obtaining justice. Poor performance in one aspect can colour the entire system. In an FGD with daily wage earners in a rural setting, the participants pointed out that 'the police is of no use to the poor section of society. They are only meant for the protection of the rich and powerful'. 'The police has no discipline and little answerability and they do as they please.' 'The police presence is quite meaningless to us. If tomorrow the police is removed or is taken away, our lot will still be the same.' According to another participant, the courts are so time consuming that they become

[3]The composite Index has not been presented in the document since the focus is on the methodology and data gaps constrain the Index figure.

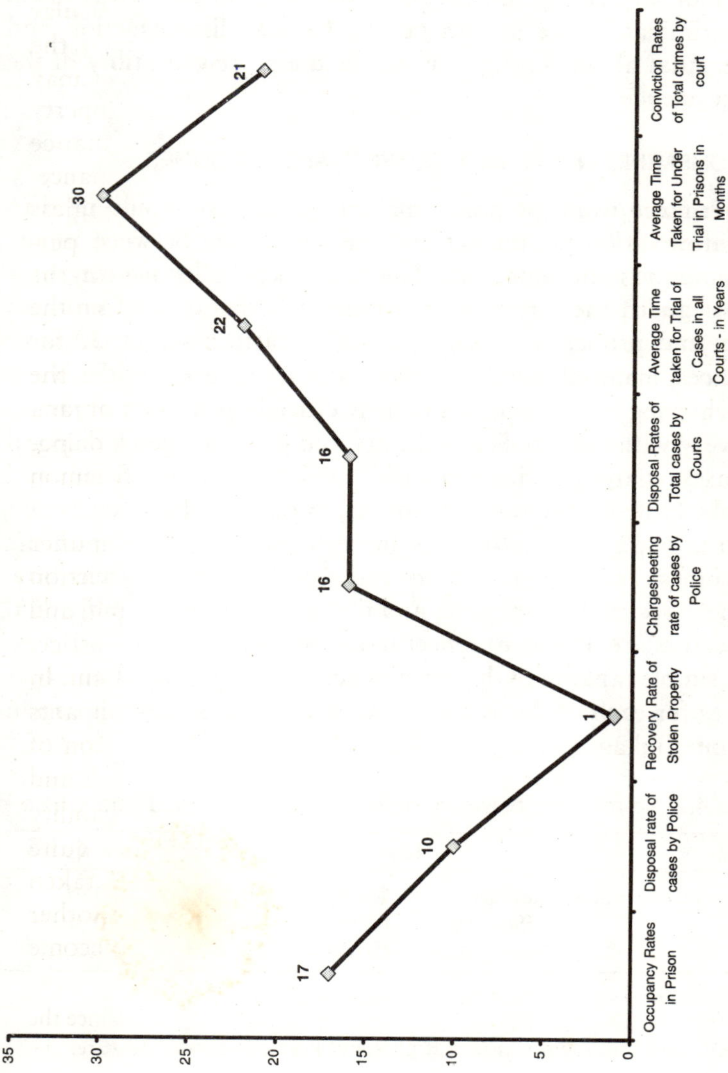

Graph 4.1: Profile of Haryana on Efficiency Indicators: An Illustration

expensive and the resolution meaningless.[4] In a narrative with the migrant community, a member revealed that the group had minimal contact with the formal justice system as members in their colony felt that the local leaders were competent to tackle disputes arising in the day-to-day life of the group and in maintaining decorum in the area. This image of the police or the judiciary in certain sections makes them shy away from the criminal justice system *per se*. Citizen dissatisfaction and perception about one agency, colour the perceived utility of the other agencies.

3. COMPARING INPUTS WITH OUTPUTS AND OUTCOMES

Governance from the policy makers perspective would need to be informed on the impact and the correlation between inputs with outputs and outcomes. The state takes collective measures to safeguard the interests of citizens in terms of protection to body and property. Outlays for the infrastructure in terms of finances, material, goods, human costs are incurred with a view to achieving certain outputs namely efficient processes of justice delivery within the police, judiciary and prisons—quick disposal of cases, chargesheeting rates and convictions to be efficient and timely. How do the resource inputs, impact on these functions? Do the outlays and efficiency in performance reflect upon the outcomes, i.e. on higher safety and security of the citizens (low crime)? Sectoral functioning and the large number of individual indicators are unable to reflect this relationship.

A simple ranking of the three indices of input, output and outcomes for each of the states and union territories reveals gap in the interlinkages.

Table 4.2: Co-relations between Resources, Efficiency and Total Crime

		Resources	Efficiency	Total Crime
Pearson Correlation	Resources	1.000	0.203	–0.012
	Efficiency	0.203	1.000	0.392*
	Total Crime	–0.012	0.392*	1.000

*Correlation is significant at the 0.05 level (2-tailed).

[4]IDC Field survey on Citizen Rights and Police Reforms, 2006.

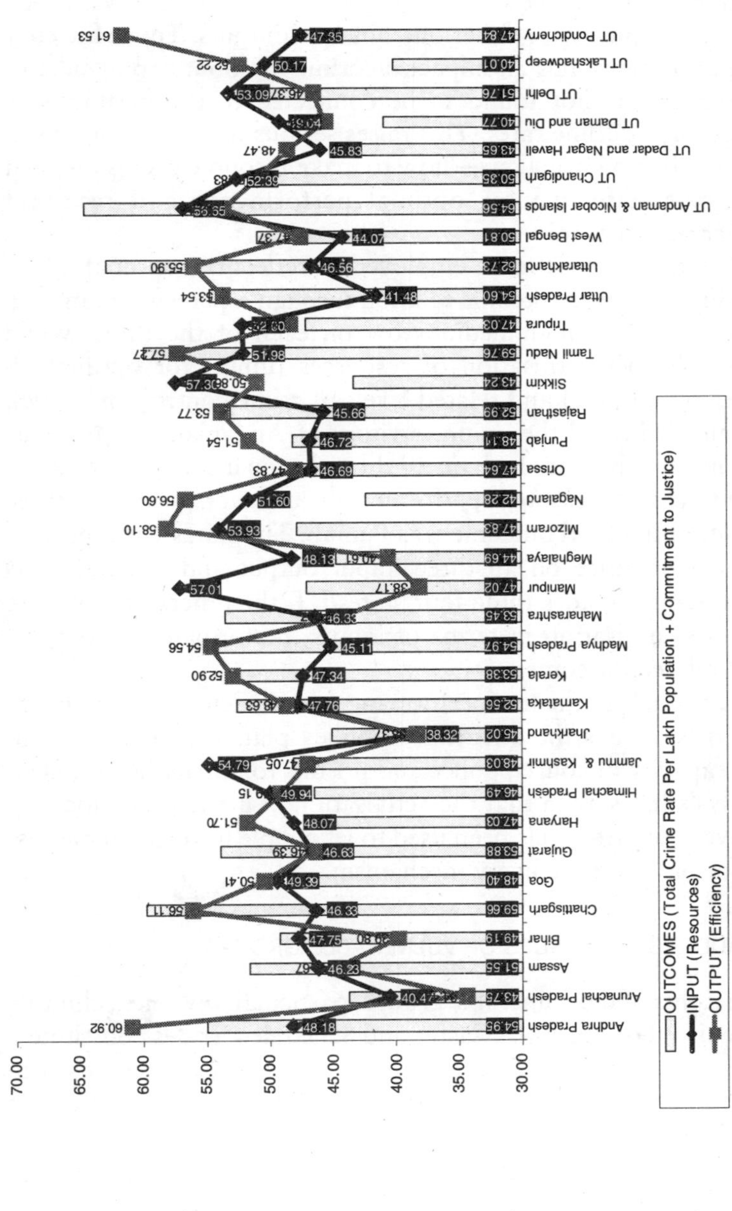

Graph 4.2: Statewise Resources, Efficiency, Total Crime and Commitment to Justice (Input, Output, Outcomes)

The interconnection can be explored further through a composite correlation or in a more disaggregate manner to gauge optimal efficacy for each state.

The correlations for the three subsets of inputs, outputs and outcomes found that there was a significant correlation between outputs and outcomes, while no significant correlation was found between inputs with either outcomes or outputs. Thus efficiency of performance has an impact on crime rate, but deployment of resources has not found to be connected to the performance levels or for crime rates. This raises serious questions for investigation by policy makers—how to make resource provisions that are most effective for optimal performance and resultant lowering of crime?

The index can also be employed to reflect the optimal use of the input-output-outcome relation through a percentile ranking. States that are high/medium/low on each of the three would show the best utilisation of resources (input) for optimal efficiency (outputs) and related levels of crime control (outcome). Tamil Nadu and the union territory of Andaman and Nicobar fall in the top band, high on all three. In the medium percentile's band where the states performed on an average on all three input, output and outcome was Punjab. The states with the lowest performance on all three, input output and outcome was Jharkhand. Besides these four states/UT, the others do not have the best utilisation in terms of inputs, performance in outputs and related outcomes.

In a nutshell, the low performance on efficiency and reduction of crime invites the attention of policy planners to supplement the capacity of courts, police and prisons to impact justice. Data analysis has shown that the activisation of alternative modes of delivery of justice has been used to let people have greater access to formal justice delivery mechanism.

4. ADDRESSING ISSUES OF VULNERABLE GROUPS

The rights of the vulnerable groups, particularly women, children and also the Scheduled Castes and Scheduled Tribes constitute a part of the political discourse. State commitment towards providing special attention to the vulnerable groups and those on the

Table 4.3: Optimal Efficacy in Input-Output-Outcomes: An Analysis Through Bands

	Input		Output		Outcomes	
	Resources T	Percentile	Efficiency T	Percentile	Total Crime + Commitment to Justice T	Percentile
HIGH BAND						
Tamil Nadu	51.98	1	57.27	1	59.76	1
UT Andaman & Nicobar Islands	60.69	1	53.44	1	64.56	1
MEDIUM BAND						
Punjab	46.72	2	51.54	2	48.11	2
LOW BAND						
Jharkhand	44.70	3	38.37	3	45.02	3

Keys: Low Band: <=33%
Medium band: > 33% and <=66%
High band: 66% and <=100%

margins is reflected in policy statements, but what are the operational initiatives undertaken and do these initiatives have an impact on improving the services to these specific groups? For instance, is the Scheduled Caste population discriminated by the agencies? Is there any difference in the chargesheeting rate related to the Scheduled Castes *vis-à-vis* the total chargesheeting rates?[5] Is the justice system gender sensitive? Are conviction rates for crimes against women higher as compared to other crimes?

A view of the index reveals that there is a significant difference in chargesheeting rates as crimes against the Scheduled Castes are much lower in states like West Bengal, Tamil Nadu and Jammu and Kashmir. On the other hand, Uttarakhand, Sikkim and Punjab are more efficient when it comes to crimes against women than their average chargesheeting rates. States of Mizoram, Tamil Nadu and Bihar reflect higher conviction rates in cases of crimes against the Scheduled Tribes. Clearly, the criminal justice system differentiates in its performance levels and thus in its accessibility to justice in accordance with the nature of the crime (like rape, molestation) and also in terms of population groups, an arena for policy makers to look into.

Such a comparison would document the state's concerns for its weaker sections, allow monitoring and promote the required changes. Graphs 4.3a and 4.3b reveal that the chargesheeting rates for women and children follow an average of the state pattern with a small range of difference, (though Nagaland and Lakshadweep are the obvious better performers). On the contrary, the difference in chargesheeting rates for Scheduled Castes and Scheduled Tribe varies much more from the state average. An area of concern would be the performance of the north-eastern states where the Scheduled Tribes are in majority. In states like Goa and Haryana, the Scheduled Tribes are in

[5]The growth of prisons, jails, and other penal institutions, in turn, has meant the stigmatisation of more and more minority youths. This stigmatisation has reinforced the image of the poor as dangerous and undeserving, an image that has been crucial in legitimating the shift from the welfare state to the security state.

Katherine Beckett and Theodore Sassion, 2000, 'War on Crime as Hegemonic Strategy: A Neo-Marxian Theory of the New Punitiveness in U.S. Criminal Justice Policy', in Sally S. Simpson (ed.), *Of Crime and Criminality*, Thousand Oaks: Pine Force Press, p. 78.

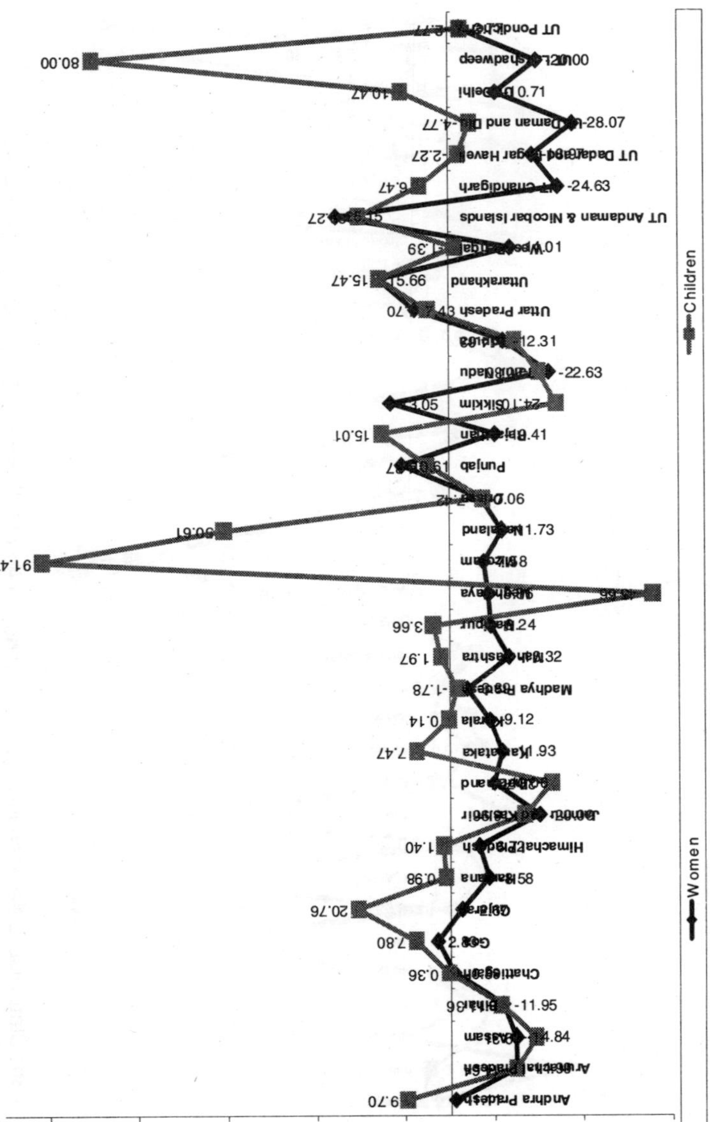

Graph 4.3a: Statewise Difference in Chargesheeting of Vulnerable Sections: Women and Children

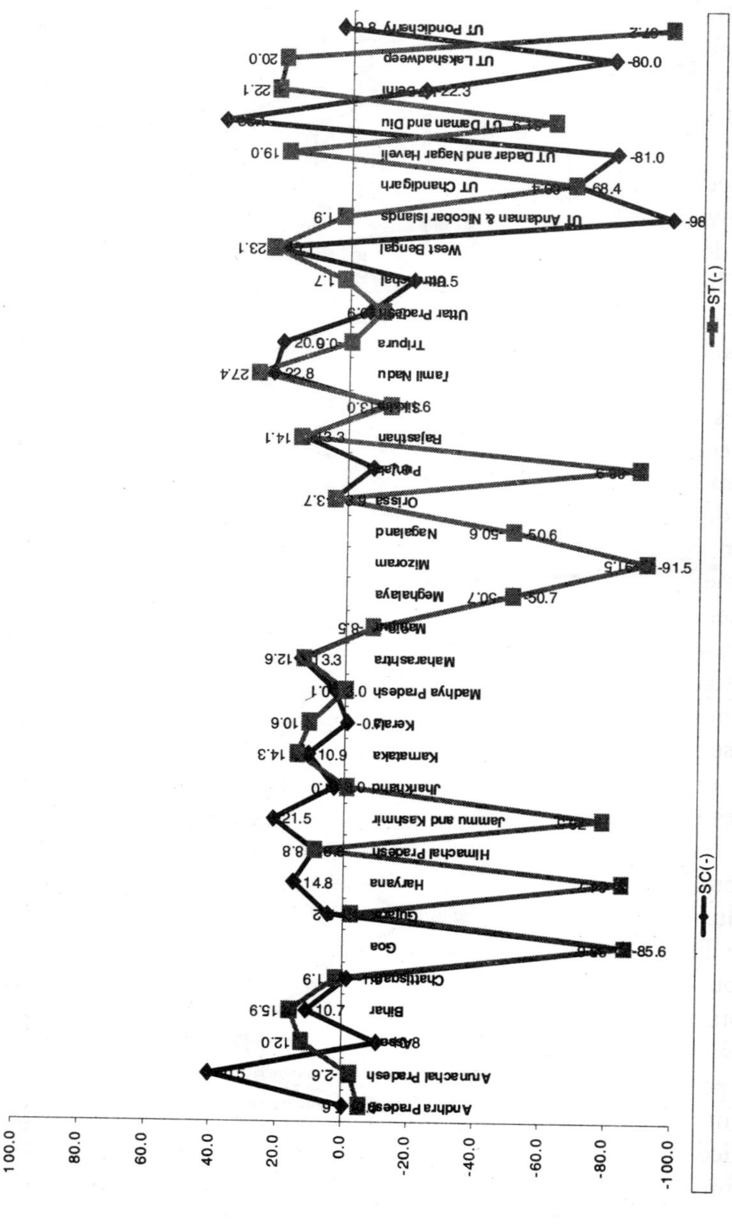

Graph 4.3b: Statewise Difference in Chargesheeting Rates of Vulnerable Sections: SCs and STs.

negligible number and the variation can be misleading. Similar is the case for Scheduled Castes in UTs of Lakshadweep, Pondicherry and the north-east.

The difference in chargesheeting rate reveals that the chargesheeting of Scheduled Castes is higher in comparison with the total chargesheeting rates in the states of Tamil Nadu, West Bengal and Jammu & Kashmir, whereas the union territories of Daman and Diu, Chandigarh and the states of Jammu & Kashmir reflect higher chargesheeting rates on crime against women, showing the states' efforts in the delivery of justice to women on gender crimes.

The point being that different groups are meted out a different justice. This can be a huge challenge to the respective state stakeholders in terms of fairness of the criminal justice system. This trend can be explored further by studying the conviction rates on these very population groups. A majority of the states reflect a higher conviction rate of the accused in crimes against women and children. The exception being the UTs of Arunachal Pradesh, Dadar and Nagar Haveli and Tripura.

In stark contrast to the stringent dealing with the accused in crime against women and children, the other weaker sections—Scheduled Castes and Tribes—face higher conviction rates as the accused. Why is this trend emerging?

Also, a clubbing of the range of initiatives for special populations would be a revealing indicator to foster confidence in these populations and can be used as advocacy data. For instance, the representation of diversity among the police staff. While certain states reflect concerns for different populations, largely for the inclusion of women in their staff, these appear to be population specific rather than more comprehensive in their inclusion for representation of the different collectivities. States like Tamil Nadu reflect the best composite representation of its population. Even here the proportionate representation of these groups only ranges between 47 to 58 per cent. Proportionate of women representation being the only exception with nearly 83 per cent representation (refer Table 6 in Annexure V). The point being that staff diversity, which is only limited to the police forces, has the most representation for women and a comparatively lesser presence of different population groups even

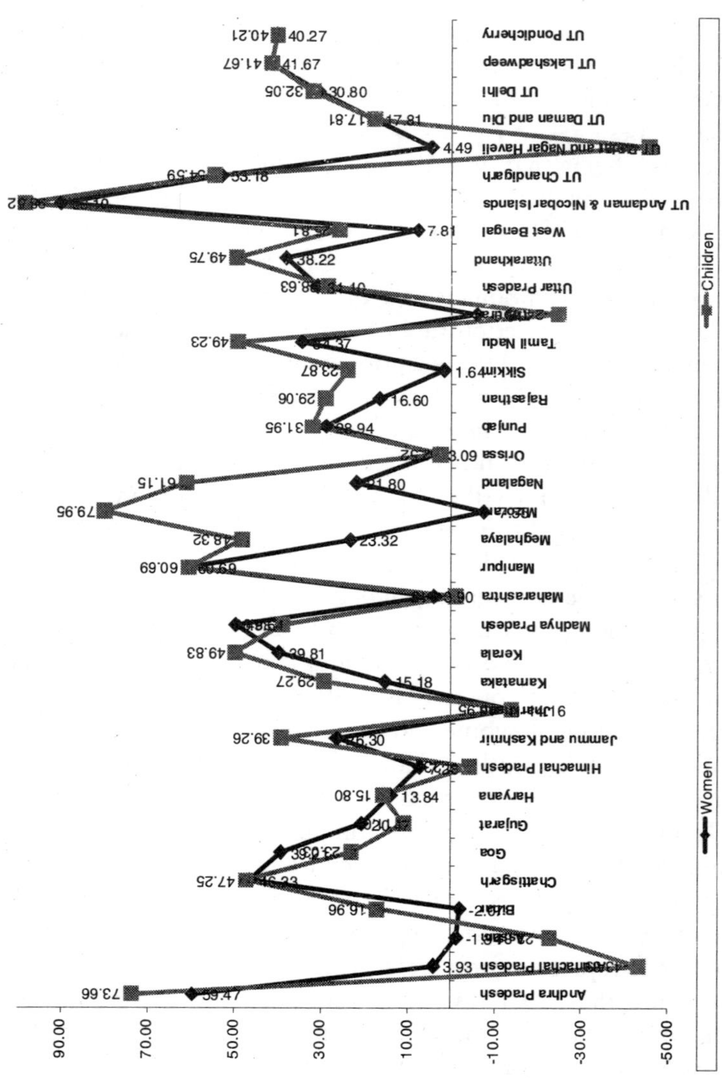

Graph 4.4a: Statewise Difference in Conviction Rates of Vulnerable Sections: Women and Children

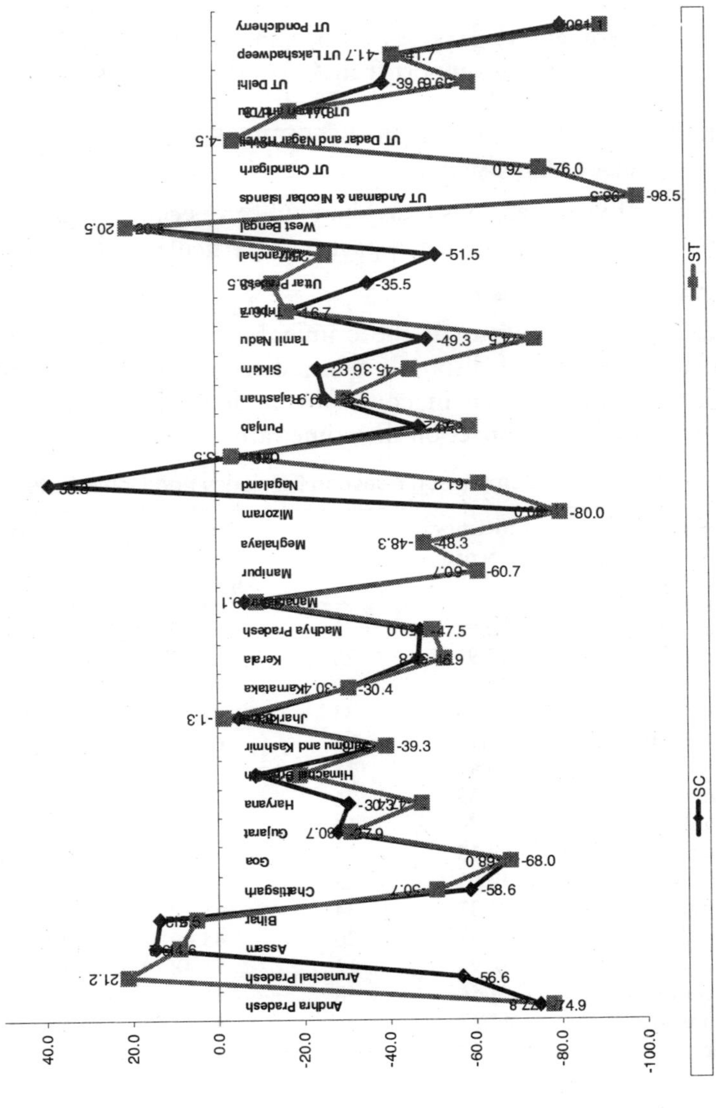

Graph 4.4b: Statewise Difference in Conviction Rates of Vulnerable Sections: SCs and STs

among those states having relatively better ranking (refer Table 6 in Annexure V). These gaps reflect on the challenges for policy makers by identifying spheres that still require special initiatives or seek support from civil society groups where gaps in certain services are identified. Stray indicators, such as rape or other forms of violence or representation of the minorities in the police force, only signify the inclination to be inclusive rather than allowing for a comprehensive strategy either in its implementation, monitoring or seeking support from informal resources.

5. IDENTIFYING INDICATORS MOST EFFECTIVE FOR PARTICULAR OUTCOMES

Within the five dimensions individual indicators can be used and clubbed to see the combined impact on a particular outcome.

(a) *Efficiency and Crime Rates*

Efficiency as an output of the criminal justice system is represented by rates of disposal, chargesheeting, conviction and the average time taken in courts by undertrials. How does efficiency make an impact on the crime rate?

Table 4.4: Statewise Comparison Between Efficiency and Crime Rate

States/UT	Efficiency T Score	Ranking	Total crime rate per lakh population	Ranking
Andhra Pradesh	60.92	2	59.47	5
Arunachal Pradesh	45.91	28	45.02	21
Assam	44.67	30	43.83	26
Bihar	39.80	33	43.06	30
Chhattisgarh	56.11	6	68.72	3
Goa	50.41	18	49.62	12
Gujarat	46.39	26	52.48	9
Haryana	51.70	14	46.88	16
Himachal Pradesh	49.15	19	46.36	18
Jammu & Kashmir	47.05	25	44.92	22
Jharkhand	38.37	34	43.37	29
Karnataka	48.63	20	45.86	19
Kerala	52.90	12	51.48	11
Madhya Pradesh	54.56	8	54.83	6
Maharashtra	44.27	31	47.64	15
Manipur	38.17	35	43.43	28

(*Contd.*)

Table 4.4 (*Contd.*)

Meghalaya	40.61	32	42.19	33
Mizoram	58.10	3	48.48	14
Nagaland	56.60	5	41.89	35
Orissa	47.83	23	44.16	24
Punjab	51.54	15	45.09	20
Rajasthan	53.77	9	46.71	17
Sikkim	50.86	16	43.98	25
Tamil Nadu	57.27	4	64.95	4
Tripura	48.26	22	42.72	31
Uttar Pradesh	53.54	10	54.64	7
Uttarakhand	55.90	7	74.29	2
West Bengal	47.37	24	42.35	32
UT Andaman & Nicobar Islands	53.44	11	86.44	1
UT Chandigarh	50.83	17	49.36	13
UT Dadar and Nagar Haveli	48.47	21	44.63	23
UT Daman and Diu	45.44	29	43.56	27
UT Delhi	46.37	27	52.36	10
UT Lakshadweep	52.22	13	42.04	34
UT Pondicherry	61.53	1	53.20	8
India	51.15		50.77	

Table 4.5: Co-relations between Efficiency and Total Crime

		Efficiency	Total Crime
Pearson Correlation	Efficiency	1.000	0.505**
	Total Crime	0.505**	1.000

Note: Efficiency is computed by taking the sum of disposal rates, charge sheeting rates, conviction rates, occupancy rates, average time taken for trials in courts and the average time spent by undertrials in prisons.

From the above table and data, the correlation between efficiency and crime rates is significant. States like Tamil Nadu, Meghalaya, Bihar, Andhra Pradesh, Orissa, etc., reflect similar ranks on these two scores underscoring the relation between the process of composite efficiency with impact of corresponding crime rates. There are a few others such as West Bengal where the efficiency rank is relatively average, but the rank on crime rate is high. And Gujarat with a similar efficiency level as West Bengal reflects much lower crime rates. Clearly, factors external to this relationship exist and these need to be explored.

(b) *Relation Between Efficiency and Staff Representation*

Table 4.6: Statewise Comparison Between Staff Representation and Efficiency

States / UT	Efficiency T Score	Ranking	Staff representation T Score	Ranking
Andhra Pradesh	60.92	2	51.76	11
Arunachal Pradesh	45.91	28	49.77	18
Assam	44.67	30	47.19	26
Bihar	39.80	33	53.51	5
Chhattisgarh	56.11	6	47.02	27
Goa	50.41	18	50.55	15
Gujarat	46.39	26	49.23	21
Haryana	51.70	14	49.71	19
Himachal Pradesh	49.15	19	52.54	8
Jammu & Kashmir	47.05	25	47.50	25
Jharkhand	38.37	34	46.45	30
Karnataka	48.63	20	52.68	7
Kerala	52.90	12	52.08	10
Madhya Pradesh	54.56	8	45.51	32
Maharashtra	44.27	31	47.66	23
Manipur	38.17	35	55.54	3
Meghalaya	40.61	32	46.63	29
Mizoram	58.10	3	52.24	9
Nagaland	56.60	5	53.42	6
Orissa	47.83	23	50.44	16
Punjab	51.54	15	44.74	33
Rajasthan	53.77	9	46.96	28
Sikkim	50.86	16	51.00	13
Tamil Nadu	57.27	4	62.63	1
Tripura	48.26	22	46.05	31
Uttar Pradesh	53.54	10	44.38	34
Uttarakhand	55.90	7	48.50	22
West Bengal	47.37	24	43.71	35
UT Andaman & Nicobar Islands	53.44	11	57.26	2
UT Chandigarh	50.83	17	50.07	17
UT Dadar and Nagar Haveli	48.47	21	51.20	12
UT Daman and Diu	45.44	29	53.52	4
UT Delhi	46.37	27	47.52	24
UT Lakshadweep	52.22	13	49.52	20
UT Pondicherry	61.53	1	50.67	14

Note: Efficiency is computed by taking the sum of disposal rates, charge-sheeting rates, conviction rates, occupancy rates, average time taken for trials in courts, average time taken for undertrials in prisons and staff representation.

Table 4.7: Co-relations between Staff Representation and Total Crime

		Staff representation	Total crime
Pearson Correlation	Staff Representation	1.000	0.288
	Total Crime	0.288	1.000

Efficiency levels and staff diversity, like representation of women, the Scheduled Castes and Tribes and Muslims do not reflect a significant correlation with correlates of efficiency and crime rate. If there are common rankings such as in Goa, that is perhaps a reflection of a larger commitment to justice where efficiency and diversity are both given relevance. This raises a strategic issue relating to the purpose of staff diversity. If this is a confidence building measure and not a direct correlate of efficiency, it may constitute a measure of commitment to justice. And the policy prescription and its implementation strategy may require a different focus in terms of mainstreaming the inclusive concepts.

6. MEASURING THE UTILITY OF ALTERNATIVES

Community policing has been initiated in most states with improved programmes seeking citizen participation in crime prevention. Lok adalats have been instituted to help relieve the pressure of cases in courts and to provide quick relief to the people. Open jails have been constituted as reformative programmes, but how do these initiatives impact on the physical security of the citizens? While these have been evaluated and improvements made, the sheer volume and its impact on crime, or on the expenditure of courts, or on occupancy rates in prisons, need to be studied to provide support as the case may be. Are alternatives then subsidising formal structures or are they improving public perception of safety in their areas?

7. IDENTIFYING PATTERNS

(a) *Sharing Expertise: Beyond State Borders*

In India, law and order is a state subject. And the responsibility to control crime and improve the performance of the criminal justice system lies with the state governments. There are certain operational aspects of crime control, which transcend the territorial boundaries. For instance, the central states of Madhya Pradesh, Rajasthan, Orissa and southern states of Andhra Pradesh and Karnataka have high crime rates against Scheduled Castes. Whereas, trafficking in women, is high in the border states of the north-east. And narcotics and drug related crimes are border area crimes, finding high representation in Punjab, Jammu & Kashmir and the north-east. Combating these crimes can use experience and expertise devised in relevant states or culturally relevant mechanisms.

(b) *Exploring the Inconsistencies*

By organising data into a framework, certain inconsistencies in the emerging patterns stand out and these can be explored both in terms of data inadequacy or gaps in linkages. For instance, a clear pattern that emerges in terms of budget expenditure of the police reveals that areas of civil unrest such as Mizoram, Nagaland and Jammu & Kashmir along with capital areas, such as Delhi or the union territory of Chandigarh rank high in terms of police expenditure per lakh population. The central states comprising West Bengal, Bihar, Orissa, Chhatisgarh, Uttar Pradesh and Rajasthan are comparable and fall in the lower range of expenditure per lakh population. Further, these states reflect a similar patterns in terms of their capital outlay for motor vehicles, per lakh population and equipments. One state that stands out in the difference in its budget and ranking *vis-à-vis* motor vehicles and equipment per lakh population, is Haryana. It falls in the average bracket of 17th rank for budget expenditure but ranks the lowest, i.e. 35th on both motor vehicles per lakh population and on equipments per lakh population. (Refer Table 7 in Annexure V.) What does this inconsistency indicate? Perhaps resources are being put to more ingenious expenses?

Another illustration that reflects the inconsistencies across the institutions pertains to the staff deployment across the institutions of the police, the judiciary and prisons. States in north-east such as Assam, Manipur, Meghalaya, Mizoram and Nagaland rank among the better placed states in terms of staff

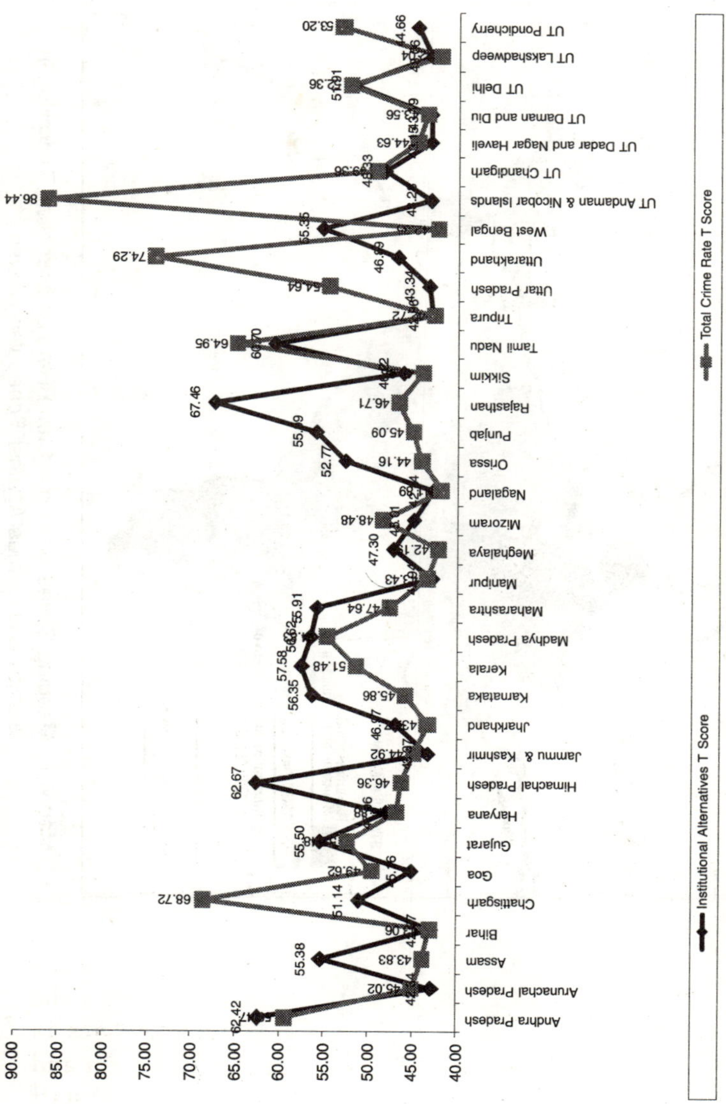

Graph 4.5: Statewise Comparison Between on Institutional Alternative and Total Crime

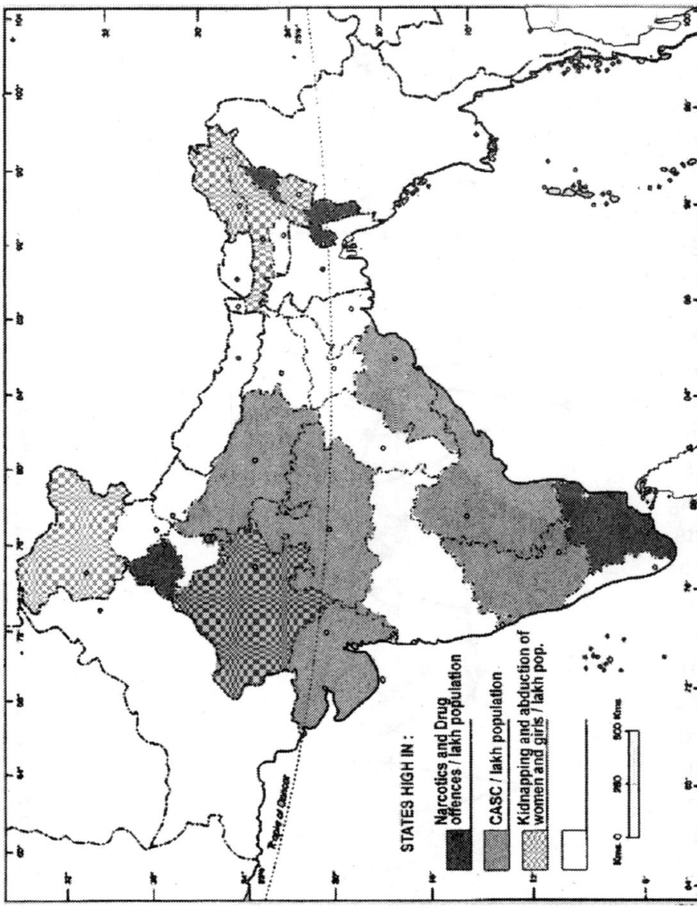

Map 4.1: Mapping States with High Crime Rate on Narcotics, Trafficking in Women and Crimes Against Scheduled Castes

density. (See Table 2 in Annexure V.) With Manipur, Meghalaya, Mizoram and Nagaland falling in top ranks in terms of jail staff after 100 inmates, but states of Meghalaya, Mizoram and Assam have a low ranking in terms of number of judges per lakh population.

If these are areas of civil strife then corresponding layers of protection as also delivery of justice needs to be compatible. Policy makers need to explore such gaps. Bolstering particular aspect of security systems without corresponding protective measures for a fair and timely delivery of justice may raise tensions within the populations affected.

8. Theme Specific Pointers

Specialists, located both in interest groups and sectoral agencies, can explore the strategies and initiatives undertaken *vis-à-vis* particular themes and accordingly review processes. A theme that stands out refers to gender considerations. A number of initiatives ranging from staff representation to special provisions such as women cells, women's rights commissions and focus on crime against women have been an urgent concern for gender activists both inside and outside policy lines. However, to what extent are these initiatives providing women safety? Compilation of the existing data where the range of initiatives is correlated to the extent of crime against women does not show any significant correlations. However, this could be due to data inadequacy or reflect inadequate measures. However, this progress can be mapped and benchmarked by employing this index.

A disaggregate analysis may provide relevant trends. For instance, a case profile of Andhra Pradesh on the gender measures and corresponding reported crime against women reflects a negative relationship. Thus gender staffing, women police stations, family courts correspond to higher rates of chargesheeting and conviction of those accused of crimes against women in a state, which reports the highest level of crime against women after Delhi. Perhaps initiatives taken to make women more secure in the state have resulted in higher confidence by women in reporting their victimisation.

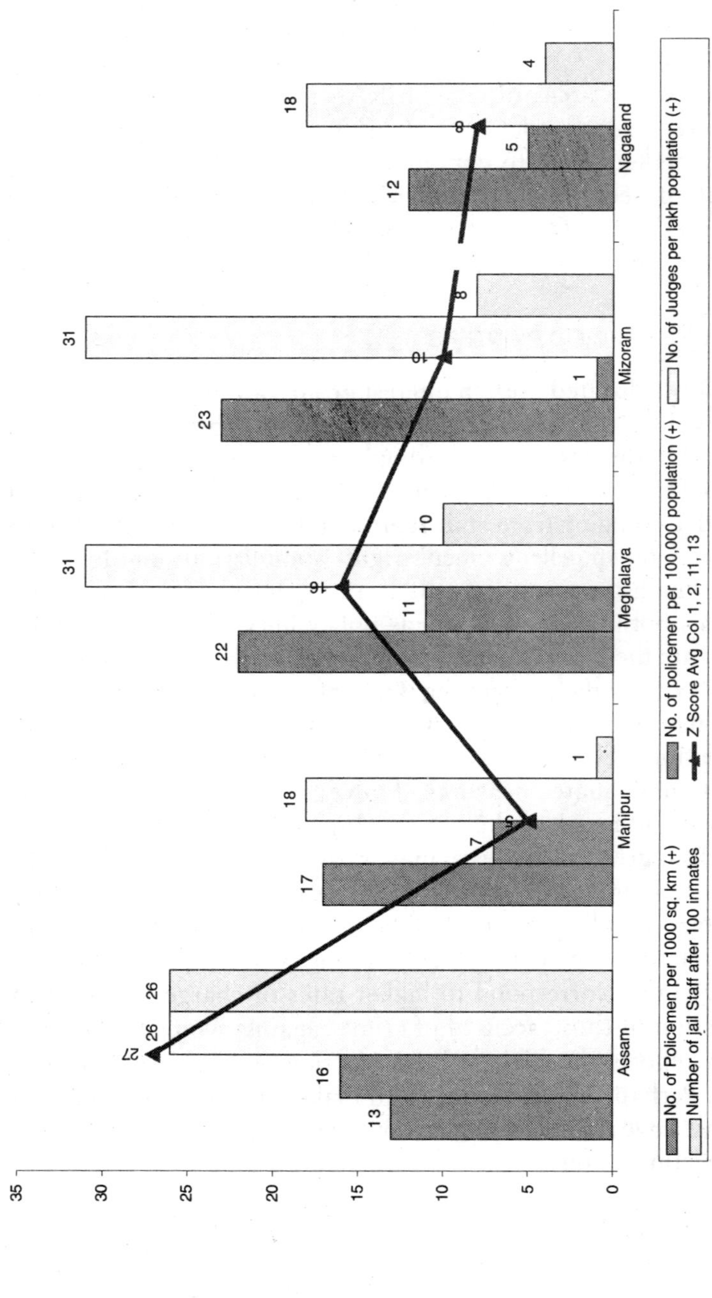

Graph 4.6: Profile and Ranking of Assam, Manipur, Meghalaya, Mizoram and Nagaland on Staffing Pattern

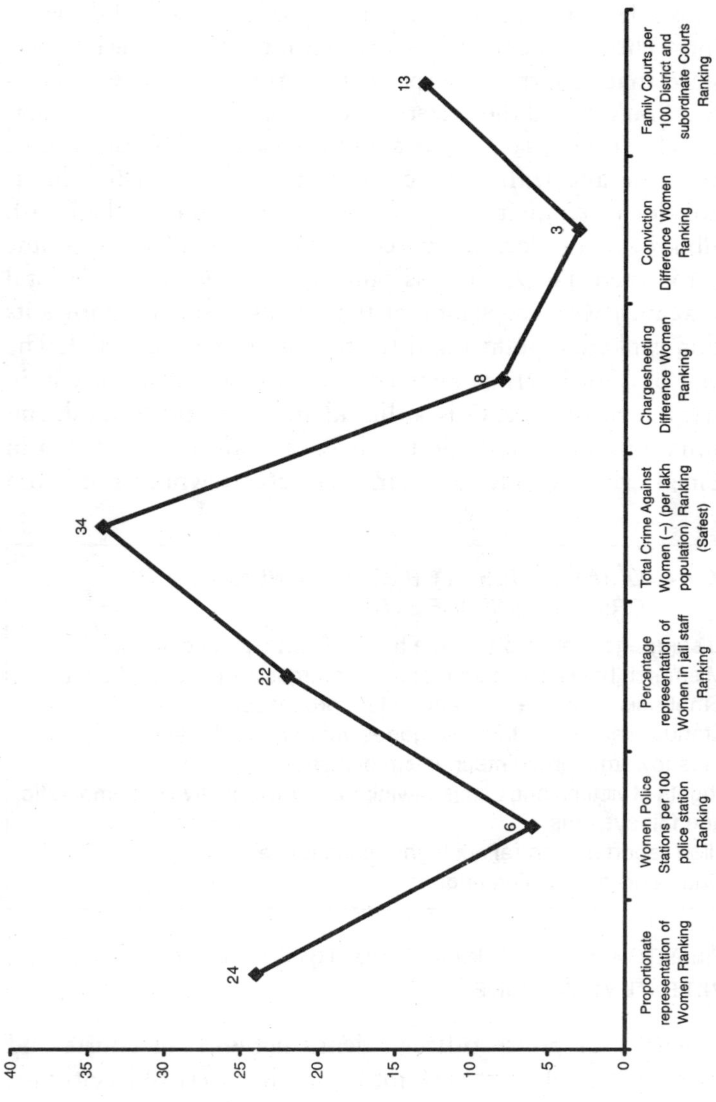

Graph 4.7: Profile of Andhra Pradesh on Gender Related Performance

Data Pointers for Strengthening the Criminal Justice System

1. Disaggregate Analysis on the Basis of Conceptual Categories

The Home Ministry through its National Bureau on Crime prepares relevant crime statistics in accordance with IPC classifications. These are not treated separately for analysis. For instance, the state that reported the maximum crime against women is Andhra Pradesh and the safest is the Union Territory of Lakshadweep. However, disaggregate analysis based on domestic crime, public crime and trafficking crime reflects the need for different policies to combat crime. Jammu & Kashmir ranked 34th on public crime, reflecting the second highest incidence of crime being reported. However, it is only ranked 19th *vis-à-vis* total crime against women. A look at the domestic spheres shows its position ranked as fourth and trafficking is least reported. The ranking of 19th in crime against women would bring it within the margins of average. Orissa, Jharkhand, Madhya Pradesh and Haryana, rate high on domestic violence against women, but in combined crime against women, these states would not stand out.

BOX 4.4: DATA POINTERS FOR STRENGTHENING THE CRIMINAL JUSTICE SYSTEM

1. Disaggregate analysis on the basis of conceptual categories
2. Mismatch between infrastructure resources and extent of crime
3. Emphasis on crime data and not on processes
4. Standardisation of data categories yet to be undertaken
5. Bias towards formal mechanism of justice
6. Rights of victims and accused/violators: Not reflective of democratic and fair systems
7. High reporting can reflect higher confidence of citizens
8. Data tools for building bridges

2. Mismatch between Infrastructure Resources and Extent of Crime

High density of police officers, dense network of courts and efficient disposal of cases may not secure the safety of its citizens.

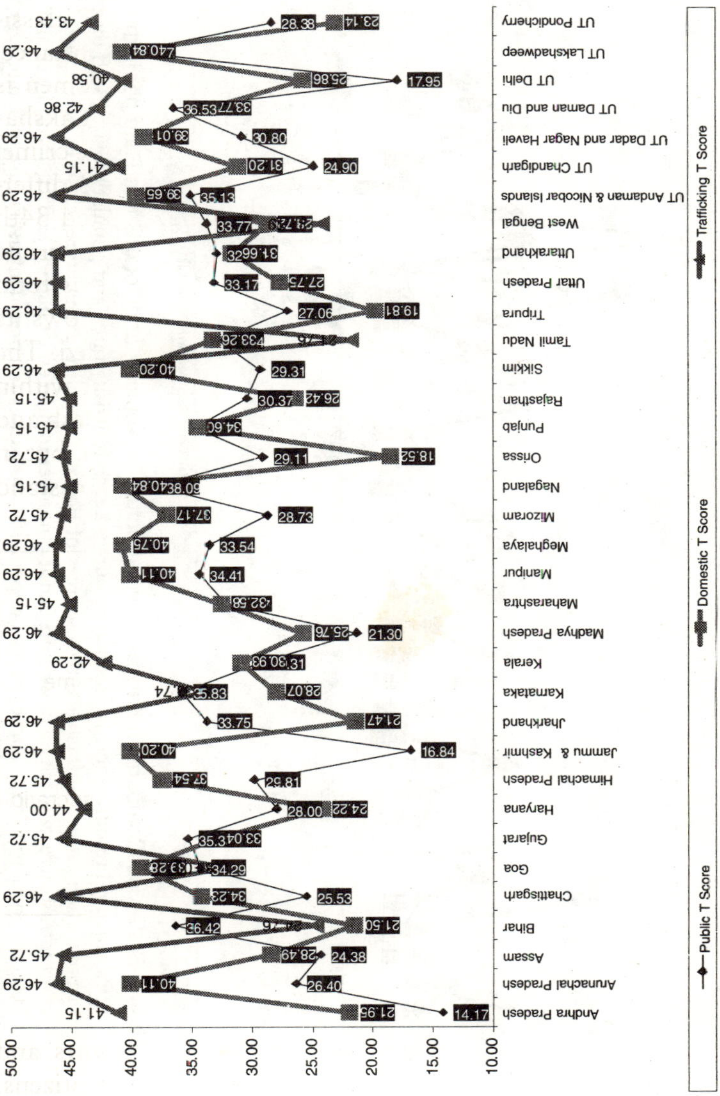

Graph 4.8: Profile of Crime Against Women in Disaggregated by Public, Domestic and Trafficking Crime

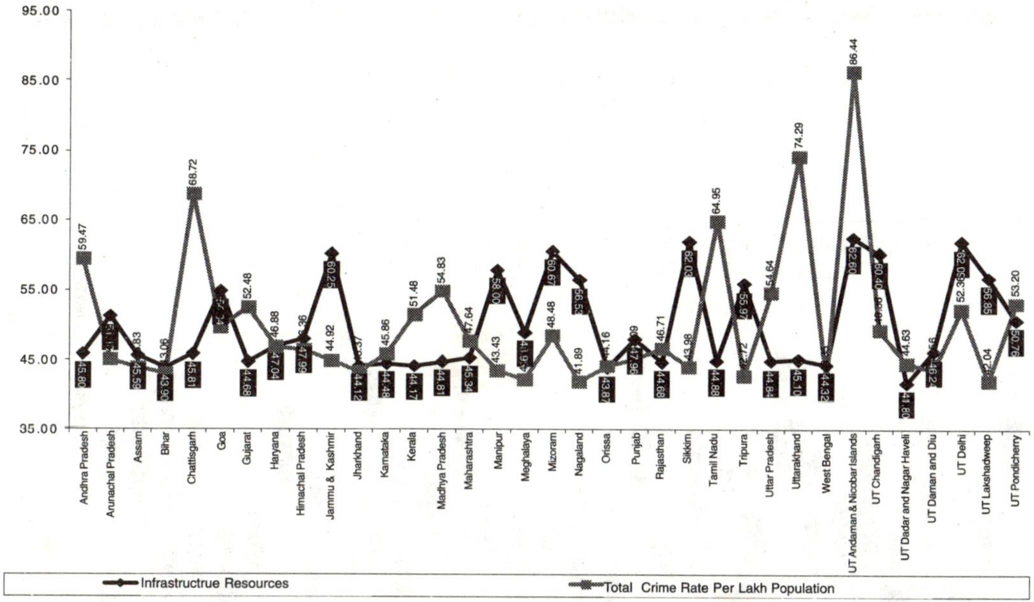

Graph 4.9: Statewise Comparison between Infrastructure Resources and Total Crime Rate per lakh Population

Note: Infrastructural resources include human resources i.e. staff density (area and populationwise), staff diversity as representative of population groups, infrastructure resources of police, i.e. police expenditure, existing equipment, women police station, court infrastructure which includes staff density (number of high court judges, district court judges and number of judges per 100,000 population and court expenditure per lakh population and prison infrastructure with number of jail staff, percentage representation and expenditure on prisons per lakh population.

For instance, Chandigarh ranks 6th in accessibility and efficiency that measures the deployment of resources, which includes both human and material resources, yet it ranks 35th on the level of physical security enjoyed by the citizens. Physical security includes not only the extent of crime, but also the rights of the accused and victims and transgressions by the police and prison personnel. West Bengal on the contrary ranked 33rd on the extent of resources available, yet it achieved the top rank of the 2nd most safe state in physical security enjoyed by its citizens. However, there are states that reflect a high correlation between resources provided and control of crime such as Punjab, Tamil Nadu and Jharkhand.

3. EMPHASIS ON CRIME DATA AND NOT ON PROCESSES

The index has a large number of indicators that pertain to efficiency of the departments both in terms of crime data (crime rate) and rates of disposal, chargesheeting and conviction). However, the processes which could be vital for improving performance such as internal controls, systems of coordination, informal justice mechanisms, including data about statutory bodies such as legal cells, is not reflected. Either these components are not well formulated or/and data are not collated or their visibility and documentation needs to be improved. Certain mismatch in resource provision and extent of crime and other anomalies could be addressed once this gap is filled.

4. STANDARDISATION OF DATA CATEGORIES YET TO BE UNDERTAKEN

Data continue to suffer from lack of standardisation with classification of categories incomplete or non-existent. For instance, representation of minorities and vulnerable group through staff diversity is reflected only in the police data and similar considerations may have yet to occur within the judiciary and also in jails other than those for women. Even among the police, representation is only for staff. Gender budgeting or documentation of women's cells is not reflected. Similarly, regarding chargesheeting and conviction rates, there is lack of total chargesheeting or conviction rates for crime against women and these have to be computed by clubbing separate conviction rates against each crime. Similarly if legal aid or lok adalats are being held, the data for this is not segregated for vulnerable populations.

5. BIAS TOWARDS FORMAL MECHANISM OF JUSTICE

The state perspective of criminal justice is reflected in its conceptualisation of justice systems being limited to those that fall within the formal sector. While a number of initiatives pertaining to statutory bodies such as legal aid, lok adalats, human rights commission and other oversights have been institutionalised, their documentation and details continue to be sketchy or non-existent. This is true of most states.

6. RIGHTS OF VICTIMS AND ACCUSED/VIOLATORS: NOT REFLECTIVE OF DEMOCRATIC AND FAIR SYSTEMS

If the policy measures and data provisions are looked into, it is interesting to note that citizens affected by crime, whether the accused or the victims, have little relevance within the existing criminal justice system. In fact the victims and accused seem to be on par with very few services recorded under facilities and services provided to them. At the national level, the constitutional measures and policy safeguard the inherent rights of the accused where they can only be arrested with warrants and there are specified days and procedures for judicial custody and remand. State level measures only reflect free legal aid. For the victims, special courts, i.e. family courts, courts for SCs/STs are included in the data that is too sketchy at times. Data pertaining to medical provisions or compensation, etc. is not widely available in the existing documents.

7. HIGH REPORTING CAN REFLECT HIGHER CONFIDENCE OF CITIZENS

Precautions need to be exercised in reading the crime rates. The crime rate refers to the extent of reporting. Higher the crime rate, higher is the state ranking on this indicator. However, higher reporting of cases can also mean that the citizens are confident that they will get justice and accordingly they report the crime.[6] For instance, women and the Scheduled Castes may not be reporting crime due to considerations such as social stigma, lack of perception of crime, etc. but high awareness of their rights, faith in the police, lack of alternative systems may raise the crime levels of that particular area/state in comparison with other states. The union territories of Chandigarh and Delhi can be such examples where community surveys have revealed that 'the police reaches within five minutes of dialling 100'. 'The police is vigilant and responds by registering cases the moment they are backed by NGOs.'

8. DATA TOOLS FOR BUILDING BRIDGES

Different data types can be useful in measuring different facets of the criminal justice system. For instance, community interface with the criminal justice system can be gauged from the application of different data. State published data can be used to measure public confidence (increase in reporting of petty crimes as compared to heinous crimes is a pointer towards increasing confidence of people in the criminal justice system), public opinion surveys to measure legitimacy, and expert surveys to measure community participation for crime prevention (expert surveys can provide analytical insights into the functioning and corresponding reforms a democratic criminal justice system).

DELIVERY OF JUSTICE: A FUNCTION OF AN INTEGRATED PROCESS

The delivery of Justice is not the exclusive domain of the police, courts, prisons, but also non-state civilian oversights both on the supply side of justice, i.e. National Human Rights Commission, National Minority Commission, National Women's Commission and on the demand side of justice civil society oversights, NGOs and the media have emerged to build bridges with state institutions.

Institutions of delivery of justice in the formal sector are largely directed by established social rules. These rules are at the most punitive. On the other hand, the non-state autonomous organ-

[6]An 'increase in crime' may in fact be because more crime is *reported*, rather than because more crime is *committed*.

John Muncie, op. cit. (2001), p. 26.

isations have focused on a correctional agenda with particular reference to marginalised groups.

The civil society organisations and media have articulated the violations by the police and cases of delayed justice. The media has often provided the much needed transparency to violation of human rights by the police.

All these institutions function around a common axis;

(a) They largely function within given societal consensus. And the given societal consensus is pregnated with unequal power and gives licence to hierarchies based on caste, minority and gender, to remain functional.

ACCOUNTABILITY STRUCTURE

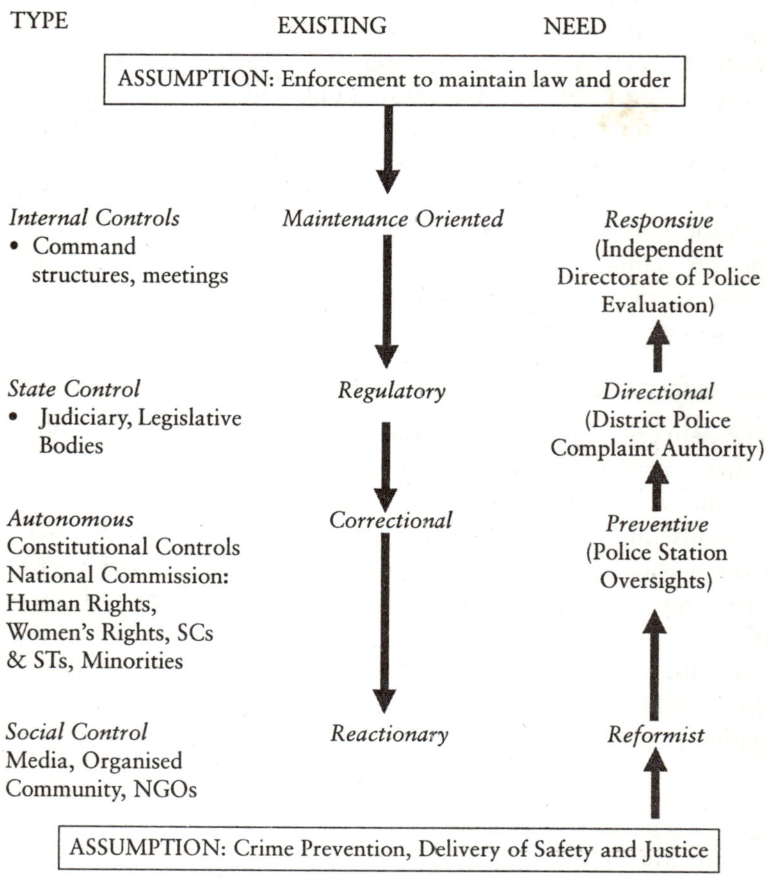

(b) Most of the violations are attributed merely to individual actors rather than to institutional arrangements, legal statutes and political and cultural factors. For example the National Human Rights Commission has suggested action against police officials functioning at the behest of 'prejudiced politics'. To quote:

> Investigations of the Gujarat riots to be purged of prejudiced, politics influenced police officials, CBI inquires to be initiated and proceedings against officers who have failed to act appropriately. (NHRC Recommendations, 2002)

These recommendations pertain to individual acts of omission or commission, while it has traced the cause of these violations to 'prejudiced politics'. Human rights should be analysed in relation to factors (in this case prejudiced politics) which have contributed to violations, rather than merely in relation to individual acts of omission or commission.

Institutions of delivery of justice have to function within the cooperative rather than competitive framework. The perspective needs to be interactive with the multi-cultural reality and responsive to the specificities of social institutions and casteism, racism, religiosity and gender relations for crime prevention and delivery of safety and justice.

The alternative framework has to take into consideration:

(a) Changing global standards and local needs leading to corresponding development of institutional mechanisms.
(b) Growing societal pressures to shift from enforcement to participatory service delivery. The need is to build such institutional accountability structures as are democratic in response, protective of rights and sensitive to multicultures.

In a nutshell, there is need for the police, the courts and prisons at the internal level to change from *status quo* maintenance to people centric response orientation. And the state regulatory to be replaced by directional and participatory mechanisms. Above all, the autonomous non-state institutions have to shift from correctional thrust to preventive. Civil society organisations and the media have to play a reformist rather reactive and sensational role. The relevance of these can be gauged by assessing the performance of multi-institutions.

ANNEXURE I

Dimensionwise T-Scores on Each Indicator

I. Accessibility and Efficiency of Criminal Justice System

States	Police infrastructure					
	Staff density (area and population wise)		Staff Diversity as proportionate representation of population group			
	No. of policemen per 100 sq. km. (+)	No. of policemen per per 100,000 population (+)	Proportionate representation of SCs in police	Proportionate representation of STs in police	Proportionate representation of women	Proportionate representation of Muslim
	1	2	3	4	5	6
Andhra Pradesh	46.82	42.04	47.18	48.15	42.43	77.14
Arunachal Pradesh	46.56	60.36	53.87	51.64	45.54	52.42
Assam	47.27	45.89	46.10	46.62	38.24	45.32
Bihar	47.12	40.14	46.34	93.51	42.53	45.55
Chattisgarh	46.68	42.27	45.49	43.57	45.12	48.13
Goa	47.62	48.40	48.48	0.00	62.24	43.66
Gujarat	46.83	42.41	53.07	50.05	47.17	55.53
Haryana	47.45	44.87	45.37	NA	45.18	62.82
Himachal Pradesh	46.72	45.75	47.59	56.83	56.68	58.61
Jammu & Kashmir	47.24	64.03	44.36	40.39	45.51	58.76

Jharkhand	46.84	41.44	0.00	0.00	39.52	NA
Karnataka	46.82	42.04	48.14	45.28	62.10	53.07
Kerala	47.80	43.48	50.77	49.94	53.69	51.58
Madhya Pradesh	46.76	42.74	45.46	41.92	46.33	48.33
Maharashtra	47.00	43.62	48.69	46.06	57.87	48.31
Manipur	47.20	62.31	45.40	45.41	42.20	69.61
Meghalaya	46.95	54.38	NA	47.83	40.89	47.20
Mizoram	46.93	77.11	NA	49.02	0.00	49.00
Nagaland	47.34	63.75	NA	50.03	0.00	39.53
Orissa	46.74	41.67	46.37	46.42	38.93	70.19
Punjab	48.15	50.30	46.09	NA	44.43	40.37
Rajasthan	46.70	42.23	47.20	49.20	43.59	45.68
Sikkim	47.06	65.74	47.85	63.07	57.35	37.13
Tamil Nadu	47.25	43.53	47.30	46.87	82.79	54.92
Tripura	48.56	62.64	46.94	47.58	40.21	42.85
Uttar Pradesh	47.23	41.39	46.79	0.00	41.10	42.24
Uttarakhand	46.74	43.57	49.37	57.80	50.26	42.04
West Bengal	47.55	41.86	45.55	46.26	42.06	43.64
UT Andaman & Nicobar Islands	46.87	70.29	0.00	52.07	62.55	65.48
UT Chandigarh	88.83	56.37	47.19	0.00	65.11	38.10
UT Dadar and Nagar Haveli	47.02	41.72	70.80	47.02	51.44	48.62
UT Daman and Diu	49.07	43.94	95.54	41.24	NA	50.75
UT Delhi	89.89	53.45	47.29	0.00	53.45	41.04
UT Lakshadweep	56.62	56.98	0.00	46.21	59.69	35.60
UT Pondicherry	51.75	47.28	49.41	0.00	53.81	46.78

States	Police infrastructure				Courts infrastructure	
	Budget/ Expenditure	Existing equipment and transport support			Staff density (population wise)	
	Expenditure on police after per lakh population of state/UTs (in lakhs)	Motor Vehicles per lakh population	Equipments per lakh population	Women police station's per 100 police station	No. of judges per lakh population (+)	Total courts budget (in lakhs) per lakh population
	7	8	9	10	11	12
Andhra Pradesh	42.25	42.49	44.82	51.12	45.45	54.58
Arunachal Pradesh	52.93	74.08	44.29	45.37	32.80	47.22
Assam	45.93	46.23	45.25	46.62	45.45	47.44
Bihar	40.97	40.54	43.99	45.37	53.03	46.49
Chattisgarh	41.52	48.44	44.96	47.94	56.83	NA
Goa	48.59	51.84	62.25	57.34	70.74	NA
Gujarat	42.22	43.00	45.19	47.85	53.03	NA
Haryana	45.87	39.29	43.16	46.75	53.03	NA
Himachal Pradesh	45.71	43.16	46.37	45.37	58.09	NA
Jammu & Kashmir	58.17	60.68	56.84	48.75	72.00	NA
Jharkhand	42.77	40.51	43.98	45.37	53.03	47.54
Karnataka	42.60	43.40	47.00	48.99	49.24	40.66
Kerala	42.96	44.51	45.59	47.33	37.86	42.26

Madhya Pradesh	42.18	42.73	47.31	48.18	49.24	NA
Maharashtra	44.01	41.59	43.99	45.37	53.03	NA
Manipur	55.59	66.19	66.05	50.41	49.24	47.32
Meghalaya	52.48	54.09	49.19	45.37	32.80	47.45
Mizoram	70.42	75.71	56.18	45.37	32.80	47.01
Nagaland	73.23	49.07	44.19	52.21	49.24	47.26
Orissa	41.01	42.22	43.61	49.18	46.71	NA
Punjab	49.71	42.74	45.35	48.74	47.98	NA
Rajasthan	41.92	42.67	45.66	50.72	49.24	NA
Sikkim	68.80	64.61	58.30	45.37	58.09	NA
Tamil Nadu	44.43	47.14	45.41	100.23	45.45	43.74
Tripura	57.63	58.38	56.52	45.37	55.56	47.26
Uttar Pradesh	41.86	40.04	45.11	47.78	54.30	NA
Uttarakhand	45.84	42.27	43.51	50.90	47.98	NA
West Bengal	40.51	41.95	43.95	45.37	41.65	51.10
UT Andaman & Nicobar Islands	73.76	66.53	44.33	59.73	58.09	65.20
UT Chandigarh	58.89	54.81	55.15	45.37	61.89	NA
UT Dadar and Nagar Haveli	43.10	45.08	47.61	45.37	32.80	NA
UT Daman and Diu	42.62	48.27	50.90	45.37	32.80	NA
UT Delhi	61.83	52.58	56.85	45.37	64.42	82.61
UT Lakshadweep	59.82	55.64	95.92	45.37	53.03	NA
UT Pondicherry	47.85	57.54	51.22	68.66	53.03	44.88

States	Prison infrastructure				Police function	
	Staff			Budget/ Expenditure	Disposal rate of cases by Police	
	Number of jail staff after 100 inmates	Occupancy rates in prison (–)	Percentage representation of women in jail staff	Expenditure on prisons per lakhs populations (in lakhs)	Total	Recovery rate stolen property (+)
	13	14	15	16	17	18
Andhra Pradesh	48.42	50.55	44.54	45.34	59.53	55.80
Arunachal Pradesh	0.00	0.00	0.00	0.00	50.47	40.43
Assam	42.59	48.20	60.24	44.24	35.95	46.13
Bihar	38.90	36.42	47.78	43.93	39.50	43.11
Chattisgarh	41.37	35.27	51.84	44.42	62.68	57.87
Goa	62.10	52.34	41.03	47.16	48.49	42.20
Gujarat	41.08	37.62	41.74	43.67	58.55	40.04
Haryana	48.08	50.10	48.44	54.55	57.27	69.36
Himachal Pradesh	48.79	50.06	50.18	49.31	54.61	51.70
Jammu & Kashmir	70.94	58.53	47.23	52.14	49.21	52.78
Jharkhand	38.52	18.90	54.46	42.47	40.53	43.89
Karnataka	43.42	48.52	58.48	45.13	48.52	41.51
Kerala	47.28	49.30	59.15	45.83	54.63	42.12
Madhya Pradesh	42.33	42.53	42.84	45.21	62.60	53.25

Maharashtra	44.58	46.94	39.65	44.88	50.61	41.90
Manipur	71.17	61.77	80.19	56.91	28.06	36.33
Meghalaya	57.33	52.52	51.88	45.91	26.83	43.93
Mizoram	58.50	58.20	65.57	81.37	50.81	64.05
Nagaland	67.00	60.92	71.91	67.67	53.84	54.03
Orissa	44.99	45.28	51.55	44.02	53.29	53.21
Punjab	46.45	48.79	44.05	53.03	49.51	66.20
Rajasthan	46.14	56.45	45.39	42.86	62.04	60.07
Sikkim	58.20	38.48	55.24	75.43	38.43	46.26
Tamil Nadu	45.56	51.13	43.68	41.41	57.82	67.15
Tripura	58.67	48.44	53.37	58.46	52.33	44.84
Uttar Pradesh	43.72	43.31	44.01	45.11	62.49	60.46
Uttarakhand	46.22	48.29	40.63	44.64	62.60	48.51
West Bengal	46.19	55.28	39.38	44.07	48.27	45.48
UT Andaman & Nicobar Islands	70.11	57.96	46.47	68.20	52.95	36.68
UT Chandigarh	51.20	62.25	54.56	56.04	50.97	50.92
UT Dadar and Nagar Haveli	36.31	60.27	43.95	40.79	48.46	64.09
UT Daman and Diu	59.08	64.85	34.71	43.27	50.02	41.86
UT Delhi	42.36	38.16	50.42	54.83	42.84	37.97
UT Lakshadweep	36.31	67.90	60.73	40.51	26.24	37.54
UT Pondicherry	56.07	54.47	34.71	47.19	59.08	68.32

States	Police function	Courts function				
	Charge sheeting rate of cases by police	Disposal rate of cases by courts	Conviction rates of total crimes by court			
	Total	Disposal rate of total cases by courts (+) total	Average time taken for trial of cases in all courts—in years (–)	Average time taken for under trial in prisons in months (–)	Total	T Score average
	19	20	21	22	23	24
Andhra Pradesh	59.88	74.18	57.17	66.98	63.27	52.61
Arunachal Pradesh	39.13	39.75	54.30	0.00	51.35	49.03
Assam	40.81	48.49	43.41	56.49	37.88	45.69
Bihar	50.15	42.32	32.65	36.96	37.27	44.98
Chattisgarh	59.70	60.33	51.76	57.94	63.31	49.88
Goa	53.62	51.25	51.43	48.57	55.41	52.13
Gujarat	57.04	40.06	52.70	42.60	42.55	46.55
Haryana	53.11	47.50	48.88	39.33	48.08	49.45
Himachal Pradesh	56.72	46.11	50.77	45.24	37.95	49.65
Jammu & Kashmir	49.70	44.67	50.73	25.58	45.19	51.97
Jharkhand	44.63	46.38	26.23	46.54	39.86	42.17
Karnataka	52.38	53.02	55.98	45.68	43.45	48.06

Kerala	55.08	50.26	50.69	68.23	52.85	49.27
Madhya Pradesh	57.90	56.27	48.58	55.87	59.52	48.55
Maharashtra	52.77	40.68	39.63	45.96	35.70	45.58
Manipur	10.85	38.61	30.43	46.48	52.80	50.46
Meghalaya	34.29	40.21	40.70	37.99	48.41	45.39
Mizoram	56.87	51.20	63.63	60.36	59.65	58.08
Nagaland	34.22	69.89	67.16	59.79	52.97	55.96
Orissa	56.66	41.85	45.18	50.22	36.97	47.10
Punjab	55.43	45.85	54.16	40.13	52.26	48.56
Rajasthan	53.41	46.75	46.39	50.12	54.93	48.61
Sikkim	48.24	68.69	59.35	49.93	57.49	54.96
Tamil Nadu	46.41	68.70	57.32	51.92	57.72	53.82
Tripura	45.29	51.65	49.97	56.41	37.19	50.70
Uttar Pradesh	60.16	56.76	37.41	46.30	61.42	48.05
Uttarakhand	60.65	68.68	43.80	48.50	66.18	49.95
West Bengal	48.80	40.33	44.99	54.08	41.73	45.22
UT Andaman & Nicobar Islands	60.53	43.92	53.32	55.88	66.24	58.05
UT Chandigarh	44.07	45.39	50.08	44.73	58.24	54.29
UT Dadar and Nagar Haveli	51.08	41.36	55.22	34.42	32.84	46.79
UT Daman and Diu	40.49	42.15	45.28	41.32	37.57	47.67
UT Delhi	49.33	42.86	50.30	57.12	52.40	53.06
UT Lakshadweep	50.51	45.46	73.21	70.87	46.05	53.34
UT Pondicherry	60.07	58.41	67.16	61.45	63.29	54.66

II. LEVEL OF PHYSICAL SECURITY ENJOYED BY THE CITIZENS

States	Roported rate of crime					
	Percentage change in IPC crime in 2005 (–)	Total crime against body (–) (per lakh population)	Total crime against property (–) (per lakh population)	Total crime against economic crimes (–) (per lakh population)	Rate of total cognizable crimes SLL (–) (per lakh population)	Total crime against women (–) (per lakh population)
	25	26	27	28	29	30
Andhra Pradesh	52.40	32.11	51.03	39.78	40.76	30.83
Arunachal Pradesh	49.91	41.01	40.34	52.18	55.67	50.07
Assam	48.95	46.88	53.46	53.90	55.65	38.26
Bihar	59.15	54.24	57.37	57.68	55.56	59.12
Chattisgarh	48.31	50.88	50.27	59.22	31.17	45.70
Goa	51.92	53.04	47.67	48.41	49.56	57.22
Gujarat	45.58	51.95	49.79	51.47	48.24	51.82
Haryana	44.29	51.45	46.63	47.69	53.48	42.20
Himachal Pradesh	51.44	50.93	56.61	56.52	54.16	50.80
Jammu & Kashmir	55.69	53.93	54.27	54.51	55.25	41.33
Jharkhand	42.04	54.15	53.79	58.30	55.54	56.05
Karnataka	49.43	45.85	50.15	51.36	55.09	52.99
Kerala	51.36	39.32	53.91	40.50	51.72	39.28
Madhya Pradesh	54.73	34.98	48.05	58.66	47.66	36.81

Maharashtra	46.70	46.22	44.29	46.89	52.56	49.93
Manipur	39.64	49.88	59.50	49.10	55.32	60.87
Meghalaya	45.98	59.14	53.52	59.82	55.69	61.16
Mizoram	17.64	59.81	24.77	47.85	52.79	54.30
Nagaland	46.30	62.30	56.50	58.64	55.36	66.41
Orissa	46.78	52.38	54.79	57.39	55.01	45.41
Punjab	46.86	51.07	57.37	36.57	53.38	57.80
Rajasthan	58.82	41.02	51.75	32.54	54.63	41.33
Sikkim	61.63	52.14	54.34	45.86	54.30	53.14
Tamil Nadu	53.61	33.99	54.02	55.06	36.39	49.49
Tripura	44.45	54.79	58.15	58.24	55.67	32.72
Uttar Pradesh	56.58	58.37	58.68	56.27	42.67	56.93
Uttarakhand	57.22	57.14	55.54	51.53	22.96	56.35
West Bengal	54.97	61.41	58.07	59.00	55.56	48.47
UT Andaman & Nicobar Islands	58.66	54.39	50.67	53.21	12.54	60.57
UT Chandigarh	44.85	59.71	15.39	20.08	53.92	38.99
UT Dadar and Nagar Haveli	46.70	52.49	50.57	41.48	55.58	54.60
UT Daman and Diu	33.37	53.26	47.79	44.88	55.75	60.57
UT Delhi	47.91	51.93	24.15	25.44	51.83	28.64
UT Lakshadweep	83.71	63.58	59.10	65.30	55.56	68.89
UT Pondicherry	52.40	14.24	47.72	54.68	53.03	50.95

States	Reported rate of crime			Percentage difference from total charge sheeting of specific population		
	Total crime against children (–) (per lakh population)	Crime against Scheduled Caste per lakh population (–)	Crime against Scheduled Tribe per lakh population (–)	Women	Children	SC (–)
	31	32	33	34	35	36
Andhra Pradesh	53.03	34.68	50.36	55.59	52.13	53.16
Arunachal Pradesh	49.06	57.07	13.75	43.55	42.86	63.88
Assam	55.87	52.23	48.57	43.68	41.07	50.47
Bihar	59.28	46.18	54.82	46.19	44.11	56.07
Chattisgarh	34.86	46.18	36.07	55.78	48.57	52.88
Goa	39.97	57.68	54.82	59.01	51.41	30.92
Gujarat	51.33	43.76	52.14	54.24	56.35	54.45
Haryana	50.76	50.41	55.71	49.11	48.81	57.16
Himachal Pradesh	47.92	52.84	53.93	50.72	48.97	55.59
Jammu & Kashmir	57.01	58.28	55.71	39.12	41.97	58.90
Jharkhand	58.15	52.23	40.54	47.83	39.77	54.08
Karnataka	58.15	38.92	53.04	46.21	51.29	56.14
Kerala	53.03	52.23	53.93	48.65	48.49	53.09
Madhya Pradesh	28.05	18.34	34.28	53.18	47.76	54.07
Maharashtra	47.36	53.44	53.93	45.00	49.19	56.77
Manipur	55.31	58.28	55.71	48.54	49.83	51.08

Meghalaya	41.11	58.28	55.71	48.86	31.02	40.03
Mizoram	59.85	58.28	55.71	49.98	83.32	29.39
Nagaland	59.85	58.28	55.71	46.38	67.74	40.06
Orissa	58.71	35.89	41.43	50.43	45.61	54.31
Punjab	55.31	55.26	55.71	65.75	50.29	51.23
Rajasthan	54.74	20.76	43.21	47.52	54.16	56.76
Sikkim	35.43	51.02	21.78	67.88	39.25	50.26
Tamil Nadu	57.58	46.78	55.71	36.92	40.70	59.24
Tripura	55.31	51.63	52.14	45.87	42.86	58.52
Uttar Pradesh	54.17	43.76	55.71	63.00	50.23	51.67
Uttarakhand	55.31	51.63	55.71	70.14	54.34	48.20
West Bengal	58.15	58.28	55.71	44.40	47.91	59.32
UT Andaman & Nicobar Islands	47.92	58.28	51.25	78.36	56.17	27.66
UT Chandigarh	27.48	58.28	55.71	35.19	50.90	35.42
UT Dadar and Nagar Haveli	48.49	53.44	48.57	40.09	47.57	32.12
UT Daman and Diu	43.38	51.63	55.71	32.20	46.62	63.24
UT Delhi	22.93	57.68	55.71	47.27	52.43	47.47
UT Lakshadweep	59.85	58.28	55.71	39.20	78.94	32.38
UT Pondicherry	55.31	49.81	55.71	54.15	47.38	54.01

States	Percentage difference from total chargesheeting of specific population	Percentage difference from total conviction rates of specific population				T Score average
	ST (–)	Women	Children	SC (–)	ST (–)	
	37	38	39	40	41	42
Andhra Pradesh	52.84	65.36	64.11	37.30	37.37	47.23
Arunachal Pradesh	53.60	41.30	28.27	43.08	68.74	46.73
Assam	57.25	39.02	34.57	65.62	64.94	50.02
Bihar	58.22	38.70	46.75	65.32	63.68	54.26
Chattisgarh	54.73	59.67	56.02	42.46	45.96	48.16
Goa	32.78	56.59	48.60	39.46	40.45	48.21
Gujarat	53.70	48.47	44.93	52.16	52.28	50.74
Haryana	33.01	45.60	46.39	51.41	46.99	48.30
Himachal Pradesh	56.45	42.75	40.26	58.19	56.04	52.01
Jammu & Kashmir	34.55	50.99	53.58	48.57	49.57	50.78
Jharkhand	54.00	33.46	37.28	59.46	61.59	50.49
Karnataka	57.83	46.18	50.52	51.38	52.39	50.99
Kerala	56.89	56.85	56.81	46.14	45.27	49.85
Madhya Pradesh	54.21	61.11	53.49	45.97	46.17	45.74
Maharashtra	57.41	41.29	41.20	58.89	59.12	50.01
Manipur	52.12	65.89	60.14	41.79	42.78	52.69

Meghalaya	41.52	49.70	56.35	45.70	46.70	50.02
Mizoram	31.31	36.33	66.03	35.69	36.67	47.04
Nagaland	41.55	49.04	60.28	73.30	42.63	55.31
Orissa	55.17	40.94	42.33	59.41	60.90	50.41
Punjab	31.96	52.14	51.34	46.04	43.27	50.67
Rajasthan	57.77	46.79	50.45	52.91	52.55	48.10
Sikkim	50.98	40.31	48.86	53.44	47.67	48.72
Tamil Nadu	61.11	54.49	56.63	45.38	38.39	49.15
Tripura	54.10	37.03	34.07	55.70	56.71	49.88
Uttar Pradesh	51.76	53.07	50.32	49.75	57.73	53.57
Uttarakhand	54.67	56.16	56.79	44.71	53.89	53.07
West Bengal	60.03	42.98	49.46	67.48	68.52	55.87
UT Andaman & Nicobar Islands	54.73	78.67	71.72	29.81	30.78	51.49
UT Chandigarh	37.10	62.64	58.27	36.94	37.93	42.87
UT Dadar and Nagar Haveli	59.00	41.55	27.62	59.58	60.59	48.24
UT Daman and Diu	38.72	47.31	47.01	55.36	56.37	49.01
UT Delhi	59.79	52.94	51.37	48.48	43.14	45.24
UT Lakshadweep	59.26	57.65	54.31	47.81	48.81	58.14
UT Pondicherry	29.87	57.05	53.87	35.32	33.42	47.00

III. RIGHTS OF POPULATIONS AFFECTED BY CRIME

States	Right of accused	Rights of victims		Violation by enforcement agencies (police/judiciaries/prisons)				
	Free legal aid beneficiaries (per lakh population)	Family Courts per 100 district and subordinate courts	Special courts for SC/ special courts for ST	No. of complaints against per 100 policemen	Percentage of police personnel convicted per 100 police complaints received during the year ***	Total death of inmates due to various causes	No. of complaints against prison staff	T Score average
	43	44	45	46	47	48	49	50
Andhra Pradesh	41	43	41	74	46	82	58	55.15
Arunachal Pradesh	NA	NA	33	56	17	58	54	43.67
Assam	NA	45	57	56	46	63	57	53.93
Bihar	NA	43	57	56	46	96	63	60.25
Chattisgarh	45	47	41	64	45	69	54	52.36
Goa	NA	NA	57	57	46	58	54	54.54
Gujarat	45	43	57	70	46	64	54	54.08
Haryana	42	NA	33	63	46	60	54	49.76
Himachal Pradesh	NA	NA	57	60	46	59	54	55.12
Jammu & Kashmir	42	NA	33	64	46	58	54	49.54
Jharkhand	NA	43	57	56	46	70	54	54.35

Karnataka	NA	45	57	57	46	69	65	56.66
Kerala	NA	71	57	65	46	65	54	59.71
Madhya Pradesh	59	43	57	108	46	77	59	64.08
Maharashtra	NA	43	57	62	46	80	54	57.10
Manipur	NA	56	57	56	46	58	54	54.45
Meghalaya	NA	NA	57	57	46	58	54	54.38
Mizoram	NA	NA	33	56	17	58	54	43.67
Nagaland	NA	58	33	56	42	58	54	50.36
Orissa	NA	43	41	56	46	65	60	51.84
Punjab	NA	77	57	67	46	74	106	71.13
Rajasthan	NA	43	49	59	46	66	66	54.96
Sikkim	NA	65	57	57	46	58	54	56.04
Tamil Nadu	67	43	57	56	45	77	82	61.18
Tripura	NA	45	57	57	46	59	54	52.92
Uttar Pradesh	NA	43	57	63	46	90	55	59.00
Uttarakhand	NA	58	57	71	46	59	54	57.49
West Bengal	NA	43	57	56	46	65	55	53.86
UT Andaman & Nicobar Islands	NA	NA	49	68	46	58	54	54.98
UT Chandigarh	NA	NA	57	65	46	58	54	56.16
UT Dadar and Nagar Haveli	NA	NA	33	56	17	58	54	43.67
UT Daman and Diu	NA	NA	49	56	17	58	54	46.88
UT Delhi	58	52	41	80	46	63	59	56.99
UT Lakshadweep	NA	NA	33	56	17	58	54	43.67
UT Pondicherry	NA	56	57	56	46	58	54	54.61

IV. COMMITMENT TO JUSTICE

States	State oversight					
	Women Cell	State Commission for Women	State Human Rights Commission	State Minority Commission	State SC Commission	T Score average
	51	52	53	54	55	56
Andhra Pradesh	31.89	55.80	60.14	61.38	42.88	50.42
Arunachal Pradesh	31.89	55.80	40.42	41.46	42.88	42.49
Assam	55.36	55.80	60.14	61.38	63.65	59.27
Bihar	55.36	55.80	40.42	61.38	63.65	55.32
Chattisgarh	55.36	33.25	60.14	61.38	42.88	50.60
Goa	55.36	55.80	40.42	41.46	42.88	47.19
Gujarat	55.36	55.80	60.14	41.46	63.65	55.28
Haryana	55.36	55.80	40.42	41.46	42.88	47.19
Himachal Pradesh	55.36	33.25	60.14	41.46	42.88	46.62
Jammu & Kashmir	55.36	55.80	60.14	41.46	42.88	51.13
Jharkhand	55.36	33.25	40.42	61.38	42.88	46.66
Karnataka	55.36	55.80	60.14	61.38	63.65	59.27
Kerala	55.36	55.80	60.14	41.46	63.65	55.28
Madhya Pradesh	55.36	55.80	60.14	61.38	42.88	55.11
Maharashtra	55.36	55.80	60.14	61.38	63.65	59.27
Manipur	55.36	33.25	60.14	61.38	42.88	50.60
Meghalaya	55.36	55.80	40.42	41.46	42.88	47.19

Mizoram	55.36	55.80	40.42	41.46	42.88	47.19
Nagaland	55.36	33.25	40.42	41.46	42.88	42.68
Orissa	55.36	55.80	60.14	41.46	42.88	51.13
Punjab	55.36	55.80	60.14	41.46	42.88	51.13
Rajasthan	55.36	55.80	60.14	61.38	63.65	59.27
Sikkim	31.89	55.80	40.42	41.46	42.88	42.49
Tamil Nadu	31.89	55.80	60.14	61.38	63.65	54.57
Tripura	55.36	55.80	40.42	41.46	63.65	51.34
Uttar Pradesh	31.89	55.80	60.14	61.38	63.65	54.57
Uttarakhand	55.36	55.80	40.42	61.38	42.88	51.17
West Bengal	55.36	55.80	60.14	61.38	63.65	59.27
UT Andaman & Nicobar Islands	55.36	33.25	40.42	41.46	42.88	42.68
UT Chandigarh	55.36	55.80	40.42	41.46	63.65	51.34
UT Dadar and Nagar Haveli	55.36	33.25	40.42	41.46	42.88	42.68
UT Daman and Diu	31.89	33.25	40.42	41.46	42.88	37.98
UT Delhi	55.36	55.80	40.42	61.38	42.88	51.17
UT Lakshadweep	31.89	33.25	40.42	41.46	42.88	37.98
UT Pondicherry	31.89	55.80	40.42	41.46	42.88	42.49

V. INSTITUTIONAL ALTERNATIVES

States	Police		Courts	Prisons		
				Alternative to prison		
	Community policing	Informal justice system	Lok Adalat (per lakh population)	Borstal school	Open jail	T Score average
	57	58	59	60	61	62
Andhra Pradesh	62.82	64.56	58.25	63.65	62.82	62.42
Arunachal Pradesh	42.42	43.33	43.14	42.88	42.42	42.84
Assam	62.82	64.56	43.82	42.88	62.82	55.38
Bihar	42.42	43.33	43.30	42.88	42.42	42.87
Chattisgarh	62.82	64.56	43.01	42.88	42.42	51.14
Goa	42.42	43.33	54.73	42.88	42.42	45.16
Gujarat	42.42	43.33	86.02	42.88	62.82	55.50
Haryana	42.42	43.33	47.99	63.65	42.42	47.96
Himachal Pradesh	62.82	64.56	59.51	63.65	62.82	62.67
Jammu & Kashmir	42.42	43.33	45.80	42.88	42.42	43.37
Jharkhand	42.42	43.33	43.01	63.65	42.42	46.97
Karnataka	62.82	43.33	49.11	63.65	62.82	56.35
Kerala	42.42	64.56	54.45	63.65	62.82	57.58
Madhya Pradesh	62.82	64.56	49.63	63.65	42.42	56.62
Maharashtra	62.82	43.33	46.92	63.65	62.82	55.91
Manipur	42.42	43.33	43.66	42.88	42.42	42.94

Meghalaya	42.42	64.56	44.22	42.88	42.42	47.30
Mizoram	42.42	43.33	53.97	42.88	42.42	45.01
Nagaland	42.42	43.33	43.12	42.88	42.42	42.84
Orissa	42.42	43.33	51.62	63.65	62.82	52.77
Punjab	62.82	43.33	47.32	63.65	62.82	55.99
Rajasthan	62.82	64.56	83.45	63.65	62.82	67.46
Sikkim	42.42	43.33	60.07	42.88	42.42	46.22
Tamil Nadu	62.82	64.56	49.64	63.65	62.82	60.70
Tripura	42.42	43.33	43.72	42.88	42.42	42.96
Uttar Pradesh	42.42	43.33	45.63	42.88	42.42	43.34
Uttarakhand	42.42	43.33	43.01	42.88	62.82	46.89
West Bengal	62.82	64.56	43.67	42.88	62.82	55.35
UT Andaman & Nicobar Islands	42.42	43.33	45.08	42.88	42.42	43.23
UT Chandigarh	62.82	43.33	50.22	42.88	42.42	48.33
UT Dadar and Nagar Haveli	42.42	43.33	44.68	42.88	42.42	43.15
UT Daman and Diu	42.42	43.33	44.88	42.88	42.42	43.19
UT Delhi	62.82	64.56	46.86	42.88	42.42	51.91
UT Lakshadweep	42.42	43.33	44.23	42.88	42.42	43.06
UT Pondicherry	42.42	43.33	52.25	42.88	42.42	44.66

ANNEXURE II

Dimensionwise Data and Ranking on Each Indicator

I. ACCESSIBILITY AND EFFICIENCY OF CRIMINAL JUSTICE SYSTEM

States	Police infrastructure					
	Staff density (area and population wise)				Staff diversity as proportionate representation of population group	
	No. of policemen per 100 sq. km. (+)	Ranking	No. of policemen per 100,000 population (+)	Ranking	Proportionate representation of SCs in Police	Ranking
	1	2	3	4	5	6
Andhra Pradesh	28.5	27	98	28	89	17
Arunachal Pradesh	6.8	35	493	8	214	3
Assam	66.4	13	181	16	69	22
Bihar	54.2	18	57	35	73	21
Chattisgarh	17.3	34	103	26	58	25
Goa	95.8	9	235	14	113	9
Gujarat	29.4	26	106	25	199	4
Haryana	82.1	11	159	18	55	28
Himachal Pradesh	20.4	32	178	17	97	12

Jammu & Kashmir	64.1	15	572	4	37	29
Jharkhand	30.8	25	85	33	NA	–
Karnataka	28.4	28	98	28	107	10
Kerala	110.9	8	129	23	156	5
Madhya Pradesh	24.1	29	113	24	57	26
Maharashtra	44.2	21	132	20	117	8
Manipur	60.9	17	535	7	56	27
Meghalaya	39.8	22	364	11	NA	–
Mizoram	38.4	23	854	1	NA	–
Nagaland	72.2	12	566	5	NA	–
Orissa	22.4	30	90	32	74	20
Punjab	140.9	7	276	13	69	23
Rajasthan	18.3	33	102	27	90	15
Sikkim	49.3	19	609	3	102	11
Tamil Nadu	64.6	14	130	22	91	13
Tripura	175.2	6	542	6	85	18
Uttar Pradesh	63.6	16	84	34	82	19
Uttarakhand	22.3	31	131	21	130	7
West Bengal	90.2	10	94	30	59	24
UT Andaman & Nicobar Islands	33.3	24	707	2	0	–
UT Chandigarh	3564	2	407	10	89	16
UT Dadar and Nagar Haveli	45.4	20	91	31	530	2
UT Daman and Diu	217.9	5	139	19	992	1
UT Delhi	3652.5	1	344	12	91	14
UT Lakshadweep	853.1	3	420	9	0	–
UT Pondicherry	443.3	4	211	15	131	6

States	Police infrastructure					
	Staff diversity as proportionate representation of population groups		Staff diversity as proportionate representation of population group		Staff diversity as proportionate representation of population group	
	Proportionate representation of STs in police	Ranking	Proportionate representation of women	Ranking	Proportionate representation of muslim	Ranking
	7	8	9	10	11	12
Andhra Pradesh	90	12	4	24	143	1
Arunachal Pradesh	117	6	5	17	59	11
Assam	78	17	2	32	34	23
Bihar	438	1	4	23	35	22
Chattisgarh	55	24	5	20	44	18
Goa	0	–	13	4	28	24
Gujarat	105	7	6	15	69	8
Haryana	NA	–	5	19	94	5
Himachal Pradesh	157	4	11	9	80	7
Jammu & Kashmir	31	27	5	18	80	6
Jharkhand	0	–	2	30	NA	–
Karnataka	68	23	13	5	61	10
Kerala	104	9	9	11	56	12
Madhya Pradesh	42	25	6	16	44	16

Maharashtra	74	21	11	7	44	17
Manipur	69	22	3	25	118	3
Meghalaya	88	13	3	28	41	19
Mizoram	97	11	0	–	47	14
Nagaland	105	8	0	–	14	31
Orissa	77	18	2	31	120	2
Punjab	NA	–	5	21	17	30
Rajasthan	98	10	4	22	35	21
Sikkim	205	2	11	8	6	33
Tamil Nadu	80	16	23	1	67	9
Tripura	86	14	3	29	26	26
Uttar Pradesh	0	–	3	27	24	27
Uttarakhand	164	3	7	14	23	28
West Bengal	76	19	3	26	28	25
UT Andaman & Nicobar Islands	120	5	13	3	103	4
UT Chandigarh	0	–	15	2	9	32
UT Dadar and Nagar Haveli	81	15	8	13	45	15
UT Daman and Diu	37	26	0		53	13
UT Delhi	0	–	9	12	19	29
UT Lakshadweep	75	20	12	6	1	34
UT Pondicherry	0	–	9	10	39	20

States	Police infrastructure					
	Budget/Expenditure		Existing equipment and transport support			
	Expenditure on police per lakh population of state/UTs (in lakhs)	Ranking	Motor vehicles per lakh population	Ranking	Equipments per lakh population	Ranking
	13	14	15	16	17	18
Andhra Pradesh	144.13	27	8.1	27	36.8	25
Arunachal Pradesh	513.72	11	63.8	2	26.8	27
Assam	271.64	16	14.7	18	44.8	21
Bihar	99.96	34	4.7	32	21.1	29
Chattisgarh	119.12	32	18.6	15	39.2	24
Goa	363.57	14	24.6	13	362.7	3
Gujarat	143.20	28	9.0	23	43.5	22
Haryana	269.46	17	2.5	35	5.5	35
Himachal Pradesh	264.14	19	9.3	22	65.6	16
Jammu & Kashmir	695.22	8	40.2	6	261.5	6
Jharkhand	162.23	24	4.6	33	20.9	31
Karnataka	156.49	26	9.7	21	77.4	15
Kerala	168.95	23	11.7	20	51.0	18
Madhya Pradesh	141.79	29	8.6	25	83.2	14
Maharashtra	205.34	21	6.6	31	21.1	30

Manipur	605.79	10	49.9	4	433.8	2
Meghalaya	498.21	12	28.6	11	118.4	12
Mizoram	1118.90	3	66.7	1	249.2	8
Nagaland	1216.30	2	19.7	14	24.9	28
Orissa	101.41	33	7.7	29	14.1	33
Punjab	402.54	13	8.6	24	46.6	20
Rajasthan	133.03	30	8.5	26	52.4	17
Sikkim	1062.96	4	47.1	5	288.8	4
Tamil Nadu	219.62	20	16.3	17	47.7	19
Tripura	676.37	9	36.2	7	255.6	7
Uttar Pradesh	130.71	31	3.8	34	42.1	23
Uttarakhand	268.57	18	7.8	28	12.3	34
West Bengal	84.15	35	7.2	30	20.4	32
UT Andaman & Nicobar Islands	1234.54	1	50.5	3	27.5	26
UT Chandigarh	720.14	7	29.9	10	229.8	9
UT Dadar and Nagar Haveli	173.77	22	12.7	19	88.9	13
UT Daman and Diu	157.14	25	18.3	16	150.4	11
UT Delhi	821.69	5	25.9	12	261.7	5
UT Lakshadweep	752.31	6	31.3	9	992.6	1
UT Pondicherry	338.18	15	34.7	8	156.4	10

States	Police infrastructure		Courts infrastructure			
	Existing building		Staff density (population wise)			
	Women police station's per 100 police station	Ranking	No. of high court judges* (per lakh population)	No. of district court judges* (per lakh population)	No. of judges per lakh population (+)	Ranking
	19	20	21	22	23	24
Andhra Pradesh	2.00	6	0.04	0.91	1.0	26
Arunachal Pradesh	0.00	21	0.10	0.00	0.0	31
Assam	0.43	20	0.10	1.00	1.0	26
Bihar	0.00	21	0.34	1.00	1.6	11
Chattisgarh	0.90	15	0.02	1.10	1.9	8
Goa	4.17	4	0.08	2.96	3.0	2
Gujarat	0.86	16	0.10	1.60	1.6	11
Haryana	0.48	19	0.10	1.20	1.6	11
Himachal Pradesh	0.00	21	0.10	1.90	2.0	5
Jammu & Kashmir	1.18	12	0.10	3.00	3.1	1
Jharkhand	0.00	21	0.03	1.60	1.6	11
Karnataka	1.26	11	0.06	1.24	1.3	18
Kerala	0.68	18	0.07	0.36	0.4	30
Madhya Pradesh	0.98	14	0.10	1.28	1.3	18
Maharashtra	0.00	21	0.60	1.60	1.6	11
Manipur	1.75	9	0.04	1.24	1.3	18

Meghalaya	0.00	21	0.10	0.30	0.0	31
Mizoram	0.00	21	0.00	0.00	0.0	31
Nagaland	2.38	5	0.10	1.30	1.3	18
Orissa	1.32	10	0.03	1.90	1.1	25
Punjab	1.17	13	0.10	1.10	1.2	23
Rajasthan	1.86	8	0.10	1.20	1.3	18
Sikkim	0.00	21	0.36	1.70	2.0	5
Tamil Nadu	19.10	1	0.06	1.10	1.0	26
Tripura	0.00	21	0.10	1.90	1.8	9
Uttar Pradesh	0.84	17	0.04	1.00	1.7	10
Uttarakhand	1.92	7	0.10	1.10	1.2	23
West Bengal	0.00	21	0.10	0.70	0.7	29
UT Andaman & Nicobar Islands	5.00	3	0.28	1.96	2.0	5
UT Chandigarh	0.00	21	0.11	2.20	2.3	4
UT Dadar and Nagar Haveli	0.00	21	0.00	0.00	0.0	31
UT Daman and Diu	0.00	21	0.00	0.00	0.0	31
UT Delhi	0.00	21	0.23	2.30	2.5	3
UT Lakshadweep	0.00	21	1.64	0.00	1.6	11
UT Pondicherry	8.11	2	0.10	1.53	1.6	11

States	Courts infrastructure		Prison infrastructure			
	Court expenditure (per lakh of population)		Staff provision		Prisons functions	
	Total courts budget per lakh population in rupees	Ranking	Number of jail Staff after 100 inmates	Ranking	Occupancy rates in prison (–)	Ranking
	25	26	27	28	29	30
Andhra Pradesh	616716.9	3	21	14	–119.1	16
Arunachal Pradesh	304744.8	11	0	33	0.0	
Assam	313818.6	7	11	26	–133.9	24
Bihar	273619.4	13	5	31	–208.0	32
Chattisgarh	NA	–	9	29	–215.2	33
Goa	NA	–	45	5	–107.9	14
Gujarat	NA	–	8	30	200.5	31
Haryana	NA	–	21	15	–121.9	17
Himachal Pradesh	NA	–	22	13	–122.2	18
Jammu & Kashmir	NA	–	61	2	–68.9	7
Jharkhand	318045.5	5	4	32	–318.2	34
Karnataka	26489.8	17	12	25	–131.9	21
Kerala	94217.0	16	19	16	–127.0	19
Madhya Pradesh	NA	–	11	28	–169.6	28
Maharashtra	NA	–	15	23	–141.8	25
Manipur	308844.2	8	61	1	–48.5	4

Meghalaya	314362.2	6	37	10	–106.7	13
Mizoram	295867.6	12	39	8	–71.0	8
Nagaland	306250.7	10	54	4	–53.9	5
Orissa	NA	–	15	22	–152.3	26
Punjab	NA	–	18	17	–130.2	20
Rajasthan	NA	–	17	20	–82.0	10
Sikkim	NA	–	38	9	–195.0	29
Tamil Nadu	157037.0	15	16	21	–115.4	15
Tripura	306295.0	9	39	7	–132.4	22
Uttar Pradesh	NA	–	13	24	–164.7	27
Uttarakhand	NA	–	17	18	–133.3	23
West Bengal	469216.6	4	17	19	–89.4	11
UT Andaman & Nicobar Islands	1066960.2	2	59	3	–72.5	9
UT Chandigarh	NA	–	26	12	–45.5	3
UT Dadar and Nagar Haveli	NA	–	0	33	–58.0	6
UT Daman and Diu	NA	–	40	6	–29.2	2
UT Delhi	1804988.1	1	11	27	–197.1	30
UT Lakshadweep	NA	–	0	33	–10.0	1
UT Pondicherry	205266.1	14	35	11	–94.4	12

States	Courts infrastructure		Prison infrastructure			
	Staff diversity		Budget/Expenditure		Disposal rate of cases by police	
	Percentage representation of women in jail staff	Ranking	Expenditure on prisons per lakh population (in lakhs)	Ranking	Total disposal rates	Ranking
	31	32	33	34	35	36
Andhra Pradesh	4.47	22	10.44	17	92.06	6
Arunachal Pradesh	0.00	33	0.00		73.59	20
Assam	11.61	5	8.41	24	43.98	32
Bihar	5.94	18	7.84	27	51.22	30
Chattisgarh	7.79	13	8.74	23	98.48	1
Goa	2.87	29	13.80	14	69.55	25
Gujarat	3.19	28	7.36	28	90.06	8
Haryana	6.24	17	27.43	9	87.45	10
Himachal Pradesh	7.03	16	17.76	12	82.03	12
Jammu & Kashmir	5.69	19	22.99	11	71.01	23
Jharkhand	8.98	10	5.14	31	53.31	29
Karnataka	10.81	7	10.06	19	69.62	24
Kerala	11.11	6	11.35	16	82.07	11
Madhya Pradesh	3.69	27	10.21	18	98.32	2
Maharashtra	2.25	31	9.59	21	73.88	19

Manipur	20.68	1	31.78	6	27.89	33
Meghalaya	7.80	12	11.49	15	25.40	34
Mizoram	14.03	3	76.91	1	74.29	18
Nagaland	16.91	2	51.64	4	80.46	13
Orissa	7.66	14	8.00	26	79.34	14
Punjab	4.25	23	24.63	10	71.63	22
Rajasthan	4.86	21	5.86	30	97.18	5
Sikkim	9.33	8	65.95	2	49.04	31
Tamil Nadu	4.08	26	3.20	32	88.57	9
Tripura	8.48	11	34.65	5	77.38	16
Uttar Pradesh	4.23	24	10.01	20	98.10	4
Uttarakhand	2.69	30	9.15	22	98.32	3
West Bengal	2.12	32	8.10	25	69.10	27
UT Andaman & Nicobar Islands	5.35	20	52.60	3	78.65	15
UT Chandigarh	9.02	9	30.17	7	74.60	17
UT Dadar and Nagar Haveli	4.20	25	2.05	33	69.49	26
UT Daman and Diu	0.00	33	6.63	29	72.67	21
UT Delhi	7.14	15	27.95	8	58.04	28
UT Lakshadweep	11.83	4	1.54	34	24.19	35
UT Pondicherry	0.00	33	13.86	13	91.14	7

States	Police functions				Courts function	
	Recovery rates		Charge sheeting rate of cases by police		Disposal rate of cases by courts	
	Stolen property (+)	Ranking	Total charge sheeting rate	Ranking	Disposal rate of total cases by courts (+) total	Ranking
	37	38	39	40	41	42
Andhra Pradesh	45.9	10	96.9	5	71.2	1
Arunachal Pradesh	10.3	30	59.5	32	6.1	34
Assam	23.5	19	62.5	30	22.6	15
Bihar	16.5	24	79.3	21	11.0	26
Chattisgarh	50.7	9	96.6	6	45.0	6
Goa	14.4	25	85.6	14	27.8	12
Gujarat	9.4	31	91.8	8	6.7	33
Haryana	77.3	1	84.7	16	20.8	16
Himachal Pradesh	36.4	15	91.2	10	18.1	19
Jammu & Kashmir	38.9	14	78.5	22	15.4	23
Jharkhand	18.3	23	69.4	28	18.6	18
Karnataka	12.8	29	83.4	18	31.2	10
Kerala	14.2	26	88.2	13	26.0	14
Madhya Pradesh	40	12	93.3	7	37.3	9
Maharashtra	13.7	27	84.1	17	7.9	30
Manipur	0.8	35	8.5	35	4.0	35

Meghalaya	18.4	22	50.7	33	7.0	32
Mizoram	65	6	91.5	9	27.8	13
Nagaland	41.8	11	50.6	34	63.1	2
Orissa	39.9	13	91.1	11	10.1	28
Punjab	70	4	88.9	12	17.7	20
Rajasthan	55.8	8	85.2	15	19.3	17
Sikkim	23.8	18	75.9	25	60.8	4
Tamil Nadu	72.2	3	72.6	26	60.8	3
Tripura	20.5	21	70.6	27	28.6	11
Uttar Pradesh	56.7	7	97.4	3	38.3	8
Uttarakhand	29	17	98.3	1	60.8	5
West Bengal	22	20	76.9	24	7.2	31
UT Andaman & Nicobar Islands	1.6	34	98.1	2	14.0	24
UT Chandigarh	34.6	16	68.4	29	16.8	22
UT Dadar and Nagar Haveli	65.1	5	81.0	19	9.2	29
UT Daman and Diu	13.6	28	61.9	31	10.7	27
UT Delhi	4.6	32	77.9	23	12.0	25
UT Lakshadweep	3.6	33	80.0	20	16.9	21
UT Pondicherry	74.9	2	97.2	4	41.4	7

States	Courts functions					
	Avarage time taken by trials				Conviction rates of total crimes by court	
	Average time taken for under trial of cases in courts (in years)	Ranking	Average time taken for under trial in prisons in months (–)	Ranking	Total conviction rate	Ranking
	43	44	45	46	47	48
Andhra Pradesh	–2.0	7	–3.9	3	90.2	5
Arunachal Pradesh	–2.3	10	0.0		56.6	19
Assam	–3.7	29	–6.2	9	18.7	29
Bihar	–5.0	33	–10.6	32	17.0	31
Chartisgarh	–2.6	14	–5.9	7	90.3	3
Goa	–2.7	15	–8.0	18	68.0	12
Gujarat	–2.5	13	–9.3	27	31.8	25
Haryana	–3.0	22	–10.1	30	47.4	21
Himachal Pradesh	–2.8	16	–8.7	25	18.9	28
Jammu & Kashmir	–2.8	17	–13.2	34	39.3	23
Jharkhand	–5.8	35	–8.5	20	24.2	27
Karnataka	–2.1	8	–8.6	24	34.4	24
Kerala	–2.8	18	–3.6	2	60.8	15
Madhya Pradesh	–3.0	23	–6.4	12	79.6	8

Maharashtra	–4.1	31	–8.6	23	12.5	34
Manipur	–5.3	34	–8.5	21	60.7	16
Meghalaya	–4.0	30	–10.4	31	48.3	20
Mizoram	–1.2	4	–5.4	5	80.0	7
Nagaland	–0.7	2	–5.5	6	61.2	14
Orissa	–3.5	26	–7.6	15	16.1	33
Punjab	–2.3	11	–9.9	29	59.2	18
Rajasthan	–3.3	24	–7.7	16	66.7	13
Sikkim	–1.7	5	–7.7	17	73.9	11
Tamil Nadu	–2.0	6	–7.3	14	74.5	10
Tripura	–2.9	21	–6.2	10	16.7	32
Uttar Pradesh	–4.4	32	–8.5	22	84.9	6
Uttarakhand	–3.6	28	–8.0	19	98.4	2
West Bengal	–3.5	27	–6.8	13	29.5	26
UT Andaman & Nicobar Islands	–2.4	12	–6.4	11	98.5	1
UT Chandigarh	–2.8	20	–8.9	26	76.0	9
UT Dadar and Nagar Haveli	–2.2	9	–11.2	33	4.5	35
UT Daman and Diu	–3.4	25	–9.6	28	17.8	30
UT Delhi	–2.8	19	–6.1	8	59.6	17
UT Lakshadweep	0.0	1	–3.0	1	41.7	22
UT Pondicherry	–0.7	3	–5.1	4	90.2	4

II. Level of Physical Security Enjoyed by the Citizens

States	Reported rate of crime					
	Total crime rate (per lakh population)	Percentage change in IPC crime in 2005 (–)	Ranking	Total crime against body (–) (per lakh population)	Ranking	Total crime against property (–) (per lakh population)
	49	50	51	52	53	54
Andhra Pradesh	834.76	1.0	12	–73.11	34	–41.07
Arunachal Pradesh	205.09	–2.1	17	–54.62	30	–77.14
Assam	153.61	–3.3	19	–42.4	26	–32.87
Bihar	119.87	9.4	3	–27.11	11	–19.68
Chattisgarh	1237.42	–4.1	20	–34.09	24	–43.62
Goa	405.71	0.4	14	–29.6	15	–52.42
Gujarat	530.18	–7.5	28	–31.87	19	–45.25
Haryana	286.35	–9.1	31	–32.9	21	–55.93
Himachal Pradesh	263.85	–0.2	15	–33.98	23	–22.25
Jammu & Kashmir	200.95	5.1	8	–27.74	13	–30.14
Jharkhand	133.61	–11.9	32	–27.29	12	–31.77
Karnataka	241.78	–2.7	18	–44.54	28	–44.03
Kerala	486.44	–0.3	16	–58.13	31	–31.35
Madhya Pradesh	632.39	3.9	10	–67.16	32	–51.11
Maharashtra	319.24	–6.1	24	–43.77	27	–63.81
Manipur	135.92	–14.9	33	–36.16	25	–12.49

Meghalaya	82.22	–7.0	27	–16.92	6	–32.67
Mizoram	355.86	–42.3	35	–15.52	4	–129.67
Nagaland	69.11	–6.6	26	–10.34	2	–22.63
Orissa	167.80	–6.0	23	–30.97	17	–28.40
Punjab	208.54	–5.9	22	–33.69	22	–19.69
Rajasthan	278.90	9.0	4	–54.60	29	–38.65
Sikkim	160.17	12.5	2	–31.48	18	–29.91
Tamil Nadu	1073.27	2.5	11	–69.20	33	–30.99
Tripura	105.28	–8.9	30	–25.96	9	–17.05
Uttar Pradesh	624.15	6.2	7	–18.52	7	–15.25
Uttarakhand	1480.27	7.0	6	–21.07	8	–25.86
West Bengal	88.93	4.2	9	–12.19	3	–17.31
UT Andaman & Nicobar Islands	2009.28	8.8	5	–26.8	10	–42.27
UT Chandigarh	394.39	–8.4	29	–15.73	5	–161.32
UT Dadar and Nagar Haveli	188.11	–6.1	24	–30.74	16	–42.62
UT Daman and Diu	141.71	–22.7	34	–29.14	14	–52.00
UT Delhi	524.92	–4.6	21	–31.91	20	–131.75
UT Lakshadweep	75.38	40	1	–7.69	1	–13.85
UT Pondicherry	561.43	1	12	–110.27	35	–52.23

States	Reported rate of crime					
	Ranking	Total crime against economic crimes (–) (per lakh population)	Ranking	Rate of total cognizable crimes SLL per lakh population (–)	Ranking	Total crime against women (–) (per lakh population)
	55	56	57	58	59	60
Andhra Pradesh	20	–11.42	31	–637.9	31	–26.1
Arunachal Pradesh	32	–5.87	18	–6.3	3	–12.9
Assam	18	–5.10	16	–7.2	5	–21.0
Bihar	6	–3.41	9	–10.9	8	–6.7
Chattisgarh	23	–2.72	3	–1044.2	33	–15.9
Goa	29	–7.56	23	–265.1	27	–8.0
Gujarat	25	–6.19	20	–321.2	28	–11.7
Haryana	30	–7.88	25	–99.2	20	–18.3
Himachal Pradesh	8	–3.93	11	–70.4	18	–12.4
Jammu & Kashmir	13	–4.83	15	–24.1	13	–18.9
Jharkhand	16	–3.13	7	–11.8	10	–8.8
Karnataka	24	–6.24	21	–30.7	14	–10.9
Kerala	15	–11.10	30	–173.4	26	–20.3
Madhya Pradesh	26	–2.97	5	–345.6	29	–22.0
Maharashtra	31	–8.24	26	–137.9	24	–13.0
Manipur	1	–7.25	22	–21.2	12	–5.5

Meghalaya	17	–2.45	2	–5.5	2	–5.3
Mizoram	33	–7.81	24	–128.2	23	–10.0
Nagaland	9	–2.98	6	–19.6	11	–1.7
Orissa	11	–3.54	10	–34.4	15	–16.1
Punjab	7	–12.86	32	–103.2	21	–7.6
Rajasthan	19	–14.66	33	–50.4	16	–18.9
Sikkim	12	–8.70	27	–64.2	17	–10.8
Tamil Nadu	14	–4.58	13	–822.9	32	–13.3
Tripura	4	–3.16	8	–6.3	3	–24.8
Uttar Pradesh	3	–4.04	12	–556.9	30	–8.2
Uttarakhand	10	–6.16	19	–1392.2	34	–8.6
West Bengal	5	–2.82	4	–10.9	8	–14.0
UT Andaman & Nicobar Islands	21	–5.41	17	–1833.5	35	–5.7
UT Chandigarh	35	–20.24	35	–80.5	19	–20.5
UT Dadar and Nagar Haveli	22	–10.66	29	–10.2	6	–9.8
UT Daman and Diu	27	–9.14	28	–2.9	1	–5.7
UT Delhi	34	–17.84	34	–168.8	25	–27.6
UT Lakshadweep	2	0.00	1	–10.8	7	0.0
UT Pondicherry	28	–4.75	14	–118.1	22	–12.3

States	Reported rate of crime					
	Ranking	Total crime against children (–) (per Lakh population)	Ranking	Crime against Scheduled Caste per lakh population (–)	Ranking	Crime against Scheduled Tribe per lakh population (–)
	61	62	63	64	65	66
Andhra Pradesh	34	–1.2	19	–3.9	33	–0.6
Arunachal Pradesh	20	–1.9	23	–0.2	12	–4.7
Assam	31	–0.7	11	–1.0	17	–0.8
Bihar	7	–0.1	4	–2.0	27	–0.1
Chattisgarh	24	–4.4	32	–2.0	27	–2.2
Goa	9	–3.5	30	–0.1	10	–0.1
Gujarat	17	–1.5	21	–2.4	29	–0.4
Haryana	26	–1.6	22	–1.3	24	0.0
Himachal Pradesh	19	–2.1	25	–0.9	16	–0.2
Jammu & Kashmir	27	–0.5	10	0.0	1	0.0
Jharkhand	12	–0.3	6	–1.0	17	–1.7
Karnataka	16	–0.3	6	–3.2	31	–0.3
Kerala	29	–1.2	19	–1.0	17	–0.2
Madhya Pradesh	32	–5.6	33	–6.6	35	–2.4
Maharashtra	21	–2.2	27	–0.8	14	–0.2
Manipur	4	–0.8	12	0.0	1	0.0
Meghalaya	3	–3.3	29	0.0	1	0.0

Mizoram	14	0.0	1	0.0	1	0.0
Nagaland	2	0.0	1	0.0	1	0.0
Orissa	25	−0.2	5	−3.7	32	−1.6
Punjab	8	−0.8	12	−0.5	13	0.0
Rajasthan	27	−0.9	17	−6.2	34	−1.4
Sikkim	15	−4.3	31	−1.2	23	−3.8
Tamil Nadu	22	−0.4	9	−1.9	26	0.0
Tripura	33	−0.8	12	−1.1	20	−0.4
Uttar Pradesh	10	−1.0	18	−2.4	29	0.0
Uttarakhand	11	−0.8	12	−1.1	20	0.0
West Bengal	23	−0.3	6	0.0	1	0.0
UT Andaman & Nicobar Islands	5	−2.1	25	0.0	1	−0.5
UT Chandigarh	30	−5.7	34	0.0	1	0.0
UT Dadar and Nagar Haveli	13	−2.0	24	−0.8	14	−0.8
UT Daman and Diu	5	−2.9	28	−1.1	20	0.0
UT Delhi	35	−6.5	35	−0.1	10	0.0
UT Lakshadweep	1	0.0	1	0.0	1	0.0
UT Pondicherry	18	−0.8	12	−1.4	25	0.0

States	Reported rate of crime	Percentage difference from total chargesheeting for specific population				
	Ranking	Women	Ranking	Children	Ranking	SC (–)
	67	68	69	70	71	72
Andhra Pradesh	26	–1.1	8	9.7	9	0.5
Arunachal Pradesh	35	–15.0	29	–14.6	29	–40.5
Assam	27	–14.8	28	–19.3	31	10.8
Bihar	17	–11.9	24	–11.4	27	–10.7
Chattisgarh	32	–0.9	7	0.4	19	1.6
Goa	17	2.8	6	7.8	10	85.6
Gujarat	23	–2.7	9	20.8	4	–4.4
Haryana	1	–8.6	15	1.0	18	–14.8
Himachal Pradesh	19	–6.7	12	1.4	17	–8.8
Jammu & Kashmir	1	–20.1	32	–17.0	30	–21.5
Jharkhand	31	–10.1	19	–22.7	33	–3.0
Karnataka	22	–11.9	23	7.5	11	–10.9
Kerala	19	–9.1	17	0.1	20	0.7
Madhya Pradesh	33	–3.9	11	–1.8	22	–3.0
Maharashtra	19	–13.3	26	2.0	16	–13.3
Manipur	1	–9.2	18	3.7	15	8.5
Meghalaya	1	–8.9	16	–45.7	35	50.7
Mizoram	1	–7.6	14	91.5	1	91.5
Nagaland	1	–11.7	22	50.6	3	50.6

Orissa	30	–7.1	13	–7.4	26	–3.9
Punjab	1	10.6	4	4.9	13	7.9
Rajasthan	29	–10.4	20	15.0	7	–13.3
Sikkim	34	13.1	3	–24.1	34	11.6
Tamil Nadu	1	–22.6	33	–20.3	32	–22.8
Tripura	23	–12.3	25	–14.6	28	–20.0
Uttar Pradesh	1	7.4	5	4.7	14	6.2
Uttarakhand	1	15.7	2	15.5	6	19.5
West Bengal	1	–14.0	27	–1.4	21	–23.1
UT Andaman & Nicobar Islands	25	25.1	1	20.3	5	98.1
UT Chandigarh	1	–24.6	34	6.5	12	68.4
UT Dadar and Nagar Haveli	27	–19.0	30	–2.3	23	81.0
UT Daman and Diu	1	–28.1	35	–4.8	25	–38.1
UT Delhi	1	–10.7	21	10.5	8	22.3
UT Lakshadweep	1	–20.0	31	80.0	2	80.0
UT Pondicherry	1	–2.8	10	–2.8	24	–2.8

States	Percentage difference from total charge sheeting for specific population			Percentage difference from total conviction rates for specific population		
	Ranking	ST (–)	Ranking	Women	Ranking	Children
	73	74	75	76	77	78
Andhra Pradesh	18	5.6	14	59.5	3	73.7
Arunachal Pradesh	35	2.6	15	3.9	27	–43.4
Assam	12	–12.0	26	–1.3	31	–22.8
Bihar	25	–15.9s	30	–2.1	32	17.0
Chattisgarh	16	–1.9	22	46.3	6	47.3
Goa	3	85.6	4	39.2	10	23.0
Gujarat	23	2.2	16	20.5	19	11.0
Haryana	29	84.7	5	13.8	23	15.8
Himachal Pradesh	24	–8.8	24	7.3	25	–4.2
Jammu & Kashmir	31	78.5	6	26.3	16	39.3
Jharkhand	21	1.0	17	–14.2	35	–14.0
Karnataka	26	–14.3	29	15.2	22	29.3
Kerala	17	–10.6	25	39.8	9	49.8
Madhya Pradesh	20	0.1	19	49.6	5	39.0
Maharashtra	28	–12.6	27	3.9	28	–1.2
Manipur	13	8.5	13	60.7	2	60.7
Meghalaya	7	50.7	9	23.3	17	48.3
Mizoram	2	91.5	2	–7.5	34	80.0
Nagaland	8	50.6	10	21.8	18	61.2
Orissa	22	–3.7	23	3.1	29	2.5

Punjab	14	88.9	3	28.9	15	32.0
Rajasthan	27	–14.1	28	16.6	21	29.1
Sikkim	11	13.0	11	1.6	30	23.9
Tamil Nadu	32	–27.4	35	34.4	12	49.2
Tripura	30	0.6	18	–5.9	33	–24.5
Uttar Pradesh	15	9.9	12	31.1	13	28.6
Uttarakhand	10	–1.7	20	38.2	11	49.8
West Bengal	33	–23.1	34	7.8	24	25.8
UT Andaman & Nicobar Islands	1	–1.9	21	90.2	1	98.5
UT Chandigarh	6	68.4	7	53.2	4	54.6
UT Dadar and Nagar Haveli	4	–19.0	31	4.5	26	–45.5
UT Daman and Diu	34	61.9	8	17.8	20	17.8
UT Delhi	9	–22.1	33	30.8	14	32.1
UT Lakshadweep	5	–20.0	32	41.7	7	41.7
UT Pondicherry	19	97.2	1	40.3	8	40.2

States	Percentage difference from total conviction rates for specific population				
	Ranking	SC (–)	Ranking	ST (–)	Ranking
	79	80	81	82	83
Andhra Pradesh	3	74.9	5	77.8	4
Arunachal Pradesh	34	56.6	9	–21.2	35
Assam	32	–14.6	33	–9.2	33
Bihar	25	–13.6	32	–5.2	32
Chattisgarh	11	58.6	8	50.7	13
Goa	23	68.0	6	68.0	7
Gujarat	27	27.9	22	30.7	20
Haryana	26	30.3	21	47.4	16
Himachal Pradesh	30	8.9	27	18.9	24
Jammu & Kashmir	14	39.3	18	39.3	19
Jharkhand	31	4.8	30	1.3	31
Karnataka	18	30.4	20	30.4	21
Kerala	7	46.9	15	52.8	12
Madhya Pradesh	15	47.5	13	50.0	14
Maharashtra	29	6.6	28	9.1	28
Manipur	5	60.7	7	60.7	9
Meghalaya	10	48.3	12	48.3	15
Mizoram	2	80.0	3	80.0	3
Nagaland	4	–38.8	35	61.2	8
Orissa	28	5.0	29	3.5	30

Punjab	17	47.3	14	59.2	11
Rajasthan	19	25.6	23	29.9	22
Sikkim	22	23.9	24	45.3	17
Tamil Nadu	9	49.3	11	74.5	6
Tripura	33	16.7	26	16.7	26
Uttar Pradesh	20	35.5	19	13.5	27
Uttarakhand	8	51.5	10	25.7	23
West Bengal	21	–20.5	34	–20.5	34
UT Andaman & Nicobar Islands	1	98.5	1	98.5	1
UT Chandigarh	6	76.0	4	76.0	5
UT Dadar and Nagar Haveli	35	4.5	31	4.5	29
UT Daman and Diu	24	17.8	25	17.8	25
UT Delhi	16	39.6	17	59.6	10
UT Lakshadweep	12	41.7	16	41.7	18
UT Pondicherry	13	81.1	2	90.2	2

III. RIGHTS OF POPULATIONS AFFECTED BY CRIME

States	Rights of accused		Right of victims			
	Free legal aid beneficiaries (per lakh population)	Ranking	Family courts per 100 district and subordinate courts	Ranking	Special courts for SC and ST	Ranking
	84	85	86	87	88	89
Andhra Pradesh	3.95	8	1	13	1	25
Arunachal Pradesh	NA	–	NA	–	0	29
Assam	NA	–	2	10	3	1
Bihar	NA	–	1	13	3	1
Chattisgarh	23.52	4	3	9	1	25
Goa	NA	–	NA	–	3	1
Gujarat	21.47	5	1	13	3	1
Haryana	11.24	7	NA	–	0	29
Himachal Pradesh	NA	–	NA	–	3	1
Jammu & Kashmir	11.32	6	NA	–	0	29
Jharkhand	NA	–	1	13	3	1
Karnataka	NA	–	2	10	3	1
Kerala	NA	–	14	2	3	1
Madhya Pradesh	86.69	2	1	13	3	1
Maharashtra	NA	–	1	13	3	1
Manipur	NA	–	7	6	3	1

Meghalaya	NA	–	NA	–	3	1
Mizoram	NA	–	NA	–	0	29
Nagaland	NA	–	8	4	0	29
Orissa	NA	–	1	13	1	25
Punjab	NA	–	17	1	3	1
Rajasthan	NA	–	1	13	2	22
Sikkim	NA	–	11	3	3	1
Tamil Nadu	127.26	1	1	13	3	1
Tripura	NA	–	2	10	3	1
Uttar Pradesh	NA	–	1	13	3	1
Uttarakhand	NA	–	8	4	3	1
West Bengal	NA	–	1	13	3	1
UT Andaman & Nicobar Islands	NA	–	NA	–	2	22
UT Chandigarh	NA	–	NA	–	3	1
UT Dadar and Nagar Haveli	NA	–	NA	–	0	29
UT Daman and Diu	NA	–	NA	–	2	22
UT Delhi	84.81	3	5	8	1	25
UT Lakshadweep	NA	–	NA	–	0	29
UT Pondicherry	NA	–	7	6	3	1

States	Violation by enforcement agencies (police/judiciaries/prisons)							
	No. of complaints against per 100 policemen (–)	Ranking	Percentage of police personnel convicted per 100 police complaints received	Ranking	Total death of inmates due to various causes (–)	Ranking	No. of complaints against prison staff (–)	Ranking
	90	91	92	93	94	95	96	97
Andhra Pradesh	–9.5	33	0.03	16	–129	33	–24	27
Arunachal Pradesh	0.0	1	100.00	1	0	1	0	1
Assam	0.0	1	0.00	19	–26	19	–15	26
Bihar	–0.1	9	0.00	19	–198	35	–54	31
Chattisgarh	–4.3	26	2.98	8	–61	26	–1	17
Goa	–0.6	19	0.00	19	–4	13	0	1
Gujarat	–7.3	31	0.74	10	–32	21	0	1
Haryana	–3.4	23	0.00	19	–15	18	0	1
Himachal Pradesh	–1.9	21	0.48	11	–6	16	–1	17
Jammu & Kashmir	–3.9	25	0.00	19	–3	10	0	1
Jharkhand	0.0	1	0.00	19	–63	28	–1	17
Karnataka	–0.5	17	0.77	9	–61	26	–66	32
Kerala	–4.6	27	0.05	15	–38	22	–2	21
Madhya Pradesh	–26.6	35	0.03	17	–101	30	–29	28
Maharashtra	–3.2	22	0.30	12	–116	32	–2	21

Manipur	0.0	1	0.00	19	0	1	0	1
Meghalaya	–0.4	16	0.00	19	–2	8	0	1
Mizoram	0.0	1	100.00	1	0	1	0	1
Nagaland	–0.1	9	12.50	6	–4	13	0	1
Orissa	–0.2	13	0.00	19	–38	22	–32	30
Punjab	–5.4	29	0.11	13	–85	29	–298	35
Rajasthan	–1.7	20	0.09	14	–45	25	–69	33
Sikkim	–0.5	17	0.00	19	0	1	0	1
Tamil Nadu	–0.2	13	3.68	7	–102	31	–161	34
Tripura	–0.3	15	0.00	19	–5	15	0	1
Uttar Pradesh	–3.4	23	0.02	18	–171	34	–4	24
Uttarakhand	–7.6	32	0.00	19	–7	17	0	1
West Bengal	–0.1	9	0.00	19	–41	24	–7	25
UT Andaman & Nicobar Islands	–6.1	30	0.00	19	–2	8	0	1
UT Chandigarh	–4.7	28	0.00	19	–3	10	–2	21
UT Dadar and Nagar Haveli	0.0	1	100.00	1	0	1	0	1
UT Daman and Diu	0.0	1	100.00	1	0	1	0	1
UT Delhi	–12.3	34	0.00	19	–26	19	–31	29
UT Lakshadweep	0.0	1	100.00	1	0	1	0	1
UT Pondicherry	–0.1	9	0.00	19	–3	10	–1	17

IV. COMMITMENT TO JUSTICE

States	Specials provisions		State oversight			
	Women Cell	Ranking	State Commission for Women	Ranking	State Human Rights Commission	Ranking
	98	99	100	101	102	103
Andhra Pradesh	0	28	1	1	1	1
Arunachal Pradesh	0	28	1	1	0	18
Assam	1	1	1	1	1	1
Bihar	1	1	1	1	0	18
Chattisgarh	1	1	0	27	1	1
Goa	1	1	1	1	0	18
Gujarat	1	1	1	1	1	1
Haryana	1	1	1	1	0	18
Himachal Pradesh	1	1	0	27	1	1
Jammu & Kashmir	1	1	1	1	1	1
Jharkhand	1	1	0	27	0	18
Karnataka	1	1	1	1	1	1
Kerala	1	1	1	1	1	1
Madhya Pradesh	1	1	1	1	1	1
Maharashtra	1	1	1	1	1	1
Manipur	1	1	0	27	1	1
Meghalaya	1	1	1	1	0	18
Mizoram	1	1	1	1	0	18

Nagaland	1	1	0	27	0	18
Orissa	1	1	1	1	1	1
Punjab	1	1	1	1	1	1
Rajasthan	1	1	1	1	1	1
Sikkim	0	28	1	1	0	18
Tamil Nadu	0	28	1	1	1	1
Tripura	1	1	1	1	0	18
Uttar Pradesh	0	28	1	1	1	1
Uttarakhand	1	1	1	1	0	18
West Bengal	1	1	1	1	1	1
UT Andaman & Nicobar Islands	1	1	0	27	0	18
UT Chandigarh	1	1	1	1	0	18
UT Dadar and Nagar Haveli	1	1	0	27	0	18
UT Daman and Diu	0	28	0	27	0	18
UT Delhi	1	1	1	1	0	18
UT Lakshadweep	0	28	0	27	0	18
UT Pondicherry	0	28	1	1	0	18

States	State oversight			
	State Minority Commission	Ranking	State SC Commission	Ranking
	104	105	106	107
Andhra Pradesh	1	1	0	13
Arunachal Pradesh	0	16	0	13
Assam	1	1	1	1
Bihar	1	1	1	1
Chattisgarh	1	1	0	13
Goa	0	16	0	13
Gujarat	0	16	1	1
Haryana	0	16	0	13
Himachal Pradesh	0	16	0	13
Jammu & Kashmir	0	16	0	13
Jharkhand	1	1	0	13
Karnataka	1	1	1	1
Kerala	0	16	1	1
Madhya Pradesh	1	1	0	13
Maharashtra	1	1	1	1
Manipur	1	1	0	13
Meghalaya	0	16	0	13
Mizoram	0	16	0	13
Nagaland	0	16	0	13
Orissa	0	16	0	13

Punjab	0	16	0	13
Rajasthan	1	1	1	1
Sikkim	0	16	0	13
Tamil Nadu	1	1	1	1
Tripura	0	16	1	1
Uttar Pradesh	1	1	1	1
Uttarakhand	1	1	0	13
West Bengal	1	1	1	1
UT Andaman & Nicobar Islands	0	16	0	13
UT Chandigarh	0	16	1	1
UT Dadar and Nagar Haveli	0	16	0	13
UT Daman and Diu	0	16	0	13
UT Delhi	1	1	0	13
UT Lakshadweep	0	16	0	13
UT Pondicherry	0	16	0	13

V. Institutional Alternatives

States	Alternative to police				Alternatives to courts	
	Community policing	Ranking	Informal justice system	Ranking	Lok Adalat (per lakh population)	Ranking
	108	109	110	111	112	113
Andhra Pradesh	1	1	1	1	21	5
Arunachal Pradesh	0	14	0	12	0	31
Assam	1	1	1	1	1	26
Bihar	0	14	0	12	0	30
Chattisgarh	1	1	1	1	0	33
Goa	0	14	0	12	16	6
Gujarat	0	14	0	12	58	1
Haryana	0	14	0	12	7	15
Himachal Pradesh	1	1	1	1	22	4
Jammu & Kashmir	0	14	0	12	4	19
Jharkhand	0	14	0	12	0	33
Karnataka	1	1	0	12	8	14
Kerala	0	14	1	1	16	7
Madhya Pradesh	1	1	1	1	9	13
Maharashtra	1	1	0	12	5	17
Manipur	0	14	0	12	1	29
Meghalaya	0	14	1	1	2	25
Mizoram	0	14	0	12	15	8

Nagaland	0	14	0	12	0	32
Orissa	0	14	0	12	12	10
Punjab	1	1	0	12	6	16
Rajasthan	1	1	1	1	55	2
Sikkim	0	14	0	12	23	3
Tamil Nadu	1	1	1	1	9	12
Tripura	0	14	0	12	1	27
Uttar Pradesh	0	14	0	12	4	20
Uttarakhand	0	14	0	12	0	33
West Bengal	1	1	1	1	1	28
UT Andaman & Nicobar Islands	0	14	0	12	3	21
UT Chandigarh	1	1	0	12	10	11
UT Dadar and Nagar Haveli	0	14	0	12	2	23
UT Daman and Diu	0	14	0	12	3	22
UT Delhi	1	1	1	1	5	18
UT Lakshadweep	0	14	0	12	2	24
UT Pondicherry	0	14	0	12	13	9

States	Prisons			
	Alternative to prison			
	Borstal school	Ranking	Open jail	Ranking
	114	115	116	117
Andhra Pradesh	1	1	1	1
Arunachal Pradesh	0	13	0	14
Assam	0	13	1	1
Bihar	0	13	0	14
Chattisgarh	0	13	0	14
Goa	0	13	0	14
Gujarat	0	13	1	1
Haryana	1	1	0	14
Himachal Pradesh	1	1	1	1
Jammu & Kashmir	0	13	0	14
Jharkhand	1	1	0	14
Karnataka	1	1	1	1
Kerala	1	1	1	1
Madhya Pradesh	1	1	0	14
Maharashtra	1	1	1	1
Manipur	0	13	0	14
Meghalaya	0	13	0	14
Mizoram	0	13	0	14
Nagaland	0	13	0	14
Orissa	1	1	1	1

Punjab	1	1	1	1
Rajasthan	1	1	1	1
Sikkim	0	13	0	14
Tamil Nadu	1	1	1	1
Tripura	0	13	0	14
Uttar Pradesh	0	13	0	14
Uttarakhand	0	13	1	1
West Bengal	0	13	1	1
UT Andaman & Nicobar Islands	0	13	0	14
UT Chandigarh	0	13	0	14
UT Dadar and Nagar Haveli	0	13	0	14
UT Daman and Diu	0	13	0	14
UT Delhi	0	13	0	14
UT Lakshadweep	0	13	0	14
UT Pondicherry	0	13	0	14

DATA SOURCES

LEVEL I

Accessibility and Efficiency of Criminal Justice System

- Column 1 to 10 and 17 to 21: Government of India, Ministry of Home Affairs 2006.
- Column 13 to 16 and 22: Government of India, Ministry of Home Affairs, 2007.
- Column 11: Annual Survey of Courts (2007), *Court News*, April-June 2007.
- Column 12: National Judicial Infrastructure Plan 2006.

LEVEL II

Level of Physical Security Enjoyed by the Citizens

- Column 1 to 17: Government of India: Ministry of Home Affairs, 2006.

LEVEL III

Rights of Populations Affected by Crime

- Column 43,44 and 59: http://lawmin.nic.in.
- Column 4 and 5: Government of India: Ministry of Home Affairs, 2006.
- Column 49: Government of India: Ministry of Home Affairs, 2007.
- Column 45: www2ohchr.org/english/bodies/cescr/docs/ AdvanceVerson/ IntConvenientEscadditionalinfo.doc

LEVEL IV

Commitment to Justice

- Column 51: www.apstatepolice.org and various other state police sites.
- Column 52: http:/ncw.nic.in/
- Column 53: http:/nhrc.nic.in and various state human rights commission.
- Column 54: http://ncm.nic.in/ministry-minority/html
- Column 55: http://ncsc.nic.in

LEVEL V

Institutional Alternatives.

- Column 57: http://bprd.nic.in/writereaddate/linkimages/community %20policing4348 180177.pdf
- Column 60 and 61: http://ncrb.nic.in/PSI/2005/chapter-1pdf.

ANNEXURE III

International Covenants and Indian Law

International Covenants and Indian Law				
1. Convention on elimination of all forms of discrimination against women 1979	2. Convention against torture and other cruel, in human or degrading treatment or punishment 1984	3. Convention on the rights of the child 1989	4. International convention on the elimination of all forms of racial discrimination 1965	5. International convention on the civil and political rights 1966
Indian Laws				
1. Dowry Prohibition Rules, 1985	Bonded Labour System (Abolition) Act, 1976	1. Commission for Protection of Child's Rights Act, 2005	1. Constitution (Scheduled Caste) Order, 1950 Amendments:	1. Madhya Pradesh Freedom of Religion Act, 1968, No. 27 (35kb)
2. National Commission for Women Act, 1990	No ratification by India yet	2. Commission for Protection of Child's Rights (Amendment) Act, 2006	2. Constitution (Scheduled Caste) Order (Amendment) Act, 1990	2. Charitable and Religious Trusts Act, 1920, No. 14 (44kb)
3. Protection of Women from Domestic Violence Act, 2005		3. Juvenile Justice (Care and Protection of Children) (Amendment) Act, 2006	3. Protection of Civil Rights Act, 1955	3. National Commission for Minorities Act, 1992, No. 19 (50kb)
		4. National Commission for	4. Protection of Civil Rights Rules, 1977	

4. Commission of Sati (Prevention) Act, 1987	Protection of Child's Rights Rules, 2006. 5. Prohibition of Child Marriage Act, 2006	5. Protection of Human Rights Act, 1933 6. Protection of Human Rights (Amendment) Act, 2006 7. National Commission for Backward Classes Act, 1993 8. National Commission for Scheduled Castes Rules, 2004 9. Scheduled Castes and Scheduled Tribes Orders (Amendment) Act, 1956 10. Scheduled Castes & Scheduled Tribes (Prevention of Atrocities) Act, 1989 Scheduled Castes & Scheduled Tribes (Prevention of Atrocities) Rules, 1995

International Covenants and Indian Law				
1. Convention on elimination of all forms of discrimination against women 1979	2. Convention against torture and other cruel, in human or degrading treatment or punishment 1984	3. Convention on the rights of the child 1989	4. International convention on the elimination of all forms of racial discrimination 1965	5. International convention on the civil and political rights 1966
Indian Laws				
			11. Employment of Manual Scavenger and Construction of dry Latrines (Prohibition Act, 1993 12. National Commission for Safai Karamchari Act, 1993 13. National Commission for Safai Karamchari (Amendment) Act, 2001	

ANNEXURE IV

Relevant Human Rights Commissions

NATIONAL COMMISSION OF SCHEDULED CASTES[1]

VARIOUS FUNCTIONS

1. FUNCTIONS AND DUTIES OF THE COMMISSION

1.1 The functions, duties and power of the Commission have been laid down in clauses (5), (8) and (9) of the Article 338 of the Constitution (Annexure II) of the handbook.

Clause (5): It shall be the duty of the Commission:

(a) to investigate and monitor all matters relating to the safeguards provided for the Scheduled Castes under this Constitution or under any other law for the time being in force or under any order of the Government and to evaluate the working of such safeguards;
(b) to inquire into specific complaints with respect to the deprivation of rights and safeguards of the Scheduled Castes;
(c) to participate and advise on the planning process of socio-economic development of the Scheduled Castes and to evaluate the progress of their development under the Functions Union and any State;
(d) to present to the President, annually and at such other times as the Commission may deem fit, reports upon the working of those safeguards;
(e) to make in such reports recommendations as to the measures that should be taken by the Union or any State for the effective implementation of those safeguards and other measures for the protection, welfare and socio-economic development of the Scheduled Castes; and
(f) to discharge such other functions in relation to the protection, welfare and development and advancement of the Scheduled Castes

[1] www.ncsc.nic.in

as the President may, subject to the provisions of any law made by Parliament, by rule specify.

Clause (8): The Commission shall, while investigating any matter referred to in sub-clause (a) or inquiring into any complaint referred to in sub-clause (b) of clause (5), have all the powers of a civil court trying a suit and in particular in respect of the following matters, namely:

(a) Summoning and enforcing the attendance of any person from any part of India and examining him on oath;
(b) Requiring the discovery and production of any documents;
(c) Receiving evidence on affidavits;
(d) Requisitioning any public record or copy thereof from any court or office;
(e) Issuing commissions for the examination of witnesses and documents;
(f) Any other matter which the President may by rule, determine;

Clause (9): The Union and every State Government shall consult the Commission on all major policy matters affecting Scheduled Castes.

2. CONSTITUTIONAL SAFEGUARDS

The important Constitutional Safeguards for Scheduled Castes is mentioned below:

(A) *Development and Protective Safeguards*

These safeguards are contained in the Directive Principles of State Policy of the Constitution and a specific provision in Article 46 which is a comprehensive provision comprising both the developmental and regulatory aspects. It reads as follows:

Article 46: "The State shall promote with special care the educational and economic interests of the weaker sections of the people, and in particular, of the Scheduled Castes and the Scheduled Tribes, and shall protect them from social injustice and all forms of exploitation."

(B) *Social Safeguards*

Article 17 "Untouchability" is abolished and its practice in any form is forbidden. The enforcement of any disability arising out of "Untouchability" shall be an offence punishable in accordance with law.

To give effect to this Article, Parliament made an enactment, viz., Untouchability (Offences) Act, 1955. To make the provisions of this Act more stringent, the Act was amended in 1976 and was also renamed as the Protection of Civil Rights Act, 1955. As provided under the Act, the Government of India also notified the Rules, viz., the PCR Rules, 1977, to carry out the provisions of this Act. As cases of atrocities on SCs/STs were not covered under the provisions of PCR Act, 1955, Parliament passed another important Act in 1989 for taking specific measures to prevent the atrocities. This Act known as the Scheduled Castes and Scheduled Tribes (Prevention of Atrocities) Act, 1989, became effective from 30-1-1990. For carrying out the provisions of this Act the Govt. of India have notified the SCs and STs (Prevention of Atrocities) Rules, 1995 on 31-3-1995. Copies of PCR Act, 1955, PCR Rules 1977, the SCs and the STs (POA) Act, 1989 and the SCs and STs (POA) Rules 1995 are placed at Annexures V, VI, VII and VIII of the handbook respectively.

Article 23 prohibits traffic in human beings and beggar and other similar forms of forced labour and provides that any contravention of this provision shall be an offence punishable in accordance with law. It does not specifically mention SCs but since majority of bounded labour belong to SCs this Article has a special significance for these communities. In pursuance of this Article, Parliament has enacted the Bonded Labour System (Abolition) Act, 1976. For effective implementation of this Act, the Ministry of Labour is running a Centrally Sponsored Scheme for identification, liberation and rehabilitation of bonded labour.

Article 24 provides that no child below the age of 14 years shall be employed to work in any factory or mine or engaged in any other hazardous employment. There are Central and State laws to prevent child labour. This Article is also significant for SCs as a substantial portion of child labour engaged in hazardous jobs belong to these groups.

Article 25(2) (b) provides that Hindu religious institutions of a public character shall be thrown open to all classes and sections of Hindus. This provision is relevant as some sects of Hindus used to claim that only members of the concerned sects had a right to enter their temples. This was only a subterfuge to prevent entry of SC persons in such temples. For the purpose of this provision the term Hindu includes Sikh, Jain and Buddhist.

(C) *Economic Safeguards*

The provisions of Articles 23, 24 and 46 mentioned above also form part of the economic safeguards for Scheduled Castes.

(D) *Educational and Cultural Safeguards*

Article 15(4) empowers the State to make any special provision for the advancement of any socially and educationally backward classes of citizens or for SCs and STs. This provision was added to the Constitution through the Constitution (First Amendment) Act, 1951, which amended several Articles. This provision has enabled the State to reserve seats for SCs and STs in educational institutions including technical, engineering and medical colleges and in Scientific & Specialised Courses. In this Article as well as in Article 16(4) the term 'backward classes' is used as a generic term and comprises various categories of backward classes, viz., Scheduled Castes, Scheduled Tribes, Other Backward Classes, De-notified Communities (Vimukta Jatiyan) and Nomadic/Semi-Nomadic communities.

(E) *Political Safeguards*

Article 164(1) provides that in the States of Bihar, Madhya Pradesh and Orissa there shall be a Minister in charge of tribal welfare who may in addition be in charge of the welfare of the Scheduled Castes and backward classes or any other work.

Article 330 provides for reservation of seats for SCs and STs in the Lok Sabha.

Article 332 provides for reservation of seats for SCs/STs in the State Vidhan Sabhas (Legislative Assemblies).

Article 334 originally laid down that the provisions relating to the reservation of seats for SCs/STs in the Lok Sabha and State Vidhan Sabhas (and the representation of the Anglo-Indian community in the Lok Sabha and the State Vidhan Sabhas by nomination) would cease to have effect on the expiration of a period of ten years from the commencement of the Constitution. This Article has been amended five times, extending the said period by ten years on each occasion. This provision will now expire in January, 2010.

Article 371A contains special provisions with respect to Nagaland.

Article 371B contains special provisions with respect to Assam.

Article 371C contains special provisions with respect to Manipur.

Article 371F contains special provisions with respect to Sikkim.

(F) *Service Safeguards*

Article 16(4) empowers the State to make "any provision for the reservation in appointments or posts in favour of any backward class of citizens which, in the opinion of the State, is not adequately represented in the services under the State".

Article 16(4A) specific that nothing in this Article shall prevent the State from making any provision for reservation in matters of promotion, "with consequent seniority" to any class or classes of posts in the services under the State in favour of the Scheduled Castes and the Scheduled Tribes which, in the opinion of the State, are not adequately represented in the services under the State".

Article 16(4B) "Specific that nothing in this Article shall prevent the State from considering any unfilled vacancies of a year which are reserved for being filled up in that year in accordance with any provision for reservation made under clause (4) or clause (4A) as a separate class of vacancies to be filled up in any succeeding year or years and such class of vacancies shall not be considered together with the vacancies of the year in which they are being filled up for determining the ceiling of fifty per cent reservation on total number of vacancies of that year."

Article 320 (4) provides that nothing in clause (3) shall require a Public Service Commission to be consulted as respects the manner in which any provision under Article 16(4A) may be made or the manner in which effect may be given to the provisions of Article 335.

Article 335 mentions that the claims of the members of the Scheduled Castes and the Scheduled Tribes shall be taken into consideration, consistently with the maintenance of efficiency of administration, in the making to appointments to services and posts in connection with the affairs of the Union or of a State.

"Provided that nothing in this Article shall prevent in making of any provision in favor of Member of SCs & STs for relaxation in qualifying marks in any examination or lowering the standards of evaluation, for reservation in matters of promotion to any class or classes of services or posts in connection with affairs of Union or of a State" *(Constitutional 82nd (Amendment) Act, 2000).*

3. STATUTES AND LEGISLATIONS

There are a number of laws, both Central and State, which provide for safeguards to SCs. Some of these emanate from the various Constitutional provisions. An illustrative list of such laws is given below:

- The Protection of Civil Rights Act, 1955 (in respect of Scheduled Castes)
- The Scheduled Castes and the Scheduled Tribes (Prevention of Atrocities) Act, 1989
- The Bonded Labour System (Abolition) Act, 1976 (in respect of Scheduled Castes)
- The Child Labour (Prohibition and Regulation) Act, 1986 (in respect of Scheduled Castes)
- The Minimum Wages Act 1948 (in respect of Scheduled Castes)
- Acts and regulations in force in different States to prevent alienation of land belonging to SCs. In some States such provision exists in the Land Revenue Code.

4. SOCIO-ECONOMIC DEVELOPMENT

4.1 *Section (9) of the Article 338 of the Constitution reads as follows:*

"The Union and every State Government shall consult the Commission on all major policy matters affecting Scheduled Castes."

The Constitution has made it mandatory for the Union and every State Government to consult the Commission on all major Policy matters affecting SCs. This is very important function of the Commission, which has to keep track of all the major policy decisions, Legislative of Executive action taken by the Government of India or any State Government.

4.2 *As per the provisions of Clause 5 (c) of Article 338,* the Commission is required to participate and advise on the planning process of socio-economic development of SCs and evaluate the progress of their development under Union and any State. The role of the Commission in these areas involve interaction at various levels, i.e. with the Planning Commission, with the Central Ministries and with the State Governments. The Commission and its officers both at Headquarters and the State offices participate in formulation of policies and the developmental programmes for SCs including Special Component Plan for Scheduled Castes.

5. PROCEDURE FOR INQUIRY

5.1 *Inquiry into Specific Complaints*

The Commission is required to inquire into specific complaints with respect to the deprivation of rights and safeguards of Scheduled Castes. In order to enable the Commission to perform this function effectively and efficiently, the Commission would like the members of Scheduled Castes to know that it will be helpful to inquire into their grievances if they substantiate their complaints with supporting documents and quote the relevant provisions of the Act or Rules directions which have been violated.

5.2 *The Following Aspects May be Kept in Mind While Filing Complaints before the Commission*

(a) The complaint should be directly addressed to the Chairman/Vice-Chairman/Secretary, National Commission for Scheduled Castes, New Delhi or the heads of its State Offices.

(b) The complaints should disclose his full identity and give his full address and should sign the representation.

(c) Complaints should be legibly written or typed and, where necessary, supported by authenticated documents.

(d) No action will be taken on matters which are subjudice. Hence subjudice matter need not be referred to the Commission as complaint(s).

(e) Cases pending in courts or cases in which a court has already given its final verdict may not be taken up afresh with the Commission.

5.3 *Inquiry into Cases of Atrocities*

5.3.1 Whenever information is received in the Commission about any incident of atrocity against a person belonging to Scheduled Castes, the Commission would immediately get in touch with the law enforcing and administrative machinery of the State and the district to ascertain the details of incident and the action taken by the district administration.

5.3.2. The Commission ensures the following while by monitoring and issuing instructions to the concerned authorities:

(i) Whether the scene of occurrence of the crime has been visited immediately by Collector and Supdt. of Police of the district on receipt of information.
(ii) Whether proper FIR is registered in local Police Station.
(iii) Whether names of all the persons involved/cited by the complainant has been included in the FIR.
(iv) Whether investigation has been taken up by a Senior Police Officer as per provisions of SCs & STs (POA) Act, 1989.
(v) Whether culprits has been apprehended and booked without loss of time.
(vi) Whether proper charge sheet is filed mentioning the relevant sections of IPC together with the PCR Act, 1955 and SCs & STs (POA) Act, 1989 in Court.
(vii) Whether the cases are tried by the Special Courts.
(viii) Whether special Public Prosecutors are appointed to handle these cases.
(ix) Whether Police assists the courts in bringing forward witnesses and see that the culprits are suitably punished by the courts.

5.3.3 The Commission will also Monitor that

(i) The victims are provided with suitable medical assistance and on time;
(ii) Adequate protection is arranged for the victims of such incidents by providing police protection by stationing a police party, by patrolling, etc.;
(iii) To see that proper compensation is paid to the victims as per provisions of law.

5.3.4 The Commission will, wherever possible depending upon the gravity and circumstances of the case, visit the place of incident to oversee the arrangements and to console and infuse confidence among the victims.

5.3.5 The Commission has laid down detailed procedure for conducting such inquiries and monitoring at all levels. Such inquiries can be conduced by the Members of the Commission or Teams of Investigators from Headquarters or State office of the Commission.

5.4 *Powers of the Commission to Act as a Civil Court*

While investigating any matter referred to in sub-clause (a) or inquiring into specific complaints under sub-clause (b) of the clause (5) of Article 338 of the Constitution, the Commission shall have the powers of a Civil Court trying a suit and in particular in respect of the following matters:

(a) Summoning and enforcing the attendance of any person from any part of India and examining him on oath;
(b) Requiring the discovery and production of any document;
(c) Receiving evidence on affidavits;
(d) Requisitioning of any public record or copy thereof from any court of office;
(e) Issuing commissions for the examination of witnesses the documents;
(f) Any other matter which the President may, by rule, determine.

5.5 *Power to Regulate its Own Procedure*

Clause 4 of the amended Article 338 of the Constitution empowers the Commission to regulate its own procedure for a meaningful performance. The Commission has framed the Rules of Procedure. A copy of the Rules of Procedure of the National Commission for Scheduled Castes as notified on 1st September 2004 at given (Annexure X) of the Handbook.

6. APPROACH AND METHODOLOGY ADOPTED BY THE COMMISSION

6.1. Keeping in view its Constitutional obligations and the issues that are now critical, after almost half a century of Independence, for the overall development and mainstreaming of the Scheduled Castes, the present Commission, constituted in February 2004 has adopted a more vigorous approach in its functioning. The meetings of the Commission are held regularly and the implementation of decisions taken is monitored keenly.

6.2 In order to monitor and evaluate the impact of development schemes, the Commission has decided to interact with the State/UT Governments more actively by holding State level review meetings with the Chief Secretaries and other senior officers and conducting field level visits. The Commission feels that as a result of these visits and meetings, the State/UT Governments will become more conscious of the genuine problems of the Scheduled Castes and would take the necessary initiative in working out remedial measures and adopting appropriate strategies.

6.3 The Commission, through its Headquarters and State Offices has also conducted field level inquiries and studies. This process has been given a renewed vigour with a view to ensure prompt relief, specially in matters, relating to crimes and atrocities on Scheduled Castes and the grant of development benefits.

6.4 The procedure for investigating into complaints, especially with reference to violation of service safeguards, has also been streamlined to ensure prompt and speedy disposal of cases and relief in genuine cases. By calling officers and concerned Liaison Officers to the Commission with all relevant records, many long pending cases are being decided in one or two sittings. The Commission has also used its powers of Civil Court to summon documents and enforcing attendance in conducting the inquiries.

6.5 The Commission is of the view that it is only through proper planning and effective implementation of appropriate schemes for development that the Scheduled Castes can hope to catch up with the rest of the population and realize their full potential. The Commission has, thus, made a beginning by actively associating itself and participating in the planning process at the National and State levels. Regular communication is being maintained with the Planning Commission, Ministry of Social Justice & Empowerment and the State/UT Governments. The Annual Plans of the Central Ministries, States and UT Governments are being analysed in the Commission to this end with the support of its State Offices.

7. CONSULTATION WITH COMMISSION

Under the amended Article 338 (9), it has been provided that the Union and State Governments shall consult the Commission on all major policy matters affecting the Scheduled Castes. The Commission has impressed upon all concerned that this provision should be strictly enforced, as a result of which many Bills and other Policy matters affecting Scheduled Castes is now being received in the Commission for its views. The Commission would like to reiterate the obligatory nature of this provision and solicit the support of all concerned to bring to its notice new policies and change in existing policies, which have a bearing on the interests of SCs.

8. COMMISSION'S REPORT

8.1 *Clause 5(d)* of Article 338 provides "to present to the President, annually and at such other times as the Commission may deem fit, reports upon the working of those safeguards" and Clause 5(e) provides "to make in such reports, recommendations as to the measures that should be taken by the Union or any State for the effective implementation of those safeguards and other measures for the protection, welfare and socio-economic development of the Scheduled Castes."

8.2 As per provision of these Clauses it is the duty of the Commission to present annually a report upon the working of Constitutional safeguards and measures taken by the Union and the States for the protection and welfare of the Scheduled Castes. In this series the erstwhile National Commission for Scheduled Castes and Scheduled Tribes has presented seven Annual Reports and four Special Reports during the period from 12th March 1992 to 19th February 2004 containing a number of recommendations.

8.3 *Clause 6 of Article 338 provides*, "The President shall cause all such reports to be laid before each House of Parliament along with a Memorandum explaining the action taken or proposed to be taken on the recommendations relating to the Union and the reasons for the non-acceptance, if any, of such recommendations.

8.4 *Clause 7 of Article 338 provides*, "Where any such report or any part thereof relates to any matter with which any State Government is concerned, a copy of such report shall be forwarded to the Governor of the State who shall cause it to be laid before the Legislature of the State along with a Memorandum explaining the action taken or proposed to be taken on the recommendations relating to the State and the reasons for non-acceptance, if any, of any of such recommendations.

9. ORGANISATIONAL SET UP OF THE SECRETARIAT OF THE COMMISSION

The National Commission for Scheduled Castes functions from the Headquarters located at New Delhi and from 12 State Offices of the

Commission located in various States/UTs. The location and jurisdiction of these Offices and designation of office heads is given at Annexure XI of the handbook.

9.1 *There are Four Wings at Hqrs*

1. Administration & Coordination Wing
2. Service Safeguards Wing
3. Atrocities and Protection of Civil Rights Wing
4. Economic & Social Development Wing

9.2 *Administration and Co-ordination Wing*

This Wing looks after personnel management of officers and staff of the Secretariat of the Commission and provide administrative support in the functioning of the Commission. The Co-ordination Wing co-ordinates the various activities being performed in the Commission, including making arrangements for holding internal meetings of the Commission as well as with State/UT Administrations for reviewing the implementation of constitutional safeguards.

9.3 *Service Safeguards Wing*

This Wing is dealing with the implementation of service safeguards provided to Scheduled Castes in the Central/State Government services as well as Central and State Government Public Sector Undertakings. All representations/complaints relating to Scheduled Castes persons about their service matters are dealt within this Wing. In addition, policy matters relating to enactment/Government orders and instructions pertaining to representation of Scheduled Castes in service, evaluation studies/surveys relating to implementation of the various Constitutional safeguards in respect of service matters are dealt in this Wing. Cases relating to false caste certificate and inclusion or exclusion of caste(s) in Scheduled Castes list are also dealt in this Wing.

9.4 *Atrocities and Protection of Civil Rights Wing*

This Wing is dealing with matters pertaining to atrocities caused on Scheduled Castes and cases relating to protection of Civil Rights Act, the Bonded Labour System (Abolition) Act, the Minimum Wages Act, etc. either on receipt of complaint from individuals or from newspapers report. Evaluation studies/surveys on these subjects are also conducted by this Wing.

9.5 *Economic and Social Development Wing*

This Wing is dealing with matters relating to development of Scheduled Castes particularly implementation and monitoring of plan schemes of the Central/State Governments. Some of the specific items of work handled by this Wing are:

(i) Special Component Plan for Scheduled Castes
(ii) National Scheduled Castes Finance and Development Corporation.
(iii) Representations/complaints made by Scheduled Castes persons regarding their grievances on matters other than atrocities, untouchability practices and service matters;
(iv) Social Research Institute and other research bodies;
(v) Land Reforms Acts and their implementation;
(vi) Education Schemes for Scheduled Castes, etc.

10. FUNCTIONS OF STATE OFFICES OF THE COMMISSION

10.1 The State Offices of the Commission work as 'eyes and ears' of the Commission. They keep a watch on the formulation of policy and issue of guidelines relating to the welfare of Scheduled Castes in the respective States/UTs under their jurisdiction and keep the Commission Headquarters informed about the developments periodically. Policy decisions taken by any State Government/UT Administration affecting the interest of the Scheduled Castes are brought to the notice of the concerned authorities for necessary modifications. The State officers are requested to liaise with the State/UT Administration for taking up evaluation and other studies to assess the working of various development programmes implemented for the welfare of the Scheduled Castes and their impact on ameliorating the socio-economic conditions of the target groups. The findings of the studies are brought to the notice of the concerned State Government for taking remedial measures. The main observations are highlighted in the Commission's Report.

10.2 The State Offices of the Commission are required to interact with the State Administrations and guide them with a view to see that the interests of the Scheduled Castes is protected and promoted while in formulating plans and policies. The State Offices also monitor the utilization of funds earmarked for plans pertaining to Scheduled Castes including keeping a watch on diversion of funds from Special Component Plan.

10.3 Each of the State Offices sends Quarterly Report to the Commission Hqrs. on the activities undertaken by them highlighting major issues relating to welfare of Scheduled Castes in each States/UT under their jurisdiction. These reports contain useful information about the developments in a State and enable the Commission to have an overall view in respect of various States as well as national situation for taking appropriate action.

NATIONAL COMMISSION FOR MINORITIES[2]

Act XIX of 1992, passed on 17.5.1992, enforced w.e.f 17.5.1993; amended by National Commission for Minorities (Amendment) Act 1995 [Act XLI of 1995 passed on 8.9.1995] for creating the post of a Vice-Chairman out of the originally six Members.

An Act to constitute a National Commission for Minorities and to provide for matters connected therewith or incidental thereto.

Be it enacted by Parliament in the Forty-third year of the Republic of India as follows:

CHAPTER I: PRELIMINARY

1. SHORT TITLE, EXTENT AND COMMENCEMENT

(i) This Act may be called the National Commission for Minorities Act, 1992.

(ii) It extends to the whole of India except the State of Jammu and Kashmir.

(iii) It shall come into force on such date as the Central Government may, by notification in Official Gazette, appoint.

2. DEFINITIONS

In this Act, unless the context otherwise requires—

(i) "Commission" means the National Commission for Minorities constituted under section 3.

(ii) "Member" means a Member of the Commission [and includes the Vice Chairperson].

(iii) "Minority", for the purposes of this Act, means a community notified as such by the Central Government.

(iv) "Prescribed" means prescribed by Rules made under this Act.

[2]www.ncm.nic.in

CHAPTER II: THE NATIONAL COMMISSION FOR MINORITIES

3. CONSTITUTION OF THE NATIONAL COMMISSION FOR MINORITIES

(i) The Central Government shall constitute a body to be known as the National Commission for Minorities to exercise the powers conferred on, and to perform the functions assigned to it under this Act.

(ii) The Commission shall consist of a Chairperson, [a Vice Chairperson and five] Members to be nominated by the Central Government from amongst persons of eminence, ability and integrity; Provided that five Members including the Chairperson shall be from amongst the Minority communities.

4. TERM OF OFFICE & CONDITIONS OF SERVICE OF CHAIRPERSON & MEMBERS

(i) The Chairperson and every Member shall hold office for a term of three years from the date he assumes office.

(ii) The Chairperson or a Member may, by writing under his hand addressed to the Central Government, resign from the office of Chairperson or, as the case may be, of the Member at any time.

(iii) The Central Government shall remove a person from the office of Chairperson or a Member referred to in sub-section (2) if that person

  (a) becomes an undischarged insolvent.

  (b) is convicted and sentenced to imprisonment for an offence which in the opinion of the Central Government involves moral turpitude.

  (c) becomes of unsound mind and stands so declared by a competent court.

  (d) refuses to act or becomes incapable of acting.

  (e) is, without obtaining leave of absence from the Commission, absent from three consecutive meetings of the Commission.

  (f) has, in the opinion of the Central Government, so abused the position of Chairperson, or Member, as to render that person's continuance in office detrimental to the interests of Minorities or the public interest:

  Provided that no person shall be removed under this clause until that person has been given a reasonable opportunity of being heard in the matter.

(iv) A vacancy caused under sub-section (2) or otherwise shall be filled by fresh nomination.

(v) The salaries and allowances payable to, and the other terms and conditions of service of, the Chairperson and Members shall be such as may be prescribed.

5. OFFICERS AND OTHER EMPLOYEES OF THE COMMISSION

(i) The Central Government shall provide the Commission with a Secretary and such other officers and employees as may be necessary for the efficient performance of the functions of the Commission under this Act.
(ii) The salaries and allowances payable to, and the other terms and conditions of service of, the officers and other employees appointed for the purpose of the Commission shall be such as may be prescribed.

6. SALARIES AND ALLOWANCES TO BE PAID OUT OF GRANTS

The salaries and allowances payable to the Chairperson and Members and the administrative expenses, including salaries, allowances and pensions payable to the officers and other employees referred to in section 5, shall be paid out of the grants referred to in sub-section (1) of section 10.

7. VACANCIES, ETC., NOT TO INVALIDATE PROCEEDINGS OF THE COMMISSION

No act or proceeding of the Commission shall be questioned or shall be invalid merely on the ground of the existence of any vacancy or defect in the constitution of the Commission.

8. PROCEDURE TO BE REGULATED BY THE COMMISSION

(i) The Commission shall meet as and when necessary at such time and places as the Chairperson may think fit.
(ii) The Commission shall regulate its own procedure.
(iii) All orders and decisions of the Commission shall be authenticated by the Secretary or any other officer of the Commission duly authorized by the Secretary on his behalf.

CHAPTER III: FUNCTIONS OF THE COMMISSION

9. FUNCTIONS OF THE COMMISSION

(i) The Commission shall perform all or any of the following functions, namely:

(a) evaluate the progress of the development of Minorities under the Union and States.

(b) monitor the working of the safeguards provided in the Constitution and in laws enacted by Parliament and the State Legislatures.

(c) make recommendations for the effective implementation of safeguards for the protection of the interests of Minorities by the Central Government or the State Governments.

(d) look into specific complaints regarding deprivation of rights and safeguards of the Minorities and take up such matters with the appropriate authorities.

(e) cause studies to be undertaken into problems arising out of any discrimination against Minorities and recommend measures for their removal.

(f) conduct studies, research and analysis on the issues relating to socio-economic and educational development of Minorities.

(g) suggest appropriate measures in respect of any Minority to be undertaken by the Central Government or the State Governments.

(h) make periodical or special reports to the Central Government on any matter pertaining to Minorities and in particular the difficulties confronted by them.

(i) any other matter which may be referred to it by the Central Government.

(ii) The Central Government shall cause the recommendations referred to in clause (c) of sub-section (1) to be laid before each House of Parliament along with a memorandum explaining the action taken or proposed to be taken on the recommendations relating to the Union and the reasons for the non-acceptance, if any, of any of such recommendations.

(iii) Where any recommendation referred to in clause (c) of sub-section (1) or any part thereof is such with which any State Government is concerned, the Commission shall forward a copy of such recommendation or part to such State Government who shall cause it to be laid before the Legislature of the State along with a memorandum explaining the action taken or proposed to be taken on the recommendations relating to the State and the reasons for the non-acceptance, if any, of any of such recommendation or part.

(iv) The Commission shall, while performing any of the functions mentioned in sub-clauses (a), (b) and (d) of sub-section (1), have all the powers of a civil court trying a suit and, in particular, in respect of the following matters, namely:

(a) summoning and enforcing the attendance of any person from any part of India and examining him on oath.
(b) requiring the discovery and production of any document.
(c) receiving evidence of affidavits.
(d) requisitioning any public record or copy thereof from any court or office.
(e) issuing commissions for the examination of witnesses and documents; and
(f) any other matter which may be prescribed.

Chapter IV: Finance, Accounts and Audit

10. Grants by the Central Government

(i) The Central Government shall, after due appropriation made by Parliament by law in this behalf, pay to the Commission by way of grants such sums of money as the Central Government may think fit for being utilized for the purposes of this Act.
(ii) The Commission may spend such sums as it thinks fit for performing the functions under this Act, and such sums shall be treated as expenditure payable out of the grants referred to in sub-section (1).

11. Accounts and Audit

(i) The Commission shall maintain proper accounts and other relevant records and prepare an annual statement of accounts in such form as may be prescribed by the Central Government in consultation with the Comptroller and Auditor-General of India.
(ii) The accounts of the Commission shall be audited by the Comptroller and Auditor-General at such intervals as may be specified by him and any expenditure incurred in connection with such audit shall be payable by the Commission to the Comptroller and Auditor-General.
(iii) The Comptroller and Auditor-General and any person appointed by him in connection with the audit of the accounts of the Commission under this Act shall have the same rights and privileges and the authority in connection with such audit as the Comptroller and Auditor-General generally has in connection with the audit of government accounts and, in particular, shall have the

right to demand the production of books, accounts, connected vouchers and other documents and papers and to inspect any of the offices of the Commission.

12. ANNUAL REPORT

The Commission shall prepare, in such form and at such time, for each financial year, as may be prescribed, its annual report, giving a full account of its activities during the previous financial year and forward a copy thereof to the Central Government.

13. ANNUAL REPORT AND AUDIT REPORT TO BE LAID BEFORE PARLIAMENT

The Central Government shall cause the Annual Report together with a memorandum of action taken on the recommendations contained therein, in so far as they relate to the Central Government, and the reasons for the non-acceptance, if any, of any of such recommendations and the audit report to be laid, as soon as may be after the reports are received, before each House of Parliament.

CHAPTER V : MISCELLANEOUS

14. CHAIRPERSON, MEMBERS & STAFF OF COMMISSION TO BE PUBLIC SERVANTS

The Chairperson, Members and employees of the Commission shall be deemed to be public servants within the meaning of section 21 of the Indian Penal Code.

15. POWER TO MAKE RULES

(i) The Central Government may, by notification in the Official Gazette, make rules for carrying out the provisions of this Act.

(ii) In particular, and without prejudice to the generality of the foregoing powers, such rules may provide for all or any of the following matters, namely:

  (a) salaries and allowances payable to, and the other terms and conditions of service of, the Chairperson and Members under sub-section (5) of section 4 and of officers and other employees under sub-section (2) of section 5;

(b) any other matter under clause (f) of sub-section (4) of section 9.

(c) the form in which the annual statement of accounts shall be maintained under sub-section (1) of section 11.

(d) the form in, and the time at, which the Annual Report shall be prepared under section 12.

(e) any other matter which is required to be, or may be, prescribed.

(iii) Every rule made under this Act shall be laid, as soon as may be after it is made, before each House of Parliament, while it is in session for a total period of thirty days which may be comprised in one session or in two or more successive sessions and if, before the expiry of the session immediately following the session or the successive sessions aforesaid, both Houses agree in making any modification in the rule, or both Houses agree that the rule should not be made, the rule shall thereafter have effect only in such modified form or be of no effect, as the case may be-so, however, that any such modification or annulment shall be without prejudice to the validity of anything previously done under that rule.

16. POWER TO REMOVE DIFFICULTIES

(i) If any difficulty arises in giving effect to the provisions of this Act, the Central Government may, by order published in the Official Gazette, make such provisions, not inconsistent with the provisions of this Act, as appear to it to be necessary or expedient for removing the difficulty:
Provided that no such order shall be made after the expiry of a period of two years from the date of commencement of this Act.

(ii) Every order made under this section shall, as soon as may be after it is made, be laid before each House of Parliament.

THE PROTECTION OF HUMAN RIGHTS ACT, 1993[3]

No. 10 of 1994 (8th January, 1994)

An Act to provide for the constitution of a National Human Rights Commission. State Human Rights Commission in States and Human Rights Courts for better protection of Human Rights and for matters connected therewith or incidental thereto.

[3]www.nhrc.nic.in

Be it enacted by the parliament in the Forty-fourth year of the Republic of India as follows:

CHAPTER I: PRELIMINARY

1. SHORT TITLE, EXTENT AND COMMENCEMENT

(1) This Act may be called the Protection of Human Rights Act, 1993.
(2) It extends to the whole of India.
Provided that it shall apply to the State of Jammu and Kashmir only in so far as it pertains to the matters relatable to any of the entries enumerated in List I or List III in the Seventh Schedule to the Constitution as applicable to that State.
(3) It shall be deemed to have come into force on the 28th day of September, 1993.

2. DEFINITIONS

(1) In this Act, unless the context otherwise requires—
   (a) "armed forces" means the naval, military and air forces and includes any other armed forces of the Union;
   (b) "Chairperson" means the Chairperson of the Commission or of the State Commission, as the case may be;
   (c) "Commission" means the National Human Rights Commission under section 3;
   (d) "human rights" means the rights relating to life, liberty, equality and dignity of the individual guaranteed by the Constitution or embodied in the International Covenants and enforceable by courts in India.
   (e) "Human Rights Court" means the Human Rights Court specified under section 30;
   (f) "International Covenants" means the International Covenant on Civil and Political Rights and the International Covenant on Economic, Social and Cultural Rights adopted by the General Assembly of the United Nations on the 16th December, 1966;
   (g) "Member" means a Member of the Commission or of the State Commission, as the case may be, and includes the Chairperson;
   (h) "National Commission for Minorities" means the National Commission for Minorities constituted under section 3 of the National Commission for Minorities Act, 1992;

(i) "National Commission for the Scheduled Castes and Scheduled Tribes" means the National Commission for the Scheduled Castes and Scheduled Tribes referred to in article 338 of the Constitution;

(j) "National Commission for Women" means the National Commission for Women constituted under section 3 of the National Commission for Women Act, 1990;

(k) "Notification" means a notification published in the official Gazette;

(l) "Prescribed" means prescribed by rules made under this Act;

(m) "Public servant" shall have the meaning assigned to it in section 21 of the Indian Penal Code;

(n) "State Commission" means a State Human Rights Commission constituted under section 21.

(2) Any reference in this Act to a law, which is not in force in the State of Jammu and Kaṣhmir, shall, in relation to that State, be construed as a reference to a corresponding law, if any, in force in that State.

CHAPTER II: THE NATIONAL HUMAN RIGHTS COMMISSION

3. CONSTITUTION OF A NATIONAL HUMAN RIGHTS COMMISSION

(1) The Central Government shall constitute a body to be known as the National Human Rights Commission to exercise the powers conferred upon, and to perform the functions assigned to it, under this Act.

(2) The Commission shall consist of:

(a) a Chairperson who has been a Chief Justice of the Supreme Court;

(b) one Member who is or has been, a Judge of the Supreme Court;

(c) one Member who is, or has been, the Chief Justice of a High Court;

(d) two Members to be appointed from amongst persons having knowledge of, or practical experience in, matters relating to human rights.

(3) The Chairpersons of the National Commission for Minorities, the National Commission for the Scheduled Castes and Scheduled Tribes and the National Commission for Women shall be deemed to be Members of the Commission for the discharge of functions specified in clauses (b) to (j) of section 12.

(4) There shall be a Secretary-General who shall be the Chief Executive Officer of the Commission and shall exercise such powers and discharge such functions of the Commission as it may delegate to him.

(5) The headquarters of the Commission shall be at Delhi and the Commission may, with the previous approval of the Central Government, establish offices at other places in India.

4. APPOINTMENT OF CHAIRPERSON AND OTHER MEMBERS

(1) The Chairperson and other Members shall be appointed by the President by warrant under his hand and seal.
Provided that every appointment under this sub-section shall be made after obtaining the recommendations of a Committee consisting of

(a)	The Prime Minister	-	Chairperson
(b)	Speaker of the House of the People	-	Member
(c)	Minister in-charge of the Ministry of Home Affairs in the Government of India	-	Member
(d)	Leader of the Opposition in the House of the People	-	Member
(e)	Leader of the Opposition in the Council of States	-	Member
(f)	Deputy Chairman of the Council of States	-	Member

Provided further that no sitting Judge of the Supreme Court or sitting Chief Justice of a High Court shall be appointed except after consultation with the Chief Justice of India.

(2) No appointment of a Chairperson or a Member shall be invalid merely by reason of any vacancy in the Committee.

5. REMOVAL OF A MEMBER OF THE COMMISSION

(1) Subject to the provisions of sub-section (2), the Chairperson or any other Member of the Commission shall only be removed from his office by order of the President on the ground of proved misbehaviour or incapacity after the Supreme Court, on reference being made to it by the President, has, on inquiry held in accordance with the procedure prescribed in that behalf by the Supreme Court, reported that the Chairperson or such other Member, as the case may be, ought on any such ground to be removed.

(2) Notwithstanding anything in sub-section (1), the President may by order remove from office the Chairperson or any other Member if the Chairperson or such other Member, as the case may be
  (a) is adjudged an insolvent; or
  (b) engages during his term of office in any paid employment out side the duties of his office: or
  (c) is unfit to continue in office by reason of infirmity of mind or body; or
  (d) is of unsound mind and stands so declared by a competent court; or
  (e) is convicted and sentenced to imprisonment for an offence which in the opinion of the President involves moral turpitude.

6. TERM OF OFFICE OF MEMBERS

(1) A person appointed as Chairperson shall hold office for a term of five years from the date on which he enters upon his office or until he attains the age of seventy years, whichever is earlier.
(2) A person appointed as a Member shall hold office for a term of five years from the date on which he enters upon his office and shall be eligible for re-appointment for another term of five years:
Provided that no Member shall hold office after he has attained the age of seventy years.
(3) On ceasing to hold office, a Chairperson or a Member shall be ineligible for further employment under the Government of India or under the Government of any State.

7. MEMBER TO ACT AS CHAIRPERSON OR TO DISCHARGE HIS FUNCTIONS IN CERTAIN CIRCUMSTANCES

(1) In the event of the occurrence of any vacancy in the office of the Chairperson by reason of his death, resignation or otherwise, the President may, by notification, authorise one of the Members to act as the Chairperson until the appointment of a new Chairperson to fill such vacancy.
(2) When the Chairperson is unable to discharge his functions owing to absence on leave or otherwise, such one of the Members as the President may, by notification, authorise in this behalf, shall discharge the functions of the Chairperson until the date on which the Chairperson resumes his duties.

8. TERMS AND CONDITIONS OF SERVICE OF MEMBERS

The salaries and allowances payable to, and other terms and conditions of service of, the Members shall be such as may be prescribed:

Provided that neither the salary and allowances nor the other terms and conditions of service of a Member shall be varied to his disadvantage after his appointment.

9. VACANCIES, ETC., NOT TO INVALIDATE THE PROCEEDINGS OF THE COMMISSION

No act or proceedings of the Commission shall be questioned or shall be invalidated merely on the ground of existence of any vacancy or defect in the constitution of the Commission.

10. PROCEDURE TO BE REGULATED BY THE COMMISSION

(1) The Commission shall meet at such time and place as the Chairperson may think fit.

(2) The Commission shall regulate its own procedure.

(3) All orders and decisions of the Commission shall be audited by the Secretary-General or any other officer of the Commission duly authorised by the Chairperson in this behalf.

11. OFFICERS AND OTHER STAFF OF THE COMMISSION

(1) The Central Government shall make available to the Commission:
   (a) an officer of the rank of the Secretary to the Government of India who shall be the Secretary-General of the Commission; and
   (b) such police and investigative staff under an officer not below the rank of a Director General of Police and such other officers and staff as may be necessary for the efficient performance of the functions of the Commission.

(2) Subject to such rules as may be made by the Central Government in this behalf, the Commission may appoint such other administrative, technical and scientific staff as it may consider necessary.

(3) The salaries, allowances and conditions of service of the officers and other staff appointed under sub-section (2) shall be such as may be prescribed.

CHAPTER III: FUNCTIONS AND POWERS OF THE COMMISSION

12. FUNCTIONS OF THE COMMISSION

The Commission shall perform all or any of the following functions, namely:

(a) inquire, *suo motu* or on a petition presented to it by a victim or any person on his behalf, into complaint of
   (i) violation of human rights or abetment thereof or
   (ii) negligence in the prevention of such violation, by a public servant;

(b) intervene in any proceeding involving any allegation of violation of human rights pending before a court with the approval of such court;

(c) visit, under intimation to the State Government, any jail or any other institution under the control of the State Government, where persons are detained or lodged for purposes of treatment, reformation or protection to study the living conditions of the inmates and make recommendations thereon;

(d) review the safeguards provided by or under the Constitution or any law for the time being in force for the protection of human rights and recommend measures for their effective implementation;

(e) review the factors, including acts of terrorism that inhibit the enjoyment of human rights and recommend appropriate remedial measures;

(f) study treaties and other international instruments on human rights and make recommendations for their effective implementation;

(g) undertake and promote research in the field of human rights;

(h) spread human rights literacy among various sections of society and promote awareness of the safeguards available for the protection of these rights through publications, the media, seminars and other available means;

(i) encourage the efforts of non-governmental organisations and institutions working in the field of human rights;

(j) such other functions as it may consider necessary for the protection of human rights.

13. POWERS RELATING TO INQUIRIES

(1) The Commission shall, while inquiring into complaints under this Act, have all the powers of a civil court trying a suit under the Code

of Civil Procedure, 1908, and in particular in respect of the following matters, namely :

(a) summoning and enforcing the attendance of witnesses and examine them on oath;
(b) discovery and production of any document;
(c) receiving evidence on affidavits;
(d) requisitioning any public record or copy thereof from any court or office;
(e) issuing commissions for the examination of witnesses or documents;
(f) any other matter which may be prescribed.

(2) The Commission shall have power to require any person, subject to any privilege which may be claimed by that person under any law for the time being in force, to furnish information on such points or matters as, in the opinion of the Commission, may be useful for, or relevant to, the subject matter of the inquiry and any person so required shall be deemed to be legally bound to furnish such information within the meaning of section 176 and section 177 of the Indian Penal Code.

(3) The Commission or any other officer, not below the rank of a Gazetted Officer, specially authorised in this behalf by the Commission may enter any building or place where the Commission has reason to believe that any document relating to the subject matter of the inquiry may be found, and may seize any such document or take extracts or copies therefrom subject to the provisions of section 100 of the Code of Criminal Procedure, 1973, in so far as it may be applicable.

(4) The Commission shall be deemed to be a civil court and when any offence as is described in section 175, section 178, section 179, section 180 or section 228 of the Indian Penal Code is committed in the view or presence of the Commission, the Commission may, after recording the facts constituting the offence and the statement of the accused as provided for in the Code of Criminal Procedure, 1973, forward the case to a Magistrate having jurisdiction to try the same and the Magistrate to whom any such case is forwarded shall proceed to hear the complaint against the accused as if the case has been forwarded to him under section 346 of the Code of Criminal Procedure, 1973.

(5) Every proceeding before the Commission shall be deemed to be a judicial proceeding within the meaning of sections 193 and 228, and for the purposes of section 196, of the Indian Penal Code, and the Commission shall be deemed to be a civil court for all the

purposes of section 195 and Chapter XXVI of the Code of Criminal Procedure, 1973.

14. INVESTIGATION

(1) The Commission may, for the purpose of conducting any investigation pertaining to the inquiry, utilise the services of any officer or investigation agency of the Central Government or any State Government with the concurrence of the Central Government or the State Government, as the case may be.

(2) For the purpose of investigating into any matter pertaining to the inquiry, any officer or agency whose services are utilised under sub-section (1) may, subject to the direction and control of the Commission.

  (a) summon and enforce the attendance of any person and examine him;

  (b) require the discovery and production of any document; and

  (c) requisition any public record or copy thereof from any office.

(3) The provisions of section 15 shall apply in relation to any statement made by a person before any officer or agency whose services are utilised under sub-section (1) as they apply in relation to any statement made by a person in the course of giving evidence before the Commission.

(4) The officer or agency whose services are utilised under sub-section (1) shall investigate into any matter pertaining to the inquiry and submit a report thereon to the Commission within such period as may be specified by the Commission in this behalf.

(5) The Commission shall satisfy itself about the correctness of the facts stated and the conclusion, if any, arrived at in the report subbed to it under sub-section (4) and for this purpose the Commission may make such inquiry (including the examination of the person or persons who conducted or assisted in the investigation) as it thinks fit.

15. STATEMENT MADE BY PERSONS TO THE COMMISSION

No statement made by a person in the course of giving evidence before the Commission shall subject him to, or be used against him in, any civil or criminal proceeding except a prosecution for giving false evidence by such statement:

Provided that the statement

(a) is made in reply to the question which he is required by the Commission to answer; or
(b) is relevant to the subject matter of the inquiry.

16. PERSONS LIKELY TO BE PREJUDICIALLY AFFECTED TO BE HEARD

If, at any stage of the inquiry, the Commission

(a) considers it necessary to inquire into the conduct of any person; or
(b) is of the opinion that the reputation of any person is likely to be prejudicially affected by the inquiry;

it shall give to that person a reasonable opportunity of being heard in the inquiry and to produce evidence in his defence:

Provided that nothing in this section shall apply where the credit of a witness is being impeached.

CHAPTER IV: PROCEDURE

17. INQUIRY INTO COMPLAINTS

The Commission while inquiring into the complaints of violations of human rights may—

(i) call for information or report from the Central Government or any State Government or any other authority or organisation subordinate thereto within such time as may be specified by it; Provided that—
  (a) if the information or report is not received within the time stipulated by the Commission, it may proceed to inquire into the complaint on its own;
  (b) if, on receipt of information or report, the Commission is satisfied either that no further inquiry is required or that the required action has been initiated or taken by the concerned Government or authority, it may not proceed with the complaint and inform the complainant accordingly;
(ii) without prejudice to anything contained in clause (i), if it considers necessary, having regard to the nature of the complaint, initiate an inquiry.

18. STEPS AFTER INQUIRY

The Commission may take any of the following steps upon the completion of an inquiry held under this Act namely:

(1) where the inquiry discloses, the commission of violation of human rights or negligence in the prevention of violation of human rights by a public servant, it may recommend to the concerned Government or authority the initiation of proceedings for prosecution or such other action as the Commission may deem fit against the concerned person or persons;

(2) approach the Supreme Court or the High Court concerned for such directions, orders or writs as that Court may deem necessary;

(3) recommend to the concerned Government or authority for the grant of such immediate interim relief to the victim or the members of his family as the Commission may consider necessary;

(4) subject to the provisions of clause (5), provide a copy of the inquiry report to the petitioner or his representative;

(5) the Commission shall send a copy of its inquiry report together with its recommendations to the concerned Government or authority and the concerned Government or authority shall, within a period of one month, or such further time as the Commission may allow, forward its comments on the report, including the action taken or proposed to be taken thereon, to the Commission;

(6) the Commission shall publish its inquiry report together with the comments of the concerned Government or authority, if any, and the action taken or proposed to be taken by the concerned Government or authority on the recommendations of the Commission.

19. PROCEDURE WITH RESPECT TO ARMED FORCES

(1) Notwithstanding anything contained in this Act, while dealing with complaints of violation of human rights by members of the armed forces, the Commission shall adopt the following procedure, namely:

   (a) it may, either on its own motion or on receipt of a petition, seek a report from the Central Government;

   (b) after the receipt of the report, it may, either not proceed with the complaint or, as the case may be, make its recommendations to that Government.

(2) The Central Government shall inform the Commission of the action taken on the recommendations within three months or such further time as the Commission may allow.

(3) The Commission shall publish its report together with its re-

commendations made to the Central Government and the action taken by that Government on such recommendations.

(4) The Commission shall provide a copy of the report published under sub-section (3) to the petitioner or his representative.

20. ANNUAL AND SPECIAL REPORTS OF THE COMMISSION

(1) The Commission shall submit an annual report to the Central Government and to the State Government concerned and may at any time submit special reports on any matter which, in its opinion, is of such urgency or importance that it should not be deferred till submission of the annual report.

(2) The Central Government and the State Government, as the case may be, shall cause the annual and special reports of the Commission to be laid before each House of Parliament or the State Legislature respectively, as the case may be, along with a memorandum of action taken or proposed to be taken on the recommendations of the Commission and the reasons for non-acceptance of the recommendations, if any.

CHAPTER V: STATE HUMAN RIGHTS COMMISSIONS

21. CONSTITUTION OF STATE HUMAN RIGHTS COMMISSIONS

(1) A State Government may constitute a body to be known as the .... (name of the State) Human Rights Commission to exercise the powers conferred upon, and to perform the functions assigned to, a State Commission under this chapter.

(2) The State Commission shall consist of
- (a) a Chairperson who has been a Chief Justice of a High Court;
- (b) one Member who is, or has been, a Judge of a High Court;
- (c) one Member who is, or has been, a district judge in that State;
- (d) two Members to be appointed from amongst persons having knowledge of, or practical experience in, matters relating to human rights.

(3) There shall be a Secretary who shall be the Chief Executive Officer of the State Commission and shall exercise such powers and discharge such functions of the State Commission as it may delegate to him.

(4) The headquarters of the State Commission shall be at such place as the State Government may, by notification, specify.

(5) A State Commission may inquire into violation of human rights only in respect of matters relatable to any of the entries enumerated

in List II and List III in the Seventh Schedule to the Constitution:
Provided that if any such matter is already being inquired into by the Commission or any other Commission duly constituted under any law for the time being in force, the State Commission shall not inquire into the said matter:
Provided further that in relation to the Jammu and Kashmir Human Rights Commission, this sub-section shall have effect as if for the words and figures "List II and List III in the Seventh Schedule to the Constitution", the words and figures "List III in the Seventh Schedule to the Constitution as applicable to the State of Jammu and Kashmir and in respect of matters in relation to which the Legislature of that State has power to make laws" had been substituted.

22. APPOINTMENT OF CHAIRPERSON AND OTHER MEMBERS OF STATE COMMISSION

(1) The Chairperson and other Members shall be appointed by the Governor by warrant under his hand and seal:
Provided that every appointment under this sub-section shall be made after obtaining the recommendation of a Committee consisting of
(a) the Chief Minister—Chairperson
(b) Speaker of the Legislative Assembly—Member
(c) Minister in-charge of the Department of Home, in that State—Member
(d) Leader of the Opposition in the Legislative Assembly—Member:
Provided further that where there is a Legislative Council in a State, the Chairman of that Council and the Leader of the Opposition in that Council shall also be members of the Committee:
Provided also that no sitting Judge of a High Court or a sitting District Judge shall be appointed except after consultation with the Chief Justice of the High Court of the concerned State.
(2) No appointment of a Chairperson or a Member of the State Commission shall be invalid merely by reason of any vacancy in the Committee.

23. REMOVAL OF A MEMBER OF THE STATE COMMISSION

(1) Subject to the provisions of sub-section (2), the Chairperson or any other member of the State Commission shall only be removed from

his office by order of the President on the ground of proved misbehaviour or incapacity after the Supreme Court, on a reference being made to it by the President, has, on inquiry held in accordance with the procedure prescribed in that behalf by the Supreme Court, reported that the Chairperson or such other Member, as the case may be, ought on any such ground to be removed.

(2) Notwithstanding anything in sub-section (1), the President may by order remove from office the Chairperson or any other Member if the Chairperson or such other Member, as the case may be -
   (a) is adjudged an insolvent; OR
   (b) engages during his term of office in any paid employment outside the duties of his office; OR
   (c) is unfit to continue in office by reason of infirmity of mind or body; OR
   (d) is of unsound mind and stands so declared by a competent court; OR
   (e) is convicted and sentenced to imprisonment for an offence which in the opinion of the President involves moral turpitude.

24. TERM OF OFFICE OF MEMBERS OF THE STATE COMMISSION

(1) A person appointed as Chairperson shall hold office for a term of five years from the date on which he enters upon his office or until he attains the age of seventy years, whichever is earlier.

(2) A person appointed as a Member shall hold office for a term of five years from the date on which he enters upon his office and shall be eligible for re-appointment for another term of five years:
Provided that no Member shall hold office after he has attained the age of seventy years.

(3) On ceasing to hold office, a Chairperson or a Member shall be ineligible for further employment under the Government of a State or under the Government of India.

25. MEMBER TO ACT AS CHAIRPERSON OR TO DISCHARGE HIS FUNCTIONS IN CERTAIN CIRCUMSTANCES

(1) In the event of the occurrence of any vacancy in the office of the Chairperson by reason of his death, resignation or otherwise, the Governor may, by notification, authorise one of the Members to act as the Chairperson until the appointment of a new Chairperson to fill such vacancy.

(2) When the Chairperson is unable to discharge his functions owing

to absence on leave or otherwise, such one of the Members as the Governor may, by notification, authorise in this behalf, shall discharge the functions of the Chairperson until the date on which the Chairperson resumes his duties.

26. TERMS AND CONDITIONS OF SERVICE OF MEMBERS OF THE STATE COMMISSION

The salaries and allowances payable to, and other terms and conditions of service of, the Members shall be such as may be prescribed by the State Government:

Provided that neither the salary and allowances nor the other terms and conditions of service of a Member shall be varied to his disadvantage after his appointment.

27. OFFICERS AND OTHER STAFF OF THE STATE COMMISSION

(1) The State Government shall make available to the Com-mission
  (a) an officer not below the rank of a Secretary to the State Government who shall be the Secretary of the State Commission; and
  (b) such police and investigative staff under an officer not below the rank of an Inspector General of Police and such other officers and staff as may be necessary for the efficient performance of the functions of the State Commission.

(2) subject to such rules as may be made by the State Government in this behalf, the State Commission may appoint such other administrative, technical and scientific staff as it may consider necessary.

(3) The salaries, allowances and conditions of service of the officers and other staff appointed under sub-section (2) shall be such as may be prescribed by the State Government.

28. ANNUAL AND SPECIAL REPORTS OF STATE COMMISSION

(1) The State Commission shall submit an annual report to the State Government and may at any time submit special reports on any matter which, in its opinion, is of such urgency or importance that it should not be deferred till submission of the annual report.

(2) The State Government shall cause the annual and special reports of the State Commission to be laid before each House of State Legislature where it consists of two Houses, or where such Legislature consists of one House, before that House along with a memorandum of action taken or proposed to be taken on the

recommendations of the State Commission and the reasons for non-acceptance of the sections, if any.

29. APPLICATION OF CERTAIN PROVISIONS RELATING TO NATIONAL HUMAN RIGHTS COMMISSION TO STATE COMMISSIONS

The provisions of sections 9, 10, 12, 13, 14, 15, 16, 17 and 18 shall apply to a State Commission and shall have effect, subject to the following modifications, namely:

(a) references to "Commission" shall be construed as refer ences to "State Commission";

(b) in section 10, in sub-section (3), for the word "Secretary General", the word "Secretary" shall be substituted;

(c) in section 12, clause (f) shall be omitted;

(d) in section 17, in clause (i), the words "Central Government or any" shall be omitted;

CHAPTER VI: HUMAN RIGHTS COURTS

30. For the purpose of providing speedy trial of offences arising out of violation of human rights, the State Government may, with the concurrence of the Chief Justice of the High Court, by notification, specify for each district a Court of Session to be a Human Rights Court to try the said offences:

Provided that nothing in this section shall apply if

(a) a Court of Session is already specified as a special court; or

(b) a special court is already constituted, for such offences under any other law for the time being in force.

31. SPECIAL PUBLIC PROSECUTOR

For every Human Rights Court, the State Government shall, by notification, specify a Public Prosecutor or appoint an advocate who has been in practice as an advocate for not less than seven years, as a Special Public Prosecutor for the purpose of conducting cases in that Court.

CHAPTER VII: FINANCE, ACCOUNTS AND AUDIT

32. GRANTS BY THE CENTRAL GOVERNMENT

(1) The Central Government shall after due appropriation made by Parliament by law in this behalf, pay to the Commission by way of

grants such sums of money as the Central Government may think fit for being utilised for the purposes of this Act.

(2) The Commission may spend such sums as it thinks fit for performing the functions under this Act, and such sums shall be treated as expenditure payable out of the grants referred to in sub-section (1).

33. GRANTS BY THE STATE GOVERNMENT

(1) The State Government shall, after due appropriation made by Legislature by law in this behalf, pay to the State Commission by way of grants such sums of money as the State Government may think fit for being utilised for the purposes of this Act.

(2) The State Commission may spend such sums as it thinks fit for performing the functions under Chapter V, and such sums shall be treated as expenditure payable out of the grants referred to in sub-section (1).

34. ACCOUNTS AND AUDIT

(1) The Commission shall maintain proper accounts and other relevant records and prepare an annual statement of accounts in such form as may be prescribed by the Central Government in consultation with the Comptroller and Auditor-General of India.

(2) The Accounts of the Commission shall be audited by the Comptroller and Auditor General at such intervals as may be specified by him and any expenditure incurred in connection with such audit shall be payable by the Commission to the Comptroller and Auditor-General.

(3) The Comptroller and Auditor-General or any person appointed by him in connection with the audit of the accounts of the Commision under this Act shall have the same rights and privileges and the authority in connection with such audit as the Comptroller and Auditor-General generally has in connection with the audit of Government accounts and, in particular, shall have the right to demand the production of books, accounts, connected vouchers and other documents and papers and to inspect any of the offices of the Commission.

(4) The accounts of the Commission as certified by the Comptroller and Auditor-General or any other person appointed by him in this behalf, together with the audit report thereon shall be forwarded only to the Central Government by the Commission and the Central

Government shall cause the audit report to be laid as soon as may be after it is received before each House of Parliament.

35. ACCOUNTS AND AUDIT OF STATE COMMISSION

(1) The State Commission shall maintain proper accounts and other relevant records and prepare an annual statement of accounts in such form as may be prescribed by the State Government in consultation with the Comptroller and Auditor-General of India.
(2) The accounts of the State Commission shall be audited by the Comptroller and Auditor-General at such intervals as may be specified by him and any expenditure incurred in connection with such audit shall be payable by the State Commission to the Comptroller and Auditor-General.
(3) The Comptroller and Auditor-General or any person appointed by him in connection with the audit of the accounts of the State Commission under this Act shall have the same rights and privileges and the authority in connection with such audit as the Comptroller and Auditor-General generally has in connection with the audit of Government accounts and, in particular, shall have the right to demand the production of books, accounts, connected vouchers and other documents and papers and to inspect any of the offices of the State Commission.
(4) The accounts of the State Commission, as certified by the Comptroller and Auditor-General or any other person appointed by him in this behalf, together with the audit report thereon, shall be forwarded annually to the State Government by the State Commission and the State Government shall cause the audit report to be laid, as soon as may be after it is received, before the State Legislature.

CHAPTER VIII: MISCELLANEOUS

36. MATTERS NOT SUBJECT TO JURISDICTION OF THE COMMISSION

(1) The Commission shall not inquire into any matter which is pending before a State Commission or any other Commission duly constituted under any law for the time being in force.
(2) The Commission or the State Commission shall not inquire into any matter after the expiry of one year from the date on which the act constituting violation of human rights is alleged to have been committed.

37. CONSTITUTION OF SPECIAL INVESTIGATION TEAMS

Notwithstanding anything contained in any other law for the time being in force, where the Government considers it necessary so to do, it may constitute one or more special investigation teams, consisting of such police officers as it thinks necessary for purposes of investigation and prosecution of offences arising out of violations of human rights.

38. PROTECTION OF ACTION TAKEN IN GOOD FAITH

No suit or other legal proceeding shall lie against the Central Government, State Government, Commission, the State Commission or any Member thereof or any person acting under the direction either of the Central Government, State Government, Commission or the State Commission in respect of anything which is in good faith done or intended to be done in pursuance of this Act or of any rules or any order made thereunder or in respect of the publication by or under the authority of the Central Government, State Government, Commission or the State Commission of any report paper or proceedings.

39. MEMBERS AND OFFICERS TO BE PUBLIC SERVANTS

Every Member of the Commission, State Commission and every officer appointed or authorised by the Commission or the State Commission to exercise functions under this Act shall be deemed to be a public servant within the meaning of section 21 of the Indian Penal Code.

40. POWER OF CENTRAL GOVERNMENT TO MAKE RULES

(1) The Central Government may, by notification, make rules to carry out the provisions of this Act.

(2) In particular and without prejudice to the generality of the foregoing power, such rules may provide for all or any of the following matters namely:

- (a) the salaries and allowances and other terms and conditions of service of the Members under section 8;
- (b) the conditions subject to which other administrative, technical and scientific staff may be appointed by the Commission and the salaries and allowances of officers and other staff under sub-section (3) of section 11;
- (c) any other power of a civil court required to be prescribed under clause (f) of sub-section (1) of section 13;

(d) the form in which the annual statement of accounts is to be prepared by the Commission under sub-section (1) of section 34; and

(e) any other matter which has to be, or may be, prescribed.

(3) Every rule made under this Act shall be laid, as soon as may be after it is made, before each House of Parliament, while it is in session, for a total period of thirty days which may be comprised in one session or in two or more successive sessions, and if, before the expiry of the session immediately following the session or the successive sessions aforesaid, both Houses agree in making any modification in the rule or both Houses agree that the rule should not be made, the rule shall thereafter have effect only in such modified form or be of no effect, as the case may be; so however, that any such modification or annulment shall be without prejudice to the validity of anything previously done under that rule.

41. POWER OF STATE GOVERNMENT TO MAKE RULES

(1) The State Government may, by notification, make rules to carry out the provisions of this Act.

(2) In particular and without prejudice to the generality of the foregoing power, such rules may provide for all or any of the following matters, namely :

(a) the salaries and allowances and other terms and conditions of service of the members under section 26;

(b) the conditions subject to which other administrative, technical and scientific staff may be appointed by the State Commission and the salaries and allowances of officers and other staff under sub-section (3) of section 27;

(c) the form in which the annual statement of accounts is to be prepared under sub-section (1) of section 35.

(3) Every rule made by the State Government under this section shall be laid, as soon as may be after it is made, before each House of the State Legislature where it consists of two Houses, or where such Legislature consists of one House, before that House.

42. POWER TO REMOVE DIFFICULTIES

(1) If any difficulty arises in giving effect to the provisions of this Act, the Central Government, may by order published in the Official Gazette, make such provisions, not inconsistent with the provisions of this Act as appear to it to be necessary or expedient for removing the difficulty:

Provided that no such order shall be made after the expiry of the period of two years from the date of commencement of this Act.

(2) Every order made under this section shall, as soon as may be after it is made, be laid before each house of Parliament.

43. REPEAL AND SAVINGS

(1) The Protection of Human Rights Ordinance, 1993 is hereby repealed.

(2) Notwithstanding such repeal, anything done or any action taken under the said Ordinance, shall be deemed to have been done or taken under the corresponding provisions of this Act.

THE NATIONAL COMMISSION FOR WOMEN ACT, 1990 (NO. 20 OF 1990)[4]

An Act to constitute a National Commission for Women and to provide for matters connected therewith or incidental thereto.

Be it enacted by Parliament in the Forty-first Year of the Republic in India as follows

CHAPTER I: PRELIMINARY

1. SHORT TITLE, EXTENT AND COMMENCEMENT[5]

(1) This Act may be called the National Commission for Women Act, 1990.

(2) It extends to the whole of India except the State of Jammu and Kashmir.

(3) It shall come into force on such date[6] as the Central Government may, by notification in the Official Gazette, appoint.

2. DEFINITIONS

In this act, unless the context otherwise requires

(a) "Commission" means the National Commission for Women constituted under section 3;

[4]www.ncsc.nic.in

[5]The Act received the assent of the President on 30.8.1990.

[6]The Act came into force on 31.1.1992, vide Notification No. S.O. 99 (E), dated 31.1.1992.

(b) "Member" means a Member of the Commission and includes the Member-Secretary;
(c) "prescribed" means prescribed by rules made under this Act.

CHAPTER II: THE NATIONAL COMMISSION FOR WOMEN

3. CONSTITUTION OF THE NATIONAL COMMISSION FOR WOMEN

(1) The Central Government shall constitute[7] a body to be known as the National Commission for Women to exercise the powers conferred on, and to perform the functions assigned to, it under this Act.
(2) The Commission shall consist of—
  (a) a Chairperson, committed to the cause of women, to be nominated by the Central Government;
  (b) five Members to be nominated by the Central Government from amongst persons of ability, integrity and standing who have had experience in law or legislation, trade unionism, management of an industry or organisation committed to increasing the employment potential of women, women's voluntary organisations (including women activists), administration, economic development, health, education or social welfare:
  Provided that at least one Member each shall be from amongst persons belonging to the Scheduled Castes and Scheduled Tribes respectively;
  (c) a Member-Secretary to be nominated by the Central Government, who shall be—
    (i) an expert in the field of management, organisational structure or sociological movement, or
    (ii) an officer who is a member of a civil service of the Union or of an all-India service or holds a civil post under the Union with appropriate experience.

4. TERM OF OFFICE AND CONDITIONS OF SERVICE OF CHAIRPERSON AND MEMBERS

(1) The Chairperson and every Member shall hold office for such period, not exceeding three years as may be specified by the Central Government in this behalf.

[7]The National Commission for Women was constituted on 31.1.1992, vide Notification No. S.O. 100(E), dated 31.1.1992.

(2) The Chairperson or a Member (other than the Member-Secretary who is a member of a civil service of the Union or of an all-India service or holds a civil post under the Union) may, by writing and addressed to the Central Government, resign from the office of Chairperson or, as the case may be, of the Member at any time.

(3) The Central Government shall remove a person from the office of Chairperson or a Member referred to in subsection (2) if that person
   (a) becomes an undischarged insolvent:
   (b) gets convicted and sentenced to imprisonment for an offence which in the opinion of the Central Government involves moral turpitude.
   (c) Becomes of unsound mind and stands so declared by a competent court;
   (d) Refuses to act or becomes incapable of acting.
   (e) Is, without obtaining leave of absence from the Commission, absent from three consecutive meetings of the Commission; or
   (f) In the opinion of the Central Government has so abused the position of Chairperson or Member as to render that person's continuance in office detrimental to the public interest;

(4) A vacancy caused under sub-section (2) or otherwise shall be filled by fresh nomination.

(5) The salaries and allowances payable to and the other terms and conditions of service of, the Chairperson and Members shall be such as may be prescribed.[8]

5. OFFICERS AND OTHER EMPLOYEES OF THE COMMISSION

(1) The Central Government shall provide the Commission with such officers and employees as may be necessary for the efficient performance of the functions of the Commission under this Act.

(2) The salaries and allowances payable to and the other terms and conditions of service of, the officers and other employees appointed for the purpose of the Commission shall be such as may be prescribed.

6. SALARIES AND ALLOWANCES TO BE PAID OUT OF GRANTS

The salaries and allowances payable to the Chairperson and Members and the administrative expenses, including salaries, allowances and

[8]The National Commission for Women (Salaries and Allowances of Chairperson and Members) Rules, 1992 [G.S.R. 74 (E) dated 31.1.1992].

pensions payable to the officers and other employees referred to in section 5 shall be paid out of the grants referred to in sub-section (1) of section 11.

7. VACANCIES, ETC., NOT TO INVALIDATE PROCEEDINGS OF THE COMMISSION

No act or proceeding of the Commission shall be questioned or shall be invalid on the ground merely of the existence of any vancancy or defect in the constitution of the Commission.

8. COMMITTEES OF THE COMMISSION

(1) The Commission may appoint such committees as may be necessary for dealing with such special issues as may be taken up by the Commission from time to time.
(2) The Commission shall have the power to co-opt as members of any committee appointed under sub-section (1) such number of persons, who are not Members of the Commission, as it may think fit and the persons so co-opted shall have the right to attend the meetings of the committee and take part in its proceedings but shall not have the right to vote.
(3) The persons so co-opted shall be entitled to receive such allowances for attending the meetings of the committee as may be prescribed.[9]

9. PROCEDURE TO BE REGULATED BY THE COMMISSION

(1) The Commission or a committee thereof shall meet as and when necessary and shall meet at such time and place as the Chairperson may think fit.
(2) The Commission shall regulate its own procedure and the procedure of the Committees thereof.
(3) All orders and decisions of the Commission shall be authenticated by the Member-Secretary or any other officer of the Commission duly authorised by the Member-Secretary in this behalf.

CHAPTER III: FUNCTIONS OF THE COMMISSION

10. FUNCTIONS OF THE COMMISSION

(1) The Commission shall perform all or any of the following functions, namely:

[9]The National Commission for Women (Allowances Payable to Co-opted Members) Rules, 1992 [G.S.R. 118(E), dated 21.2.1992].

(a) investigate and examine all matters relating to the safeguards provided for women under the Constitution and other laws;

(b) present to the Central Government, annually and at such other times as the Commission may deem fit, reports upon the working of those safeguards;

(c) make in such reports recommendations for the effective implementation of those safeguards for improving the conditions of women by the Union or any State;

(d) review, from time to time, the existing provisions of the Constitution and other laws affecting women and recommend amendments thereto so as to suggest remedial legislative measures to meet any lacunae inadequacies or shortcomings in such legislations;

(e) take up the cases of violation of the provisions of the Constitution and of other laws relating to women with the appropriate authorities;

(f) look into complaints and take suo moto notice of matters relating to:

   (i) deprivation of women's rights;

   (ii) non-implementation of laws enacted to provide protection to women and also to achieve the objective of equality and development;

   (iii) non-compliance of policy decisions, guidelines or instructions aimed at mitigating hardships and ensuring welfare and providing relief to women.

   and take up the issues arising out of such matters with appropriate authorities;

(g) call for special studies or investigations into specific problems or situations arising out of discrimination and atrocities against women and identify the constraints so as to recommend strategies for their removal.

(h) undertake promotional and educational research so as to suggest ways of ensuring due representation of women in all spheres and identify factors responsible for impeding their advancement, such as, lack of access to housing and basic services, inadequate support services and technologies for reducing drudgery and occupational health hazards and for increasing their productivity;

(i) participate and advise on the planning process of socio-economic development of women;

(j) evaluate the progress of the development of women under the Union and any State;

(k) inspect or cause to be inspected a jail, remand home, women's institution or other place of custody where women are kept as prisoners or otherwise, and take up with the concerned authorities for remedial action, if found necessary;

(l) fund litigation involving issues affecting a large body of women;

(m) make periodical reports to the Government on any matter pertaining to women and in particular various difficulties under which women toil;

(n) any other matter which may be referred to it by Central Government.

(2) The Central Government shall cause all the reports referred to in clause (b) of sub-section (1) to be laid before each House of Parliament along with a memorandum explaining the action taken or proposed to be taken on the recommendations relating to the Union and the reasons for the non-acceptance, if any, of any of such recommendations.

(3) Where any such report or any part thereof relates to any matter with which any State Government is concerned, the Commission shall forward a copy of such report or part to such State Government who shall cause it to be laid before the Legislature of the State along with a memorandum explaining the action taken or proposed to be taken on the recommendations relating to the State and the reasons for the non-acceptance, if any, of any of such recommendations,

(4) The Commission shall, while investigating any matter referred to in clause (a) or sub-clause (i) of clause (f) of sub-section (1), have all the powers of a civil court trying a suit and, in particular in respect of the following matters, namely:

(a) summoning and enforcing the attendance of any person from any part of India and examining him on oath;

(b) requiring the discovery and production of any document;

(c) receiving evidence on affidavits;

(d) requisitioning any public record or copy thereof from any court or office;

(e) issuing commission for the examination of witnesses and documents; and

(f) any other matter which may be prescribed.

CHAPTER IV: FINANCE, ACCOUNTS AND AUDIT

11. GRANTS BY THE CENTRAL GOVERNMENT

(1) The Central Government shall, after due appropriation made by Parliament by law in this behalf, pay to the Commission by way of

grants such sums of money as the Central Government may think fit for being utilised for the purposes of this Act.

(2) The Commission may spend such sums as it thinks fit for performing the functions under this Act, and such sums shall be treated as expenditure payable out of the grants referred to in sub-section (1).

12. ACCOUNTS AND AUDIT

(1) The Commission shall maintain proper accounts and other relevant records and prepare an annual statement of accounts in such form as may be prescribed by the Central Government in consultation with the Comptroller and Auditor-General of India.

(2) The accounts of the Commission shall be audited by the Comptroller and Auditor-General at such intervals as may be specified by him and any expenditure incurred in connection with such audit shall be payable by the Commission to the Comptroller and Auditor-General.

(3) The Comptroller and Auditor-General and any person appointed by him in connection with the audit of the accounts of the Commission under this Act shall have the same rights and privileges and the authority in connection with such audit as the Comptroller and Auditor-General generally has in connection with the audit of Government accounts and, in particular, shall have the right to demand the production of books, accounts, connected vouchers and other doucments and papers and to inspect any of the offices of the Commission.

13. ANNUAL REPORT

The Commission shall prepare in such form and at such time, for each financial year, as may be prescribed, its annual report, giving a full account of its activities during the previous financial year and forward a copy thereof to the Central Government.

14. ANNUAL REPORT AND AUDIT REPORT TO BE LAID BEFORE PARLIAMENT

The Central Government shall cause the annual report together with a memorandum of action taken on the recommendations contained therein, in so far as they relate to the Central Government and the reasons for the non-acceptance if any, of any of such recommendations and the audit report to be laid as soon as may be after the reports are received, before each House of Parliament.

CHAPTER V: MISCELLANEOUS

15. CHAIRPERSON, MEMBERS AND STAFF OF THE COMMISSION TO BE PUBLIC SERVANTS

The Chairperson, the Members, officers and other employees of the Commission shall be deemed to be public servants within the meaning of section 21 of the Indian Penal Code (45 of 1860).

16. CENTRAL GOVERNMENT TO CONSULT COMMISSION

The Central Government shall consult the Commission on all major policy matters affecting women.

17. POWER TO MAKE RULES

(1) The Central Government may, by notification in the Official Gazette, make rules for carrying out the provisions of this Act.

(2) In particular, and without prejudice to the generality of the foregoing power, such rules may provide for all or any of the following matters, namely:

   (a) salaries and allowances payable to and the other terms and conditions of service of, the Chairperson and Members under sub-section (5) of section 4 of officers and other employees under sub-section (2) of section 5;

   (b) allowances for attending the meetings of the committee by the co-opted persons under sub-section (3) of section 8;

   (c) other matters under clause (f) of sub-section (4) of section 10;

   (d) the form in which the annual statement of accounts shall be maintained under sub-section (1) of section 12;

   (e) the form in, and the time at, which the annual report shall be prepared under section 13;

   (f) any other matter which is required to be, or may, prescribed.

(3) Every rule made under this Act shall be laid, as soon as may be after it is made, before each House of Parliament, while it is session, for a total period of thirty days which may be comprised in one session or in two or more successive sessions, and if, before the expiry of the session immediately following the session or successive

sessions aforesaid, both Houses agree in making any modification in the rule or both Houses agree that the rule should not be made, the rule shall thereafter have effect only in such modified form or be of no effect, as the case may be; so, however, that any such modification or annulment shall be without prejudice to the validity of anything previously done under that rule.

ANNEXURE V

Graph and Tables

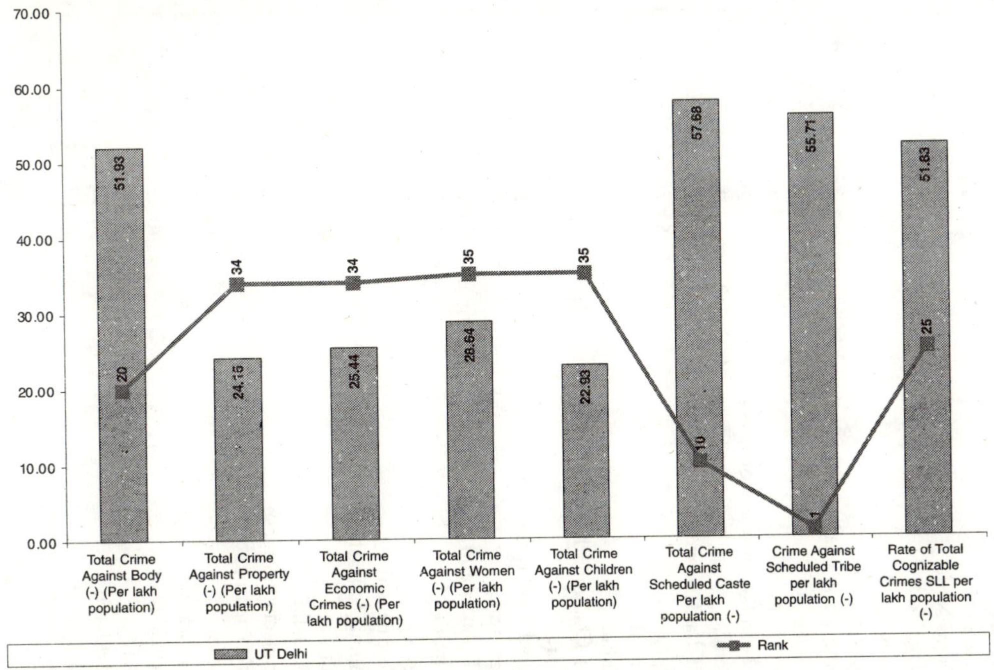

Graph 1: Delhi Crime Ranking Profile Ranking on Different Crime Types

Table 1: T of Efficiency Ranking

State/UT	Efficiency T	Ranking
UT Pondicherry	61.53	1
Andhra Pradesh	60.92	2
Mizoram	58.10	3
Tamil Nadu	57.27	4
Nagaland	56.60	5
Chattisgarh	56.11	6
Uttarakhand	55.90	7
Madhya Pradesh	54.56	8
Rajasthan	53.77	9
Uttar Pradesh	53.54	10
UT Andaman & Nicobar Islands	53.44	11
Kerala	52.90	12
UT Lakshadweep	52.22	13
Haryana	51.70	14
Punjab	51.54	15
Sikkim	50.86	16
UT Chandigarh	50.83	17
Goa	50.41	18
Himachal Pradesh	49.15	19
Karnataka	48.63	20
UT Dadar and Nagar Haveli	48.47	21
Tripura	48.26	22
Orissa	47.83	23
West Bengal	47.37	24
Jammu & Kashmir	47.05	25
Gujarat	46.39	26
UT Delhi	46.37	27
Arunachal Pradesh	45.91	28
UT Daman and Diu	45.44	29
Assam	44.67	30
Maharashtra	44.27	31
Meghalaya	40.61	32
Bihar	39.80	33
Jharkhand	38.37	34
Manipur	38.17	35

Table 2: Staff density (Area and Populationwise)

State/UT	No. of policemen per 100 sq. km.(+)	No. of policemen per 100,000 population (+)	T Score Avg. col. 1 – 2	Ranking
Andhra Pradesh	46.82	42.04	44.43	29
Arunachal Pradesh	46.56	60.36	53.46	11
Assam	47.27	45.89	46.58	16
Bihar	47.12	40.14	43.63	35
Chattisgarh	46.68	42.27	44.48	27
Goa	47.62	48.40	48.01	15
Gujarat	46.83	42.41	44.62	26
Haryana	47.45	44.87	46.16	19
Himachal Pradesh	46.72	45.75	46.24	18
Jammu & Kashmir	47.24	64.03	55.63	7
Jharkhand	46.84	41.44	44.14	34
Karnataka	46.82	42.04	44.43	30
Kerala	47.80	43.48	45.64	20
Madhya Pradesh	46.76	42.74	44.75	24
Maharashtra	47.00	43.62	45.31	22
Manipur	47.20	62.31	54.76	10
Meghalaya	46.95	54.38	50.67	12
Mizoram	46.93	77.11	62.02	3
Nagaland	47.34	63.75	55.54	9
Orissa	46.74	41.67	44.21	33
Punjab	48.15	50.30	49.23	14
Rajasthan	46.70	42.23	44.46	28
Sikkim	47.06	65.74	56.40	6
Tamil Nadu	47.25	43.53	45.39	21
Tripura	48.56	62.64	55.60	8
Uttar Pradesh	47.23	41.39	44.31	32
Uttarakhand	46.74	43.57	45.16	23
West Bengal	47.55	41.86	44.70	25
UT Andaman & Nicobar Islands	46.87	70.29	58.58	4
UT Chandigarh	88.83	56.37	72.60	1
UT Dadar and Nagar Haveli	47.02	41.72	44.37	31
UT Daman and Diu	49.07	43.94	46.51	17
UT Delhi	89.89	53.45	71.67	2
UT Lakshadweep	56.62	56.98	56.80	5
UT Pondicherry	51.75	47.28	49.51	13

Table 3: Statewise Ranking of Total Crime Rate Per Lakh Population

State/UT	Total crime rate (per lakh population)	Ranking
Andhra Pradesh	834.76	5
Arunachal Pradesh	205.09	21
Assam	153.61	26
Bihar	119.87	30
Chattisgarh	1237.42	3
Goa	405.71	12
Gujarat	530.18	9
Haryana	286.35	16
Himachal Pradesh	263.85	18
Jammu & Kashmir	200.95	22
Jharkhand	133.61	29
Karnataka	241.78	19
Kerala	486.44	11
Madhya Pradesh	632.39	6
Maharashtra	319.24	15
Manipur	135.92	28
Meghalaya	82.22	33
Mizoram	355.86	14
Nagaland	69.11	35
Orissa	167.80	24
Punjab	208.54	20
Rajasthan	278.90	17
Sikkim	160.17	25
Tamil Nadu	1073.27	4
Tripura	105.28	31
Uttar Pradesh	624.15	7
Uttarakhand	1480.27	2
West Bengal	88.93	32
UT Andaman & Nicobar Islands	2009.28	1
UT Chandigarh	394.39	13
UT Dadar and Nagar Haveli	188.11	23
UT Daman and Diu	141.71	27
UT Delhi	524.92	10
UT Lakshadweep	75.38	34
UT Pondicherry	561.43	8

Table 4: Statewise ranking of complaints against personnel

States	No. of complaints against per 100 policemen (–)	No. of complaints against prison staff (–)	Avg. T Score	Ranking
Andhra Pradesh	37.62	49.80	43.71	31
Arunachal Pradesh	56.04	53.98	55.01	1
Assam	56.04	51.37	53.70	15
Bihar	55.84	44.58	50.21	25
Chattisgarh	47.70	53.81	50.75	22
Goa	54.87	53.98	54.43	13
Gujarat	41.89	53.98	47.93	28
Haryana	49.45	53.98	51.71	19
Himachal Pradesh	52.35	53.81	53.08	16
Jammu & Kashmir	48.48	53.98	51.23	21
Jharkhand	56.04	53.81	54.92	7
Karnataka	55.07	42.49	48.78	27
Kerala	47.12	53.63	50.38	23
Madhya Pradesh	4.48	48.93	26.71	34
Maharashtra	49.83	53.63	51.73	18
Manipur	56.04	53.98	55.01	1
Meghalaya	55.26	53.98	54.62	11
Mizoram	56.04	53.98	55.01	1
Nagaland	55.84	53.98	54.91	8
Orissa	55.65	48.41	52.03	17
Punjab	45.57	2.10	23.83	35
Rajasthan	52.74	41.97	47.35	30
Sikkim	55.07	53.98	54.52	12
Tamil Nadu	55.65	25.95	40.80	32
Tripura	55.45	53.98	54.72	10
Uttar Pradesh	49.45	53.28	51.36	20
Uttarakhand	41.31	53.98	47.64	29
West Bengal	55.84	52.76	54.30	14
UT Andaman & Nicobar Islands	44.21	53.98	49.10	26
UT Chandigarh	46.93	53.63	50.28	24
UT Dadar and Nagar Haveli	56.04	53.98	55.01	1
UT Daman and Diu	56.04	53.98	55.01	1
UT Delhi	32.20	48.58	40.39	33
UT Lakshadweep	56.04	53.98	55.01	1
UT Pondicherry	55.84	53.81	54.82	9

Table 5: Statewise Ranking of Complaints Related to Conviction and Death Rates

State/UT	No. of complaints against per 100 policemen (–)	Percentage of police personnel convicted per 100 police complaints (+)	Total death of inmates due to various causes (–)	No. of complaints agaisnt prison staff (–)	Avg. T score	Ranking
Andhra Pradesh	37.62	45.79	32.84	49.80	41.51	32
Arunachal Pradesh	56.04	74.10	57.61	53.98	60.43	1
Assam	56.04	45.78	52.62	51.37	51.45	14
Bihar	55.84	45.78	19.59	44.58	41.45	33
Chattisgarh	47.70	46.62	45.90	53.81	48.51	24
Goa	54.87	45.78	56.84	53.98	52.87	12
Gujarat	41.89	45.99	51.47	53.98	48.33	25
Haryana	49.45	45.78	54.73	53.98	50.98	17
Himachal Pradesh	52.35	45.91	56.46	53.81	52.13	13
Jammu & Kashmir	48.48	45.78	57.03	53.98	51.32	15
Jharkhand	56.04	45.78	45.51	53.81	50.28	20
Karnataka	55.07	46.00	45.90	42.49	47.36	27
Kerala	47.12	45.79	50.31	53.63	49.21	23
Madhya Pradesh	4.48	45.79	38.21	48.93	34.35	34
Maharashtra	49.83	45.86	35.33	53.63	46.17	28
Manipur	56.04	45.78	57.61	53.98	53.35	7
Meghalaya	55.26	45.78	57.23	53.98	53.06	10
Mizoram	56.04	74.10	57.61	53.98	60.43	1
Nagaland	55.84	49.32	56.84	53.98	54.00	6
Orissa	55.65	45.78	50.31	48.41	50.04	21

Punjab	45.57	45.81	41.29	2.10	33.69	35
Rajasthan	52.74	45.81	48.97	41.97	47.37	26
Sikkim	55.07	45.78	57.61	53.98	53.11	9
Tamil Nadu	55.65	46.82	38.02	25.95	41.61	31
Tripura	55.45	45.78	56.65	53.98	52.97	11
Uttar Pradesh	49.45	45.78	24.77	53.28	43.32	30
Uttarakhand	41.31	45.78	56.27	53.98	49.33	22
West Bengal	55.84	45.78	49.74	52.76	51.03	16
UT Andaman & Nicobar Islands	44.21	45.78	57.23	53.98	50.30	19
UT Chandigarh	46.93	45.78	57.03	53.63	50.84	18
UT Dadar and Nagar Haveli	56.04	74.10	57.61	53.98	60.43	1
UT Daman and Diu	56.04	74.10	57.61	53.98	60.43	1
UT Delhi	32.20	45.78	52.62	48.58	44.79	29
UT Lakshadweep	56.04	74.10	57.61	53.98	60.43	1
UT Pondicherry	55.84	45.78	57.03	53.81	53.12	8

Table 6: Staff Diversity as Proportionate Representation of Population Groups

State/UT	Proportionate representation of SCs in police	Proportionate representation of STs in police	Proportionate representation of women	Proportionate representation of Muslim	T score avg. cols. 3–6	Ranking
Andhra Pradesh	47.18	48.15	42.43	77.14	53.73	6
Arunachal Pradesh	53.87	51.64	45.54	52.42	50.87	12
Assam	46.10	46.62	38.24	45.32	44.07	25
Bihar	46.34	93.51	42.53	45.55	56.98	3
Chattisgarh	45.49	43.57	45.12	48.13	45.58	19
Goa	48.48	0.00	62.24	43.66	38.59	27
Gujarat	53.07	50.05	47.17	55.53	51.45	9
Haryana	45.37	NA	45.18	62.82	51.12	11
Himachal Pradesh	47.59	56.83	56.68	58.61	54.93	4
Jammu & Kashmir	44.36	40.39	45.51	58.76	47.26	17
Jharkhand	0.00	0.00	39.52	NA	13.17	35
Karnataka	48.14	45.28	62.10	53.07	52.15	7
Kerala	50.77	49.94	53.69	51.58	51.50	8
Madhya Pradesh	45.46	41.92	46.33	48.33	45.51	20
Maharashtra	48.69	46.06	57.87	48.31	50.23	15
Manipur	45.40	45.41	42.20	69.61	50.66	13
Meghalaya	NA	47.83	40.89	47.20	45.31	21
Mizoram	NA	49.02	0.00	49.00	32.67	32
Nagaland	NA	50.03	0.00	39.53	29.85	34
Orissa	46.37	46.42	38.93	70.19	50.48	14
Punjab	46.09	NA	44.43	40.37	43.63	26

Rajasthan	47.20	49.20	43.59	45.68	46.42	18
Sikkim	47.85	63.07	57.35	37.13	51.35	10
Tamil Nadu	47.30	46.87	82.79	54.92	57.97	2
Tripura	46.94	47.58	40.21	42.85	44.40	23
Uttar Pradesh	46.79	0.00	41.10	42.24	32.53	33
Uttarakhand	49.37	57.80	50.26	42.04	49.87	16
West Bengal	45.55	46.26	42.06	43.64	44.38	24
UT Andaman & Nicobar Islands	0.00	52.07	62.55	65.48	45.02	22
UT Chandigarh	47.19	0.00	65.11	38.10	37.60	28
UT Dadar and Nagar Haveli	70.80	47.02	51.44	48.62	54.47	5
UT Daman and Diu	95.54	41.24	NA	50.75	62.51	1
UT Delhi	47.29	0.00	53.45	41.04	35.45	30
UT Lakshadweep	0.00	46.21	59.69	35.60	35.37	31
UT Pondicherry	49.41	0.00	53.81	46.78	37.50	29

Table 7: Statewise Ranking of Infrastructure (Budget/Expenditure/Existing Equipment and Transport Support) Per Lakh Population for Police

STATE/UT	Budget/ Expenditure	Existing equipment and transport support		Average	
	Expenditure on police after per lakh population of state/UT's (in lakhs)	Motor vehicles per lakh population	Equipments per lakh population	T score avg. cols. 7–9	Ranking
Andhra Pradesh	42.25	42.49	44.82	43.19	29
Arunachal Pradesh	52.93	74.08	44.29	57.10	8
Assam	45.93	46.23	45.25	45.80	17
Bihar	40.97	40.54	43.99	41.83	35
Chattisgarh	41.52	48.44	44.96	44.97	21
Goa	48.59	51.84	62.25	54.23	12
Gujarat	42.22	43.00	45.19	43.47	26
Haryana	45.87	39.29	43.16	42.77	30
Himachal Pradesh	45.71	43.16	46.37	45.08	20
Jammu & Kashmir	58.17	60.68	56.84	58.56	6
Jharkhand	42.77	40.51	43.98	42.42	31
Karnataka	42.60	43.40	47.00	44.33	23
Kerala	42.96	44.51	45.59	44.35	22
Madhya Pradesh	42.18	42.73	47.31	44.07	24
Maharashtra	44.01	41.59	43.99	43.20	28
Manipur	55.59	66.19	66.05	62.61	4
Meghalaya	52.48	54.09	49.19	51.92	14

Mizoram	70.42	75.71	56.18	67.44	2
Nagaland	73.23	49.07	44.19	55.50	11
Orissa	41.01	42.22	43.61	42.28	33
Punjab	49.71	42.74	45.35	45.93	16
Rajasthan	41.92	42.67	45.66	43.42	27
Sikkim	68.80	64.61	58.30	63.90	3
Tamil Nadu	44.43	47.14	45.41	45.66	18
Tripura	57.63	58.38	56.52	57.51	7
Uttar Pradesh	41.86	40.04	45.11	42.34	32
Uttarakhand	45.84	42.27	43.51	43.88	25
West Bengal	40.51	41.95	43.95	42.14	34
UT Andaman & Nicobar Islands	73.76	66.53	44.33	61.54	5
UT Chandigarh	58.89	54.81	55.15	56.28	10
UT Dadar and Nagar Haveli	43.10	45.08	47.61	45.26	19
UT Daman and Diu	42.62	48.27	50.90	47.26	15
UT Delhi	61.83	52.58	56.85	57.08	9
UT Lakshadweep	59.82	55.64	95.92	70.46	1
UT Pondicherry	47.85	57.54	51.22	52.21	13

ANNEXURE VI

Important Oversight Actions: NHRC

I. Police Inaction Against Scheduled Castes

(a) The commission called for report on the following:
Report from Senior Superintendent of Police, Varanasi, Uttar Pradesh on alleged police inaction on physically challenged dalit youth being set ablaze (January 2005).

(b) The commission took *suo motu* cognizance based on media report of torching a number of houses belonging to dalits by a mob in a district in Haryana and ask the Haryana Government to respond within four weeks to this violation on dalits (September 2005)

II. Police Conduct Under Scrutiny

(a) Taking cognizance of a media report the NHRC seeks report from Director General of Police, Delhi on media report of police control room van having hit and killed a person and then trying to escape. The name of the driver as well as occupant were asked for as also and if they were on the duty (January 2005).
Also a report was to be provided on police excesses (lathi charge—beating crows with batons) on the crowd that gathered around a police party after people were asked to leave since no one from their homes was killed.

(b) NHRC has asked special reporteur to investigate and present a report on the allegations of police excess (lathi charge on tribals in Orissa). The tribals were stated to gather to protest against non-payment of dues for land acquired by the state government and delay in rehabilitation. They were said to have been brutally assaulted by police which left four tribals including two children dead (June 2005)

(c) The commission strongly recommended Government of Haryana to undertake an independent investigation of assault on agitating workers of an industrial company which was widely publicised by print and electronic media. The report has since been received from the SP, Gurgaon and were being examined on last available information (July 2005)

(d) Censor punishment awarded to Uttar Pradesh police in torture and extortion case by NHRC
The DGP directed to personally look into the disciplinary action taken on officer in which a minor penalty was awarded to the erring officer and not commensurate to the gravity of misconduct of the unlawful torture and extortion for money to the victim. This was after the commission in March 2002 had directed the district police officer to look into a complaint and submit proper action report (November 2005).

III. Violence Against Women

(a) The commission has taken suo moto cognizance of a complaint filed by a NGO and ask Delhi Police Commissioner to enquire and report on the collision between pimps, brothel owners and police officers in trafficking of girls (January 2005)

(b) Director General of Police, Uttar Pradesh has been asked to submit a report on the news reporting of disabled girl raped at home and alleged intimidation by police to disallow first investigation report (complaint) to be lodged against the miscreants who were stated to have political clout (January 2005).

(c) The commission has asked DGP, Punjab to comment on the alleged media report of a young woman being paraded naked in the police complex (June 2005)

(d) Commission seeks comments from Meerut police on crackdown against female behaviour thought improper in public places. Responding to the media reports the commission has asked for SSP, Meerut, Uttar Pradesh to reply within two weeks to the television and print media reports showing police beating/slapping women found together with boys at public places for alleged improper behaviour. In fact, 'Operation Majnu' was undertaken by the police in Meerut against girls expressing pubic display of a boyfriend (December 2005).

IV. Police Excesses

(a) The Director General of Police, Uttar Pradesh has been asked to comment on the media story that alleged police were responsible for torturing in custody and the resultant death of three rag pickers who were nabbed by private security in a residential area (April 2005).

(b) Issue a notice to Director General of Police, Punjab and Superintendent of Police, District Kapurthala, Punjab on an alleged custodial death in Kapurthala in May 2005.

(c) The commission took *suo motu* cognizance of a media report of killing of students in police firing in Meghalaya and have asked the Meghalaya Government to respond on the alleged police excess.

(d) NHRC has asked Director General of Police to comment on the alleged torture of a young man reported in the electronic and print media.

Glossary of Terms

Aggregate

An aggregate is a sum of individual characteristics, experiences, or behaviours that is used to reflect a collective phenomenon for an entire population.

Chargesheeeting

Chargesheeting cases refer to such cases where charges are filed by the police and fall under the final report. Reports cancelled due to the withdrawal by the complainant or where evidence is lacking, fall under the category of case fault or untraced reports. Only the final report is chargesheeted by the police.

Conviction Rates

This reflects the ratio of cases convicted to the total number of cases tried by courts in a year.

Data Standardisation

The process of reaching agreement on common data definitions, formats, representation and structures of all data layers and elements

Disposal Rate

The total number of cases investigated by the police is referred to as the disposal rate of the police and the total number of cases tried by the courts in a year refers to the disposal rate of the courts.

Efficiency

Efficiency is computed by taking the sum of disposal rates, charge sheeting rates, recovery of stolen property, conviction rate, occupancy rates, average time taken for trials in courts and average time taken for undertrials in prisons.

INDIAN PENAL CODE (IPC)

Provides a penal code (laws that deal with defining elements and particular crimes and specifying the punishment for each crime) for all of India. The code applies to any offence committed by an Indian citizen anywhere.

INDICATORS

An Indicator is a measure that helps answer the question of how much, or whether, process is being made towards a certain objective.

INDICES

Indices combine multiple indicators into single measures. In order to generate an Index, the separate measures must be assigned individual weights based on their relative importance to the concept represented by the Index.

LOK ADALAT

Lok Adalat has the jurisdiction to settle, by way of effecting compromise between the parties, any matter which may be pending before any court, as well as matters at pre-litigative stage, i.e. disputes which have not yet been formally instituted in any court of law.

OUTPUTS AND OUTCOMES

Outputs are the goods and services produced and outcomes as the impacts of the delivery of outputs on social, economic and other indicators.

RECOVERY RATE

The stolen property that is recovered by the police against the total reported stolen property is measured under recovery rate.

RIGHT TO INFORMATION ACT

To provide freedom of information to the citizens as a basic right. It recognises the need for building institutional accountability structures, which are democratic and transparent.

Special and Local Laws (SLL)

All reported cognisable crimes dealt by the police in which a police officer may arrest a person without a warrant are broadly categorised under the 'special and local laws (SLL)' includes Arms Act, Narcotic Drugs and Psychotrophic Substances Act, Prohibition Act, Terrorist and Disruptive Activities Act, Dowry Prohibition Act, etc.

Stakeholder

A Stakeholder is defined as any individual community, group or organisation with an interest in the outcome of an activity either as a result of being affected by it positively or negatively, or by being able to influence the activity in a positive or negative manner.

*For sources of these terms please refer to main text.

Bibliography

Anderson, P.R. and D.J. Newman, 1998, *Introduction to Criminal Justice*, New York: McGraw Hill.

Beckett, Katherine and Theodore Sassion, 2000, 'War on Crime as Hegemonic Strategy: A Neo-Marxian Theory of the New Punitiveness in U.S. Criminal Justice Policy', in Sally S. Simpson (ed.), *Of Crime and Criminality*, Thousand Oaks: Pine Force Press.

Bennett, Richard R. and James P. Lynch 1990, 'Does a Difference Make a Difference? Comparing Cross-national Crime Indicators', *Criminology* 28 (1), 153-81.

Bruce, David and Rachel Neild, 2005, *The Police That We Want: A Handbook for Oversight of Police in South Africa*, Johannesburg: Centre for the Study of Violence and Reconciliation.

Carrabine, Eamonn et al., 2004, *Criminology: A Sociological Introduction*, London: Routledge.

Chopra, Harsh, 2007, *Alternate Dispute Resolution: A Case Study of Rajasthan, India*, Chandigarh: Institute for Development and Communication.

Crawford, Adam, 1999, *Local Governacne of Crime: Appeals to Community and Partnership*, New York: Oxford University Press.

Dagar, Rainuka, 2001, *Combating Violence Against Women in Punjab*. Chandigarh: Institute for Development and Communication.

———, 2002, *Policing and Gender Sensitisation: A Strategy*, Chandigarh: Institute for Development and Communication.

Daruwala, Maza and Tessa Boyd-Caine, 2007, *Stamping Out Rights: Impact of Anti-Terrorism Laws on Policing*, New Delhi: Commonwealth Human Rights Initiative.

Eck, John E. and Dennis P. Rosenbaum, 1994, 'New Police Order: Effectiveness, Equity, and Efficiency in Community Policing', in Dennis P. Rosenbaum (ed.), *Challenge of Community Policing: Testing the Promises*, Thousand Oaks: Sage Publications.

Fairchild, Erika S., 1993, *Comparative Criminal Justice Systems*, Belmont, C.A: Wadswoth.

Government of India, 2001, The Dowry Prohibition Act, 1961, Delhi: Universal Law Publisher.

———, 2003, The Pre-conception and Pre-natal Diagnostic Technique (Prohibition of Sex Selection) Act, 1994, Delhi: Universal Law Publisher.

———, Ministry of Home Affairs, 2006, *Crime in India 2005*, New Delhi: National Crime Records Bureau.

———, Ministry of Home Affairs, 2007, *Prison Statistics India 2005*, New Delhi: National Crime Records Bureau.

Guidance on Local Safety Audits: Compendium of International Practice, Paris, France: European Forum for Urban Safety (EFUS), 2007. www.urbansecurity.org/fileadmin/efus/secutopics/efus_safety_Audit_e_web.pdf

Hagan, F.E., 2003, *Research Methods in Criminal Justice and Criminology*, Boston: Allyn & Bacon.

Hickey, T., 1998, *Criminal Procedure*, New York: McGraw-Hill.

Huang, W.S. Wilson and Wellford Charles F., 1989, 'Assessing Indicators of Crime among International Crime Data Series', *Criminal Justice Policy Review* 3(1), 28-48.

IDC Field Survey on Citizen Rights and Police Reforms, 2006.

IDC Field Survey on Haryana Police Station Walkthrough, 2004.

Jary, David and Jilia Jary, 1991, *Collins Dictionary of Sociology*, London: Harper Collins.

Johnson, H., 1997, *Criminal Justice Indicators* (internal report), Ottawa: Canadian Centre for Justice Statistics.

Kumar, Pramod, 1997, *Social Policing: Case of Prohibition in Haryana, India*, Chandigarh: Institute for Development and Communication.

———, 1998, *Youth for Social Harmony: Ek Aur Manthan: Facilitator Manual*, Chandigarh: Institute for Development and Communication.

———, 2005, 'Mapping Police Accountability Spectrum: Issues for building Quality Oversights with a Multicultural Framework ', in Pramod Kumar (ed.), *Dimensions of Police Accountability in India*, Chandigarh: Institute for Development and Communication.

Kumar, Pramod and Rainuka Dagar, 1995, *Atrocities Against Women in Punjab*, Chandigarh: Institute for Development and Communication.

Kumar, Pramod, Rainuka Dagar and Neerja, 2001, *Victims of Militancy: Punjab*, New Delhi: Unicef www.idcindia.org/conflictstudies/conflict.htm

Muncie, John, 2001, 'The Construction and Deconstruction of Crime', in John Muncie and Eugene McLaughlin (eds.), *The Problem of Crime*, Thousand Oaks: Sage Publications.

National Judicial Infrastructure Plan: Draft, 10 November 2006, www.supremecourtofindia.nic.in/NJIP.doc

Newman, Graeme and Gregory J. Howard, 1999, 'Introduction: Data Sources and Their Use', in Graeme Newman (ed.), *Global Report on Crime and Justice*, New York: Oxford University Press, for United Nations; Office for Drug Control and Crime Prevention, Centre for International Crime Prevention.

Newman, Graeme, Debra Cohen and Adam C. Bouloukus (eds.), 1996, *International Factbook & Criminal Justice Systems,* US Bureau of Justice Statistics. http: www. Ojp. Usdoj. Gov/bjs/abstract/wfcj.htw.

North, Douglas C., 1990, *Institutions, Institutional Change and Economic Performance*, Cambridge: Cambridge University Press.

'Notion of Masculinity in Functioning of Panchayat', Chandigarh: Institute for Development and Communication, 2003, unpublished.

OECD, *Glossary of Statistical Terms.* http://stats.OECD.org/glossary/search.asp

Police Station Visitors Week: Global Report 2006, The Hague: Altus Global Alliance Secretariat.

Police Station Visitors Week: Report of Results in India—2006, IDC-Altus Global Alliance.

Raghavan, R.K and Mangai Natarasan, 1996, 'India' in Graeme Newman, Debra Cohen and Adam C. Bouloukos (eds.), *International Factbook of Criminal Justice Systems*, US Bureau of Justice Statistics.

Smith, Philip and Kristin Natalier, 2005, *Understanding Criminal Justice: Sociological Perspective*, London: Sage Publications.

Spohn, C.S., 2002, *How Do Judges Decide? The Search for Fairness and Justice in Punishment.* Thousand Oaks: Sage Publications.

Tarver, M., S. Walker and H. Wallace, 2002, *Multicultural Issues in the Criminal Justice System*, Boston: Allan & Bacon.

Travis, G. et al., 1995, 'The International Crime Surveys: Some Methodological Concerns', *Current Issues in Criminal Justice,* 6: 336-46.

Tuck, M., 1991, 'Community and the Criminal Justice System', *Policy Studies,* 12(3) : 22-37.

United Nations, Economic and Social Council, 2002, *Guidelines for the Prevention of Crime*, New York: United Nations.

United Nations, 1999, *Guide for Policy Makers*, New York: United Nations.

Walker, S., 2001, *Police Accountability: The Role of Citizen Oversight* Belmont, CA: Wadsworth.

———, 2005, *The New World of Police Accountability*, Thousand Oaks: Sage Publications.

'War on Terror Equals War on Minorities', *IPS*, 8 September 2006 www.ipsnews.net/print.asp? Idnews = 34652

World Bank, 2004, *Resuming Punjab's Prosperity: The Opportunities and Challenges Ahead*, Delhi: The World Bank.

Index